IMAGES
of America

PICKENS COUNTY

IMAGES
of America

PICKENS COUNTY

Piper Peters Aheron

ARCADIA
PUBLISHING

Copyright © 2000 by Piper Peters Aheron
ISBN-13 978-0-7385-0606-7

Published by Arcadia Publishing
Charleston, South Carolina

Printed in the United States of America

Library of Congress Catalog Card Number: 00-105333

For all general information contact Arcadia Publishing at:
Telephone 843-853-2070
Fax 843-853-0044
E-mail sales@arcadiapublishing.com
For customer service and orders:
Toll-Free 1-888-313-2665

Visit us on the Internet at www.arcadiapublishing.com

"It ought never be forgotten that the past is the parent of the present . . ."

—John C. Calhoun, Pickens County District

CONTENTS

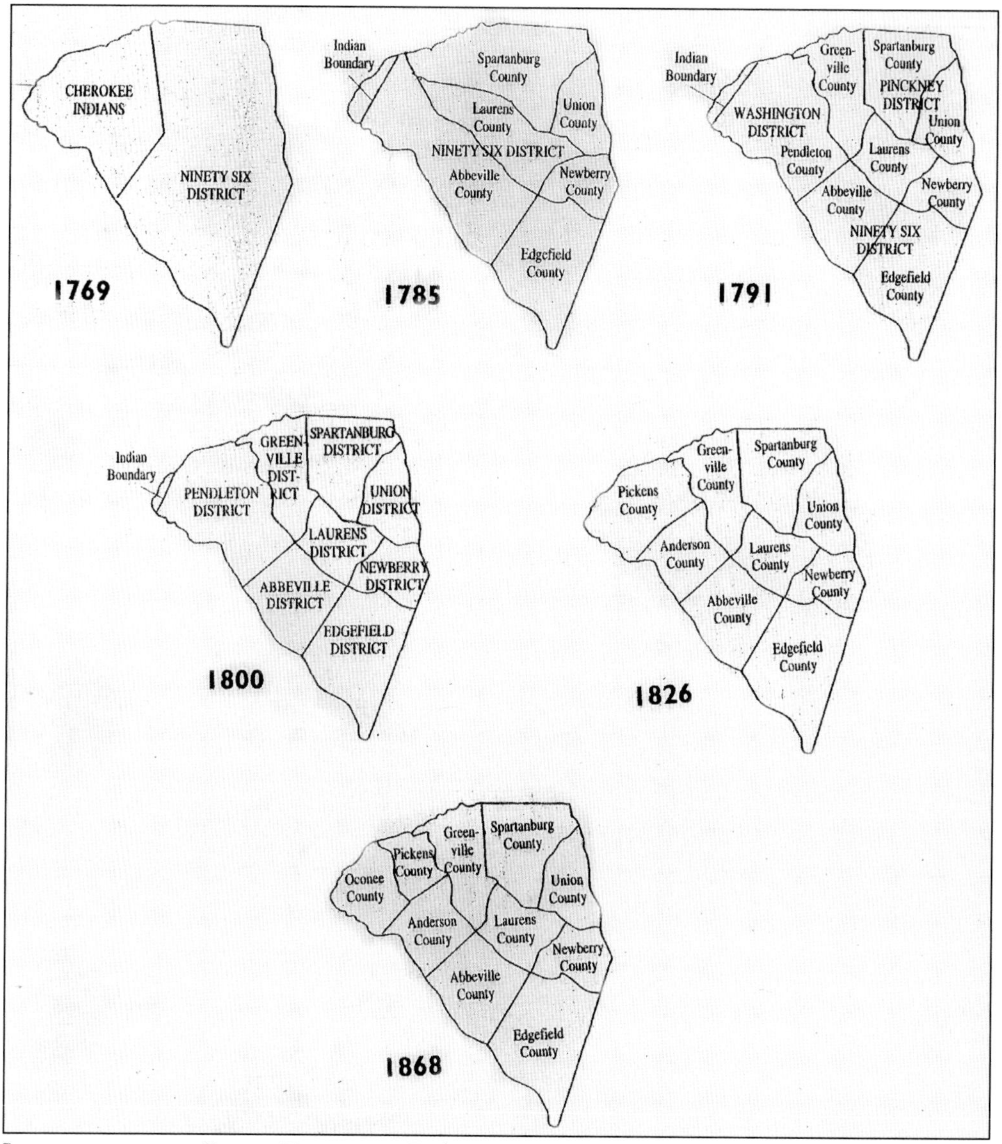

ILLUSTRATION OF COURT DISTRICTS. Pickens County, named in honor of Revolutionary War hero Andrew Pickens, was a part of an ancient Cherokee hunting preserve. In 1784 the region opened for settlement. At first the South Carolina frontier was segmented, named, and renamed in conjunction with its circuit court districts. Pickens County was in the Ninety Six District (1785–1791), the Washington District (1791–1800), and later the Pendleton District (1800–1826). From 1826 to 1868, the Pickens County District included land that would become Oconee County. Eventually, through a series of legislative acts, the land east of the Seneca River became present-day Pickens County. The western portion was renamed Oconee, a word borrowed from the American Indians who had lived in the region. From 1868 to 1968, Clemson University was a part of Oconee. Today the college's address is in Pickens County. Such dates and names depicted on these maps may prevent confusion concerning Pickens County, its origins, and its heritage. (Map courtesy of the Pendleton District Historical, Recreational, and Tourism Commission (PDHRT)).

INTRODUCTION

Sunlight dances on the trickling waters of stream-laced hills, a stead of pine, beech, and oak stranded between two spurs of solitary granite. The smaller monadnock is Glassy located southeast of the Oolonoy Valley a few miles from the Saluda River. The other is the towering Table Rock. Southwest of the Table Rock is the muddy rill called Twelve Mile, and west of Twelve Mile is the pristine Keowee River, its fertile glens fragrant with sweet berries and muscadines.

Cherokee Indians hunted game on this land east of the river Keowee. Before the push of European immigrants into the region, the Cherokee thrived in a village on the river's west bank. It was the center of the Lower Cherokee Nation until the 1700s.

The Cherokee were allies of Great Britain in the 18th century. Like many North American tribes, the Cherokee suffered from a dwindling population due to diseases unintentionally spread by European explorers from the 1500s. With few warriors, the Cherokee found it difficult to protect themselves from Creek Indians, allied with the French. Gov. James Glen of the colonial Carolinas saw opportunity in the Cherokee's predicament. He pledged his assistance and built Fort Prince George on the east bank of the river across from the Cherokee village in 1753.

At Keowee, the British offered colonial commerce, an unprofitable menace to the Cherokee. Quarrels over trading practices escalated. Colonists began stealing Cherokee property, hunting their game, and squatting on tribal lands. By 1759, bitter war had broken out, and by 1776, the Patriots had defeated Great Britain and their ally, the exploited Cherokee. The Cherokee retreated into Tennessee, and the Upcountry prospered as a part of the United States.

In the early years of American Independence, South Carolina's local government processes abided in judicial districts rather than county seats. Ninety Six District, now Greenwood County, served the Upcountry in legal activities—both civil and criminal— and in spring 1784 the first deeds for land in the river valleys of Keowee and Twelve Mile were issued to white settlers. Among the early recipients was Andrew Pickens, a hero of the Battle of Cowpens (near Gaffney) where a ragtag militia defeated an elite corps of British soldiers in 1781. Another recipient was John Ewing Colhoun from Long Cane, or Abbeville. In 1792, Sen. John E. Colhoun created his Upcountry seat at the site of the village of Keowee where a small group of farmers had settled. Colhoun's sister, Mrs. Andrew Pickens, lived nearby at Hopewell. His daughter Floride married her cousin, John C. Calhoun, and immigrants continued to move into the region.

In 1789, the Pendleton District, which included present-day Pickens, Oconee, and Anderson Counties, was abstracted from the Ninety Six District. In less than 35 years, Pendleton District became overwhelmed by the judicial demands of a growing public. Again the territory split into Pickens (inclusive of present-day Oconee) and Anderson Counties. The Pickens County District, created in 1826, stretched all the way from the Saluda River to the Chattooga River on the Georgia line. Pickens County was seated on the Keowee River where Duke Power Nuclear Complex sits today. A courthouse and hotels were constructed and the frontier town incorporated in 1847, only to be abandoned after the Civil War when Pickens and Oconee were split into counties, not judicial districts, in 1868. Walhalla, founded in 1850, served Oconee as a seat while the town of Pickens relocated 14 miles east of the Keowee River to its present location, geographically centered within the new county.

In the 1870s, the railroad boom created towns like Calhoun (Clemson), Central, Norris, Liberty, and Easley. Railroads promoted industry and Norris Cotton Mill was constructed in 1895. Clemson and Southern Wesleyan Universities also brought in a new population in the late 1800s and as the cotton economy of the Old South faded, the people of Pickens County adapted while remaining mindful of the mountains that shaped Pickens' rural and communal traditions.

In the 1960s, the landscape dramatically changed when the U.S. Corps of Engineers dammed the Seneca River and created the man-made Lake Hartwell. Then in 1968, waters of the man-made Lake Keowee, a project of Duke Energy's Keowee-Toxaway Project, flooded the ancient Cherokee lands within the Keowee River Valley. At the same time, Clemson University abstracted from Oconee and rejoined Pickens County.

This book is a brief pictorial compilation designed to provide the reader with a sense of Pickens County's evolution. Some of the photographs have been published, many appear here for the first time, but in all, the images recount the intriguing stories of hardships and accomplishments of the area's pioneering families.

It is my hope that from beginning to end, both young and old, residents and newcomers alike will find this book a delight and that they will explore their local libraries, historical sites, and museums to learn more about this beautiful area called Pickens County.

—Piper Peters Aheron

One

Frontiers and Farms

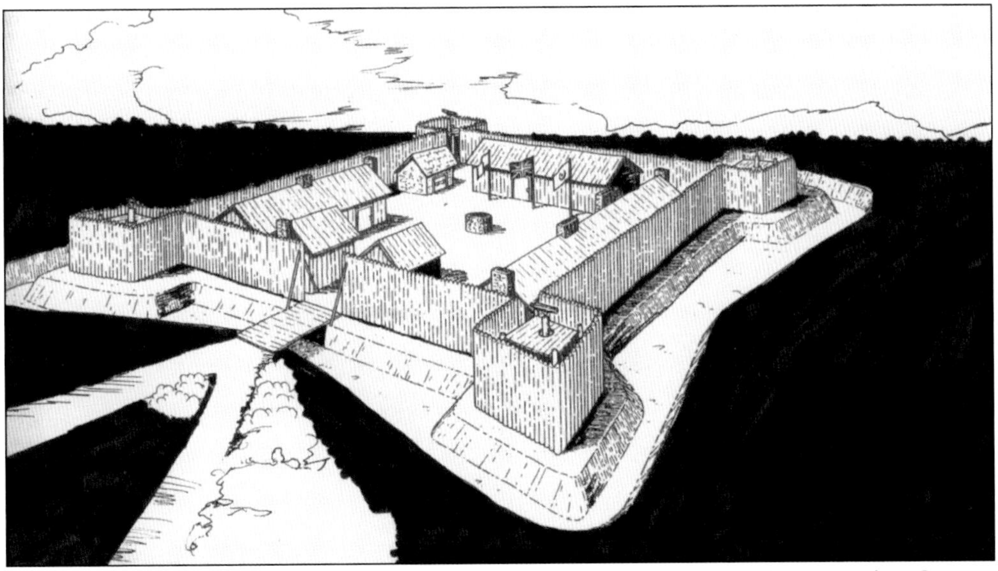

Illustration of Fort Prince George. The Cherokee, residents of present-day Oconee County, utilized Pickens County as part of a vast hunting preserve until the 1700s, when European explorers unintentionally spread diseases among them. With a diminished population, the Cherokee found it increasingly difficult to protect their territory from Creek Indian raids. Gov. James Glen of the colonial Carolinas saw opportunity in the Cherokee's predicament. He pledged his assistance by building a series of forts throughout the Southern Appalachian Mountains. Fort Prince George, located on the eastside of the Keowee River in 1753, was one of the first constructed. Presently, Fort Prince George is inundated by the Keowee-Toxaway Project. A tablet erected on the site of the outpost has been relocated to the Pickens County Museum along with Native-American relics from the 1966–1968 excavations of the Keowee-Jocassee river basin directed by the University of South Carolina and Duke Power researchers. (Illustration courtesy of Duke Power.)

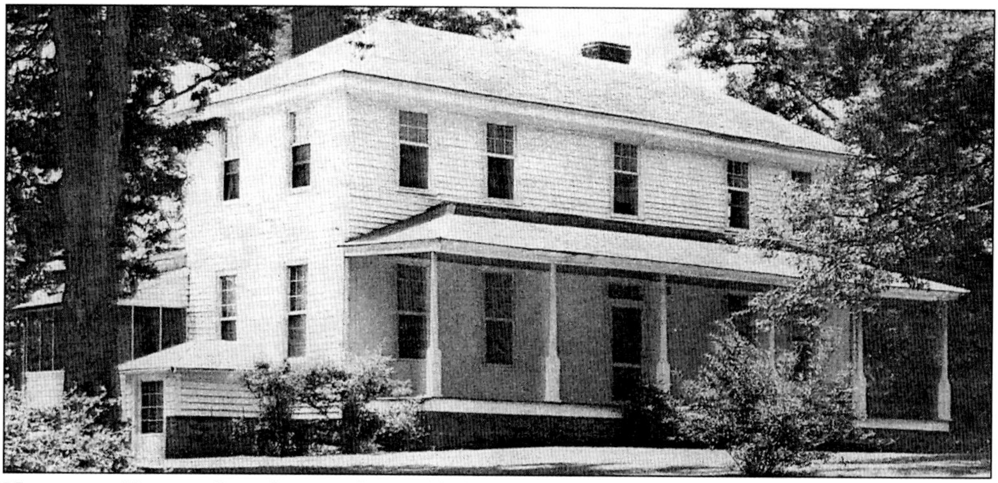

Hopewell House. Gov. James Glen published a book, *Description of South Carolina*, in 1761 after he toured the frontier in 1746. Glen personally led a group to build Fort Prince George, one of several outposts designed to fully exploit American-Indian trade while splitting the French Empire between Louisiana and Canada. The Cherokee living in the small villages along the Keowee and Tugaloo Rivers welcomed the British until they began stealing Cherokee property. Tempers flared over trading practices. Bloody rampages were attributed to both sides, and in May 1777 at DeWit's Corner, the Cherokees ceded tribal lands along the Keowee River to South Carolina. The region became a part of the Ninety Six District, and Andrew Pickens obtained a knoll overlooking the Seneca River. The Hopewell House stands near Clemson University. It eventually became the property of Andrew Pickens Jr. in the early 1800s. It is also the childhood home of Gov. Francis Wilkinson Pickens. (Photo courtesy of PDHRT.)

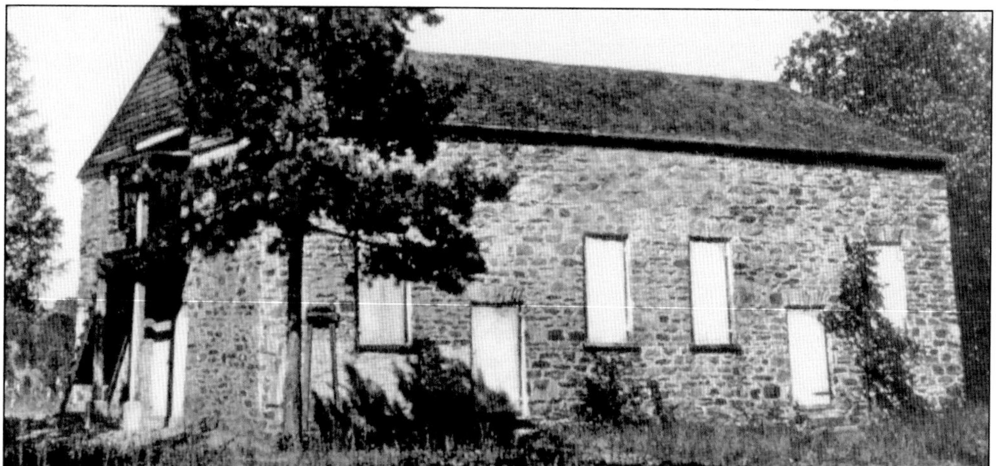

Old Stone Church. Pickens, Oconee, and Anderson Counties share history. This fact is most evident at the Old Stone Church built by John Rusk (*c.* 1800) for the Hopewell Presbyterian congregation. Located near U.S. 76 between Clemson and Pendleton, this sturdy sanctuary sits next to the cemetery where many Revolutionary soldiers who farmed the bounty lands are now buried. Among those buried are Robert Anderson and Andrew Pickens. In 1791 both Anderson and Pickens served as members of the commission to determine the site for the Washington District Courthouse, or Pickensville, near present-day Easley. Anderson and Pickens fought in the Battle of Cowpens in Cherokee County where a ragtag militia brought down an elite corps of British soldiers on January 17, 1781. (Photo courtesy of PDHRT.)

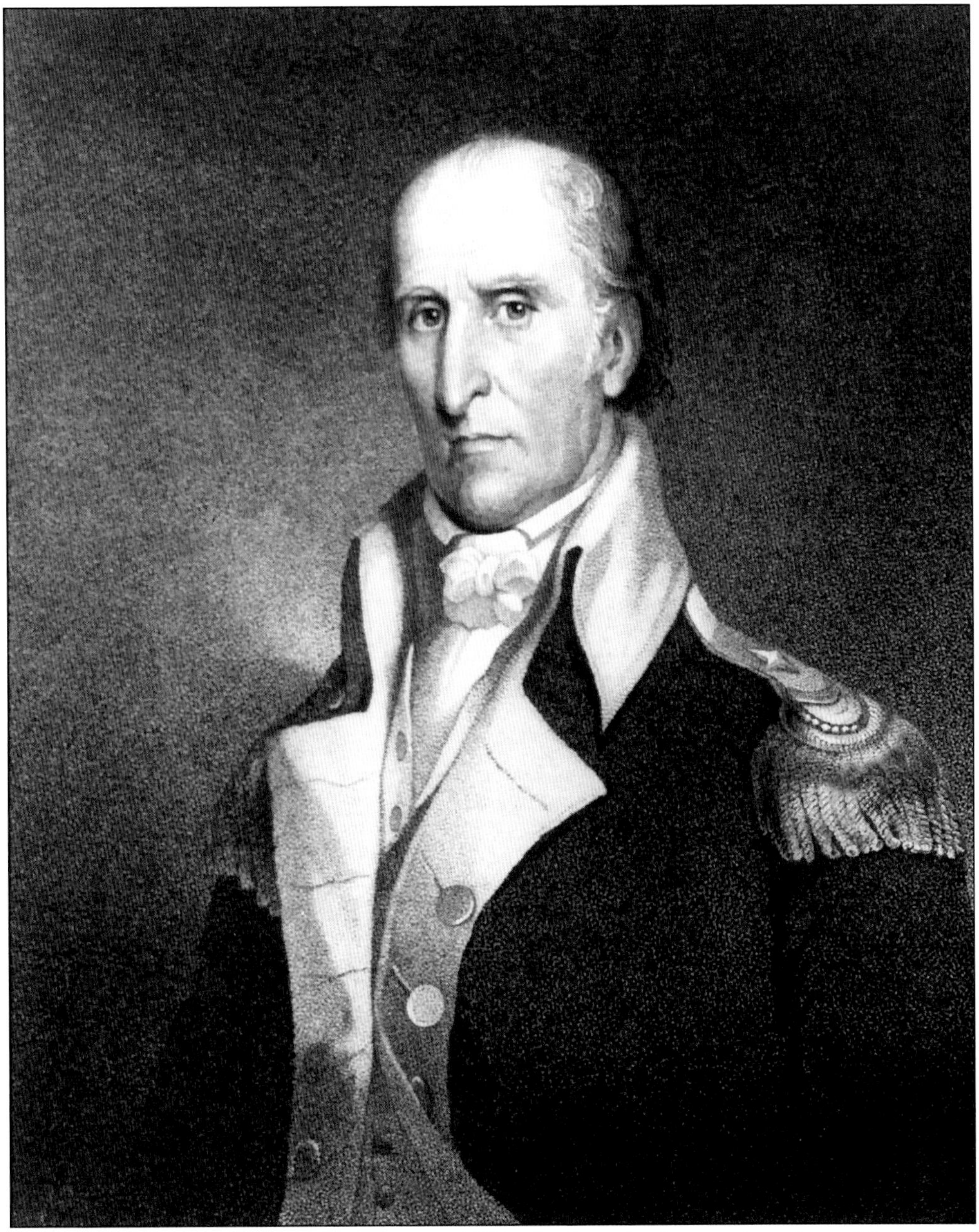

Portrait of Andrew Pickens. In spring 1784, the first deeds were issued to white settlers in the valleys of Keowee and Twelve Mile Rivers. Among the early recipients was Andrew Pickens. Pickens County, inclusive of present-day Oconee County, was established in 1826. It was named for Revolutionary War Brig.-Gen. Andrew Pickens (1739–1817). Pickens, also a South Carolina legislator and congressman, married pioneer Rebecca F. Calhoun, a relative of statesman John C. Calhoun, at Long Canes in 1765. The two settlers survived backcountry hostilities, and Pickens worked to bring law and order to the regions that are now called Anderson, Oconee, and Pickens Counties. (Portrait courtesy of the South Caroliniana Library.)

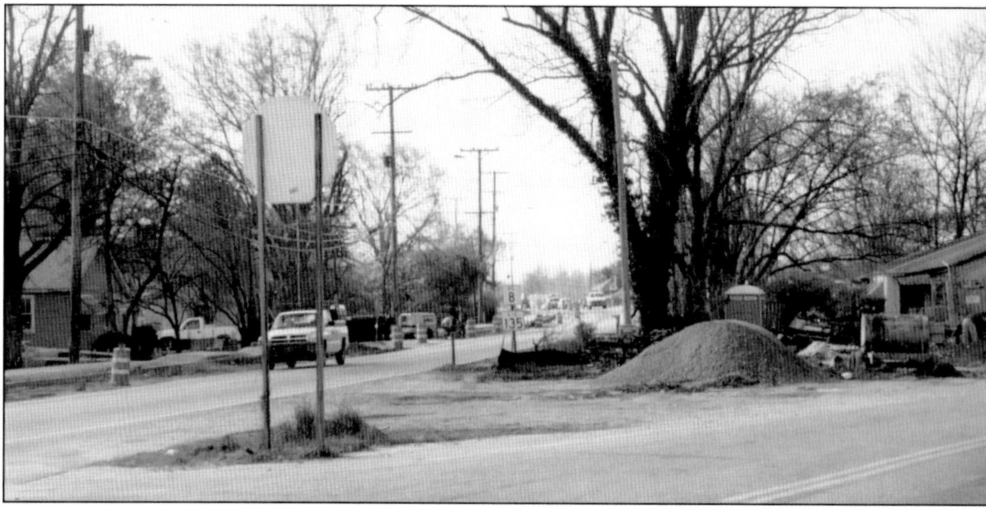

PICKENSVILLE. About 1/2 mile south of S.C. 123, at the junction of S.C. 8 and S.C. 135 (Pelzer Highway and Cherish Drive), stood the frontier community of Rockville. Rockville was renamed Pickensville to honor Gen. Andrew Pickens, and a courthouse was built to serve the Washington District (1791–1800). Deeds and wills were not maintained at Pickensville, but a state appointed judge would listen to criminal and civil cases twice a year for 6 days. Meanwhile, magistrate courts, or county courts, flourished within the villages of Greenville and Pendleton, both a part of the Washington District. Greenville and Pendleton handled the bulk of county transactions, both civil and criminal, and this factor probably led to the declining importance of the Pickensville courthouse. Presently, Easley's urban expansion projects have leveled the rocky ruins of Pickensville and a contemporary marker erected by the Fort Prince George Chapter, DAR, which designated the hamlet's location. (Photo by P.E. Peters.)

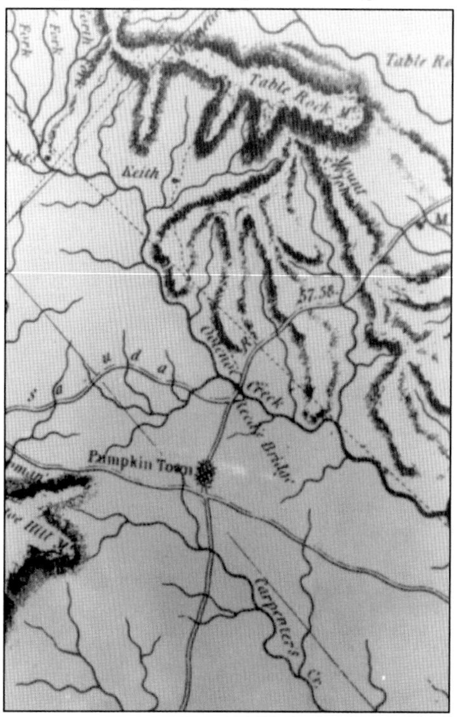

MAP OF PUMPKINTOWN/OOLONOY VALLEY. Ancient maps depict Pumpkin Town in the Oolenoy Valley, an area with a sketchy history since colonial Carolina land grants beyond the American-Indian boundary line were declared null and void after the Revolutionary War. One of two frontier towns in Pickens County during the organization of the Washington District (the other was Pickensville), Pumpkin Town received its name around 1791. (Map courtesy of PDHRT.)

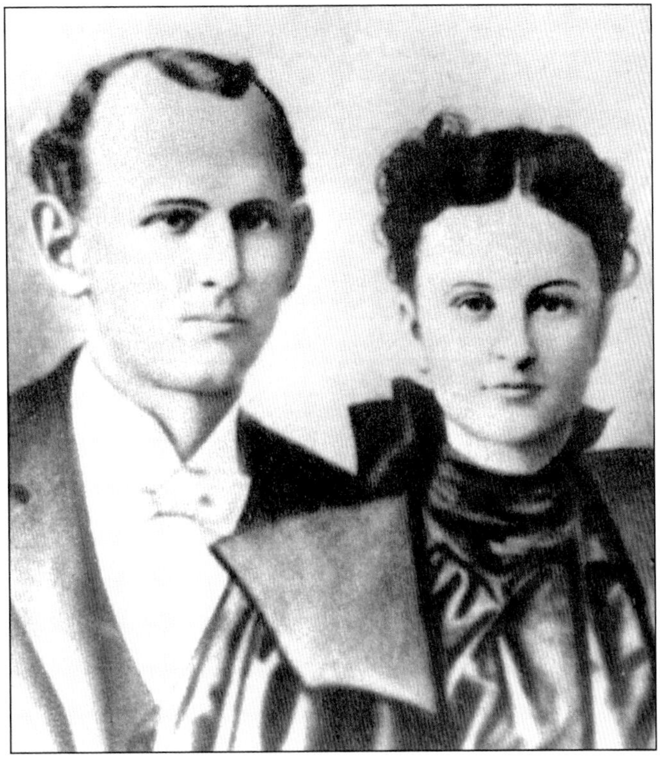

Hendrick's Couple Portrait. Moses Hendricks' kindred settled in the Oolenoy and Cross Roads area of Pickens County. In time, Hendricks became a member of the state legislature (1860–1864). He assisted in the formation of present-day Pickens County. Pictured are Mr. and Mrs. George H. Hendricks, descendants of Moses. (Portrait courtesy of the Pickens County Library.)

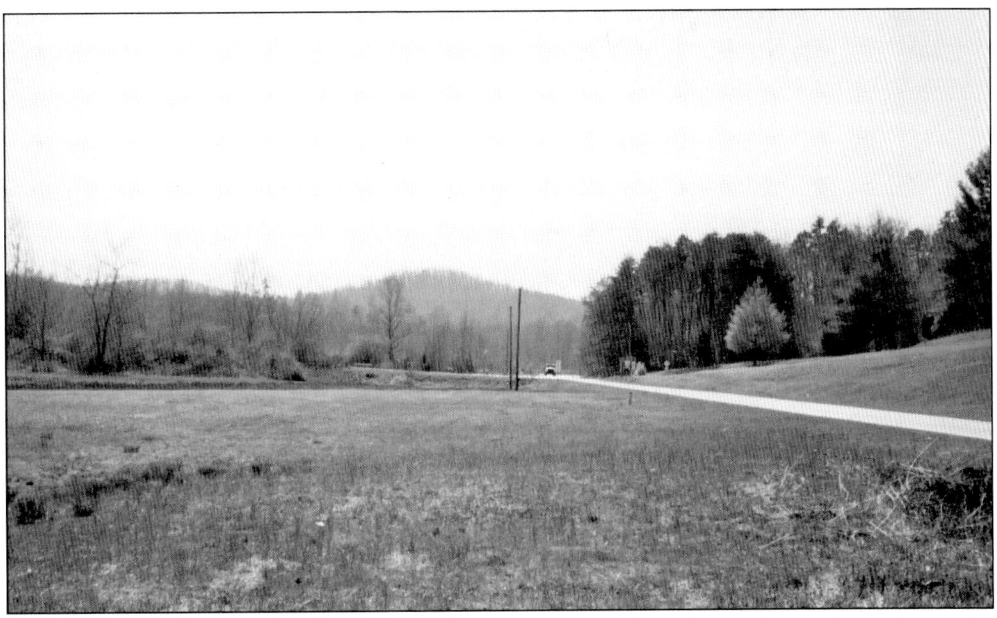

Oolonoy Valley 2000. A drunken Irishman impressed by a field of pumpkins declared a zone surrounding the intersection of S.C. 288 and S.C. 8 Pumpkin Town, or Pumpkintown (according to Dr. Claude H. Neuffer's report on Carolina township names and pronunciations). The beautiful Oolonoy Valley, where Pumpkintown is located, also became the home for a few African Americans after the Civil War. The former slaves worked their own farmlands around "Little Liberia," an early settlement that is now nearly deserted. (Photo by P.E. Peters.)

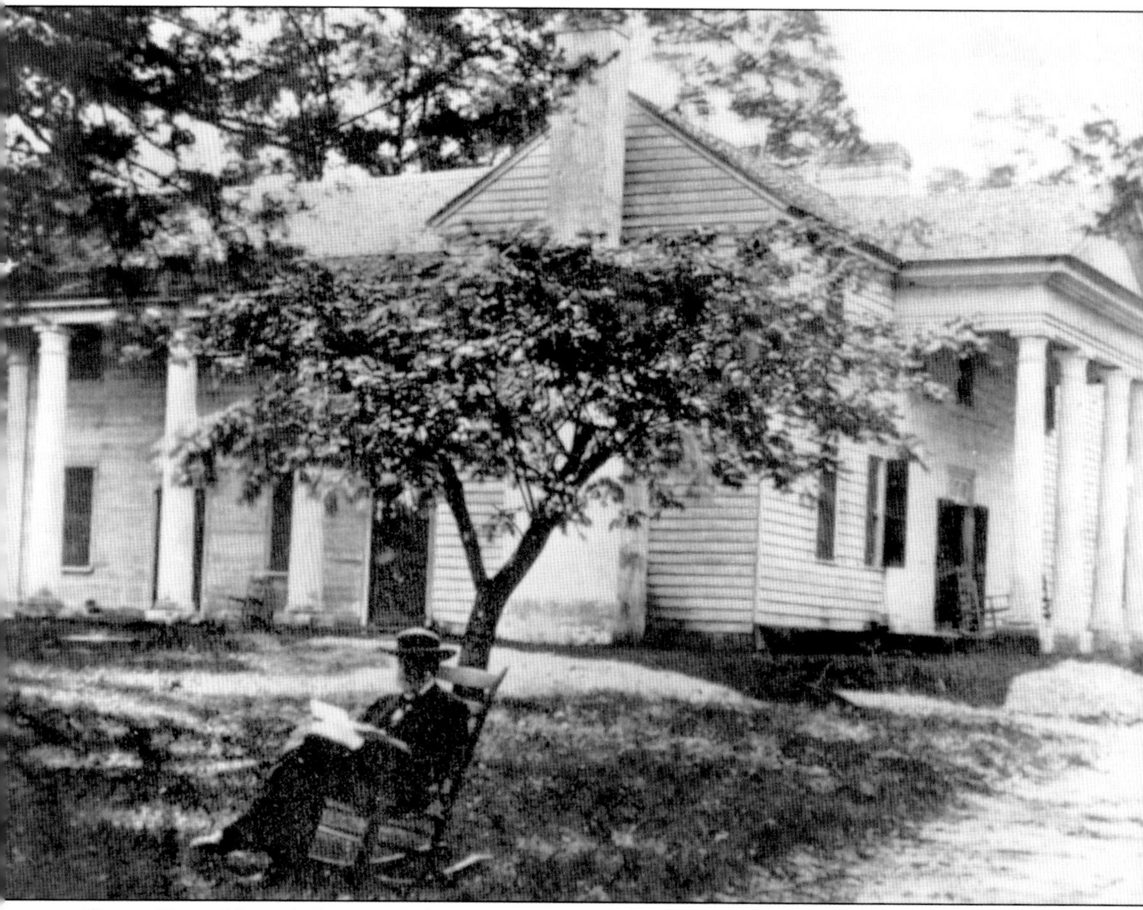

FORT HILL. United States of America property deeds for lands along the rivers Keowee and Twelve Mile were legally issued beginning in 1784. The Ninety Six District's Bratcher Index lists land recipients including families like the Colhouns. Born in Virginia in 1751, John Ewing Colhoun relocated to Long Canes (Abbeville) in 1756. He served the militia during the Revolutionary War, and in 1782 Colhoun, a Charleston lawyer, was appointed as commissioner of forfeited estates. In 1792, state legislator and senator Colhoun created his Upcountry seat at the site of Keowee near S.C. 133, 1.7 miles north of its junction at Clemson with U.S. 123. Colhoun's sister, Mrs. Andrew Pickens, lived nearby at Hopewell. His daughter Floride married her cousin, John C. Calhoun, and the couple lived at Clergy Hill, a structure erected about 1803 by Dr. James McElhenny, pastor of the Old Stone Church. The Calhouns enlarged the house and renamed it Fort Hill in honor of a fort built on the land in 1776. John Ewing Colhoun died at Keowee in 1802. His son inherited Colhoun's estate, but it is John C. Calhoun's Fort Hill at Clemson that stands as the prominent plantation of Pickens County. A part of an 1,100-acre frontier farm, Fort Hill has 14 rooms, 3 piazzas, a separate kitchen, and a restored springhouse on the north lawn. It was home to John C. Calhoun beginning in 1825. The house is furnished with Calhoun and Clemson family heirlooms. Pictured above is Thomas G. Clemson in 1875. Thomas G. Clemson, Calhoun's son-in-law, bequeathed a cash fortune and land tracts for the development of the Clemson Agricultural College of South Carolina (Clemson University), which regularly impacts Pickens and provides educational opportunities throughout the world. (Photo courtesy of Clemson University and the Strom Thurmond Institute.)

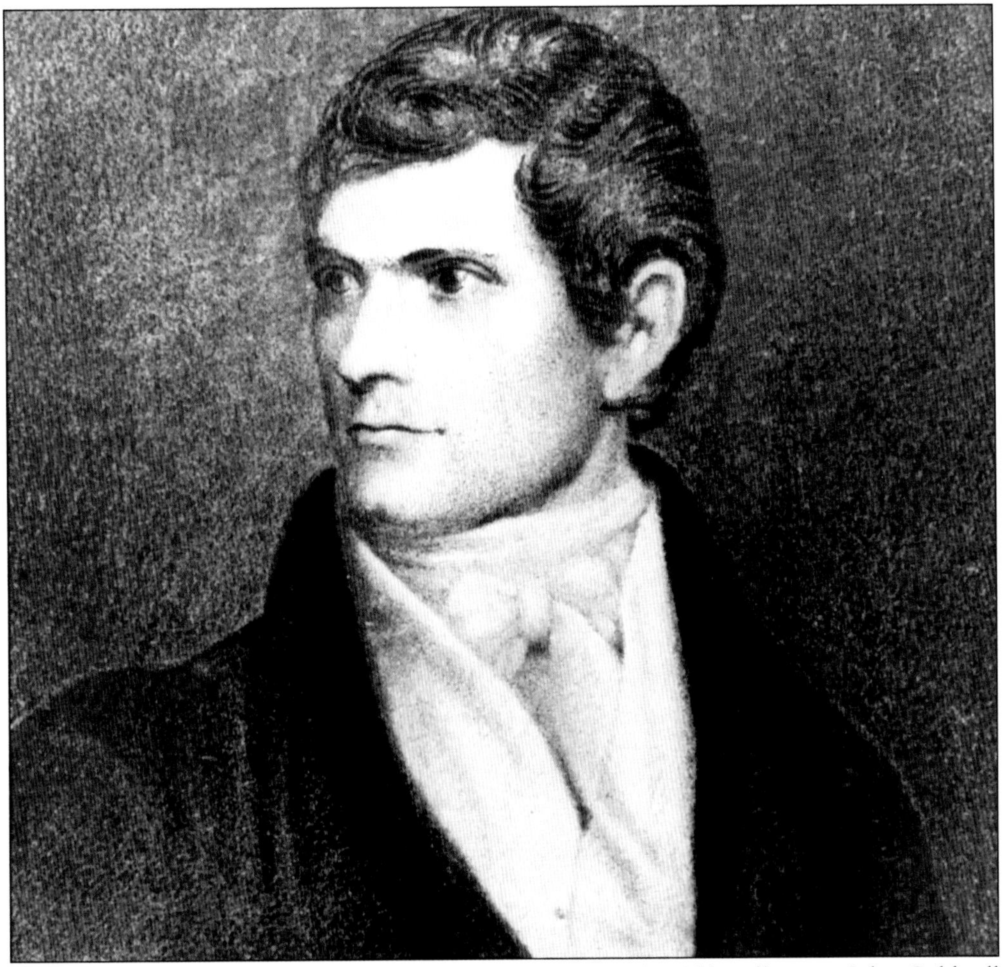

John Caldwell Calhoun's Portrait. Born in 1782 in the Abbeville area, John Caldwell Calhoun entered Yale as a junior in 1804. He studied law, and prior to his death in 1850, Calhoun served as a congressman (1811–1817), secretary of war (1817–1825), vice president of the United States (1825–1832), senator (1832–1843 and 1845–1850), and secretary of state (1844–1845). In 1810 Calhoun led a group of Congressmen referred to as the "War Hawks." In 1812 their enemy became England and Canada. The U.S. failed to invade Canada, but a nationalist mood swept the country, and Calhoun and William Lowndes convinced Congress to pass the Tariff of 1816, a tax created to protect infant northern industries until the United States became a self-sufficient society. By the mid-1820s, the growing number of tariffs issued to benefit northern industrialists outraged Carolina planters. To fuel their fury, cotton lands in the southwest expanded. Carolina farmers witnessed cotton prices shrink from 31¢ a pound in 1818 to 8¢ a pound in 1831. South Carolina's wealth declined, and Calhoun became troubled by the Tariff of 1828. Convinced that the Tariff of 1828 was unconstitutional, Vice President Calhoun backed the Theory of Nullification and sought a method of amendment as a way to save the Union. He found none, and died prior to the Civil War. The war and its economic depression squelched Calhoun's 1836 plans to complete a railroad system through the hills and valleys of Pickens, which included present-day Oconee. John C. Calhoun is buried at St. Philip's Churchyard in Charleston. (Photo courtesy of the South Caroliniana Library, University of South Carolina, Columbia.)

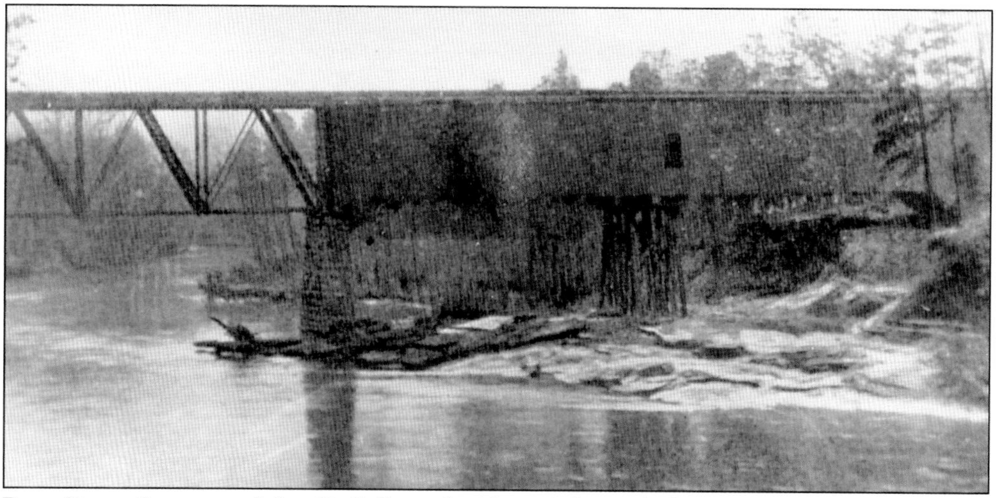

Blue Ridge Railroad. John C. Calhoun had hoped that rails from Charleston to Cincinnati would pass through the Pickens District. In 1852 the Charleston City Council approved funds for the newly chartered Blue Ridge Railroad. In 1854 the South Carolina General Assembly authorized $1 million for the project with the promise of additional funds to come during the construction phase. Construction began November 1853, but only 45 miles of track and 3 tunnels were built. Remnants of the line's right-of-way exist in Walhalla, S.C. This 1915 image depicts the dilapidated Blue Ridge Railroad Bridge spanning the Seneca River into Clemson territory. The Pickens Railroad Company would fare better than its predecessor. (Photo courtesy of PDHRT.)

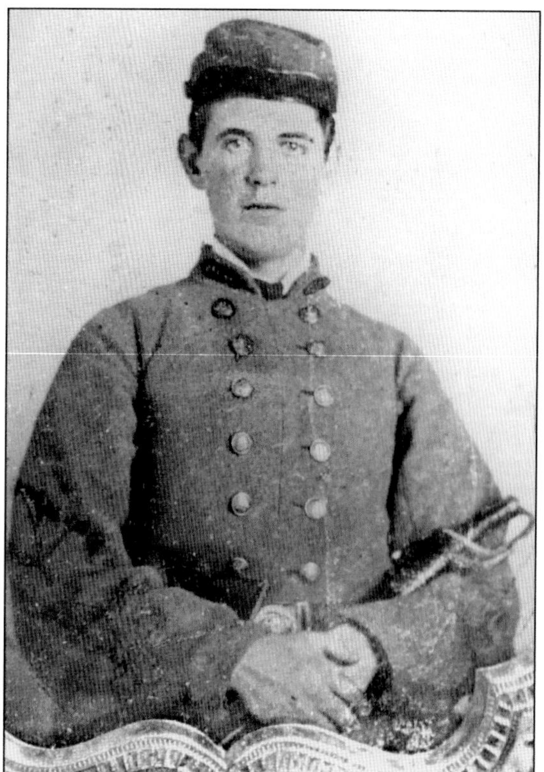

T.J. Holland, Confederate Soldier. In an effort to more efficiently serve the demands of a growing population, the state legislature divided the Pendleton District in 1826. The southeastern half became present-day Anderson County. The northern section was called Pickens,with a courthouse erected on the west bank of the Keowee River. When T.J. Holland fought for the Confederacy, Pickens County would have included territory within present-day Oconee County. The Civil War left Pickens County destitute despite the fact that northern troops did not regularly occupy the lands. (Photo courtesy of PDHRT.)

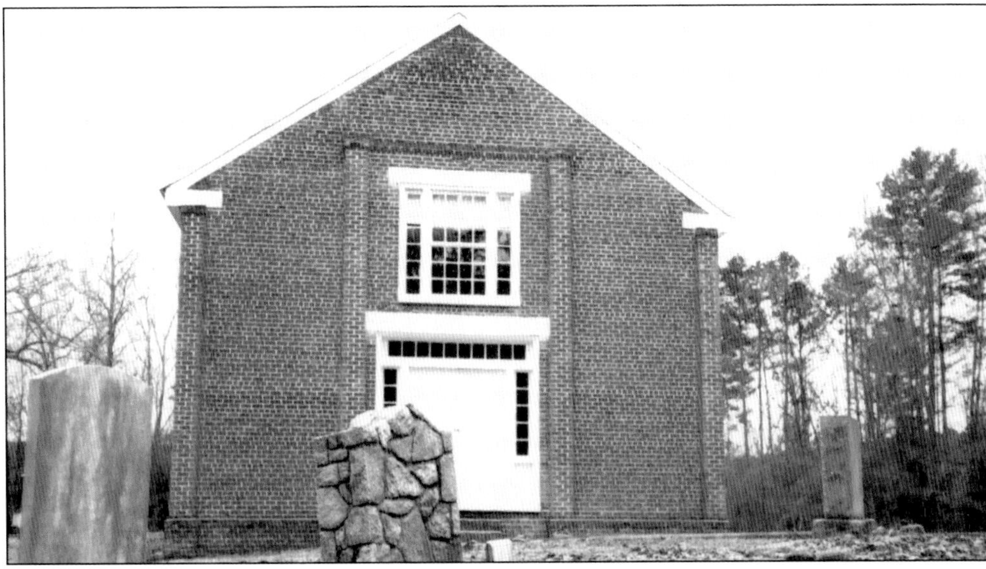

OLD PICKENS PRESBYTERIAN CHURCH. On Highway 183 near the Oconee Nuclear Station stands Old Pickens Presbyterian Church, near the original site of Pickens Courthouse (Old Pickens), a town incorporated in 1847. With the dividing of Pickens into Pickens County and Oconee County in 1868, Old Pickens residents moved 14 miles east. They abandoned a courthouse, several hostelries, and the church pictured here that was built between 1849 and 1851. Many structures associated with Old Pickens have been demolished or relocated, but the brick church, now renovated, still stands on its original foundation in the woodlands that protect the cemetery. Pioneers have been laid to rest in the cemetery. Some were relocated out of Craig cemetery, a graveyard inundated in 1968 when man-made Lake Keowee was formed. The church and cemetery are now in Oconee County. (Photo by P.E. Peters.)

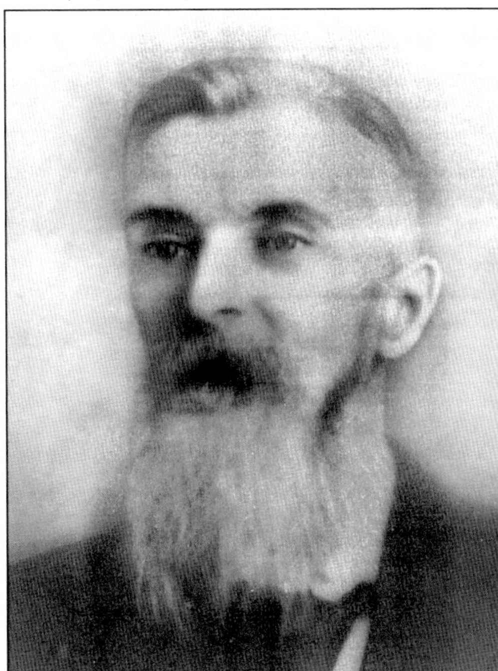

PORTRAIT OF E. SMITH GRIFFIN. Elihu Smith Griffin was the son of Elihu Griffin (1800–1877), a farmer with large land holdings between present-day Easley, Pickens, and Liberty. Smith Griffin served in the 4th Georgia Calvary under Colonel Avery. Smith Griffin survived 4 years of turmoil to marry Sarah Mildred in 1867. Eventually, Smith Griffin became a county commissioner and assisted in the planning and the construction of the Pickens County Court House built in the 1890s. An oil painting of Elihu Griffin is housed at the Pickens County Museum. (Photo courtesy of the Pickens County Library.)

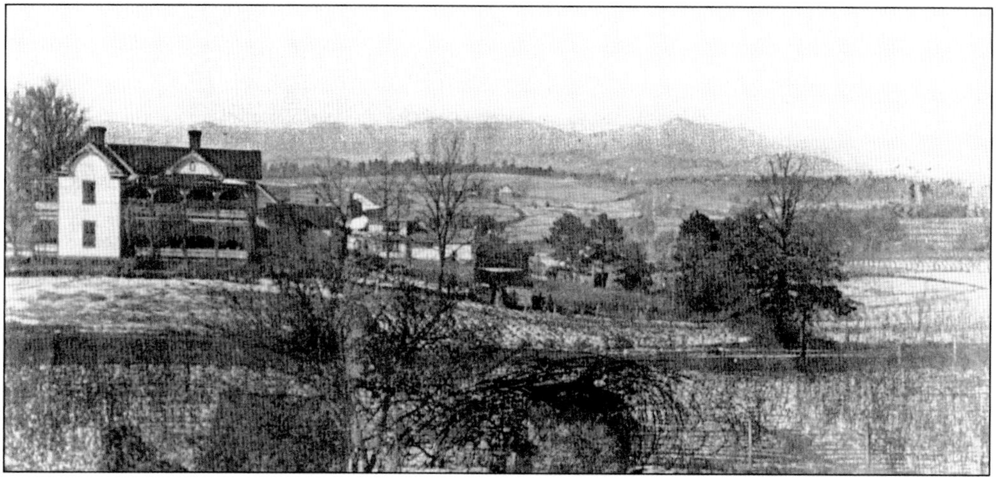

Griffin Homestead. State delegates of the 1868 Constitutional Convention passed an ordinance dividing Pickens into two counties, and therefore new government headquarters had to be chosen. In May, Oconee's Board of Commissioners designated Walhalla, founded in 1850, as that county's seat. Pickens County Commissioners, however, abandoned Old Pickens. They selected this frontier farm, property of Elihu Griffin, as the location for a new courthouse town. Town Creek was nearby, and Elihu H. Griffin received $270 for 94 acres. J. Fergerson (Ferguson) sold 18 acres for $18, W.B. Allgood sold 15 acres for $75, and W.G. Blassingame sold 24 acres for $125. The combined acreage created 151 acres of adjoining land suitable for a new county seat. The Elihu Griffin House at the left still stands on Ann Street in the city of Pickens. (Photo courtesy of the Pickens County Library.)

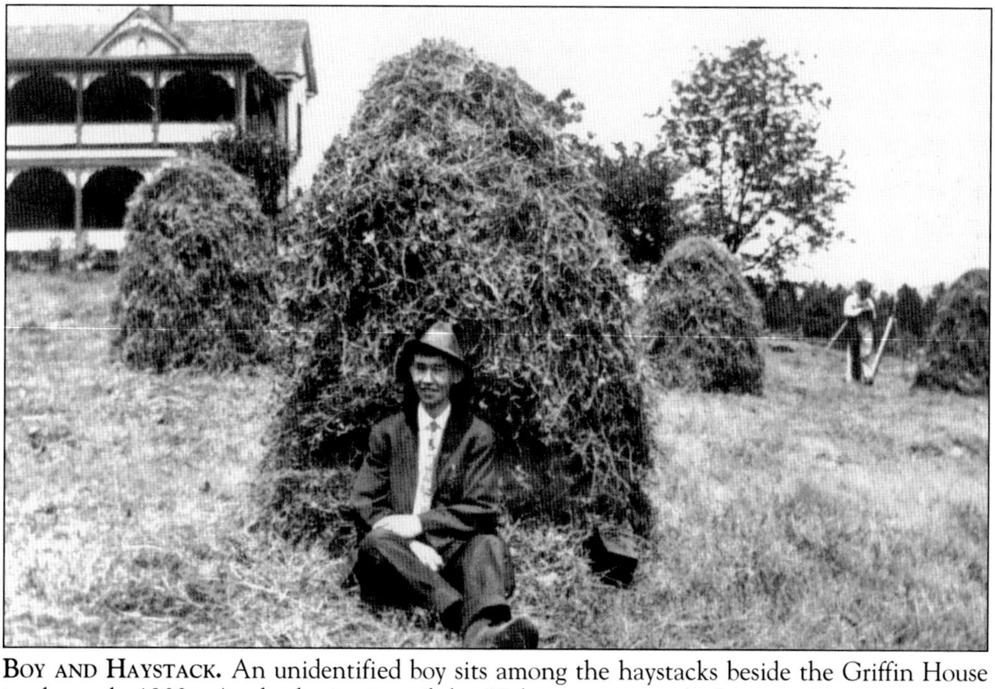

Boy and Haystack. An unidentified boy sits among the haystacks beside the Griffin House in the early 1900s. At the beginning of the 20th century, costly farm machinery remained unobtainable for landowners. Many farmers would not utilize hay bailers until the mid-1950s. (Photo courtesy of PDHRT and the Pickens County Library.)

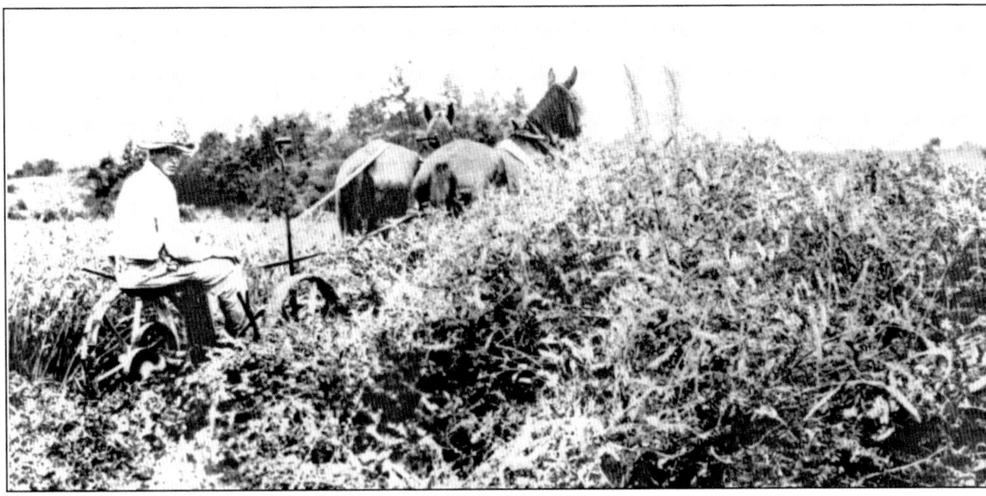

Jenkins and Hay Per Acre. The new county of Pickens relied on an agrarian economy dependent on the family farm. Mike Jenkins apparently succeeded more than most for the photographer noted on the image that Mike produced more hay per acre than any other Pickens County farmer. (Photo courtesy of the Pickens County Library.)

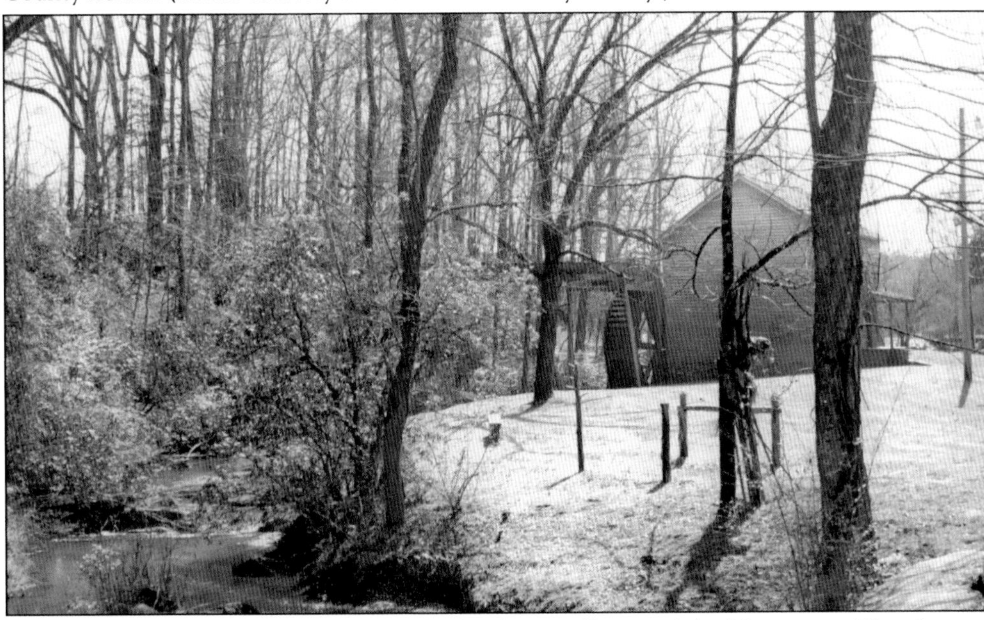

Hagood Gristmill. At one time, hundreds of gristmills served the Upcountry. They hugged the creeks of Pickens County, providing gathering places for locals to discuss the latest community news as corn was processed. Today, many of these gristmills lie in ruins. Few of the mills were as grand as Hagood Mill (pictured) or the Golden Creek Mill. Privately owned Golden Creek Mill is located on Enon Church Road not far from S.C. 8 and Easley. Hagood Mill, on U.S. 178, is 2 miles north of the city of Pickens. In 1845 Hagood Mill began operating beside a tributary of the Twelve Mile River. It has a wooden water wheel, 20 feet in diameter and 4 feet wide, which produces 22 horsepower of energy. The two granite millstones weigh approximately 1,600 pounds. Hagood Mill, which temporarily closed in the 1960s, has reopened to the public. Volunteers and members of the Pickens County Museum maintain it. (Photo by P.E. Peters.)

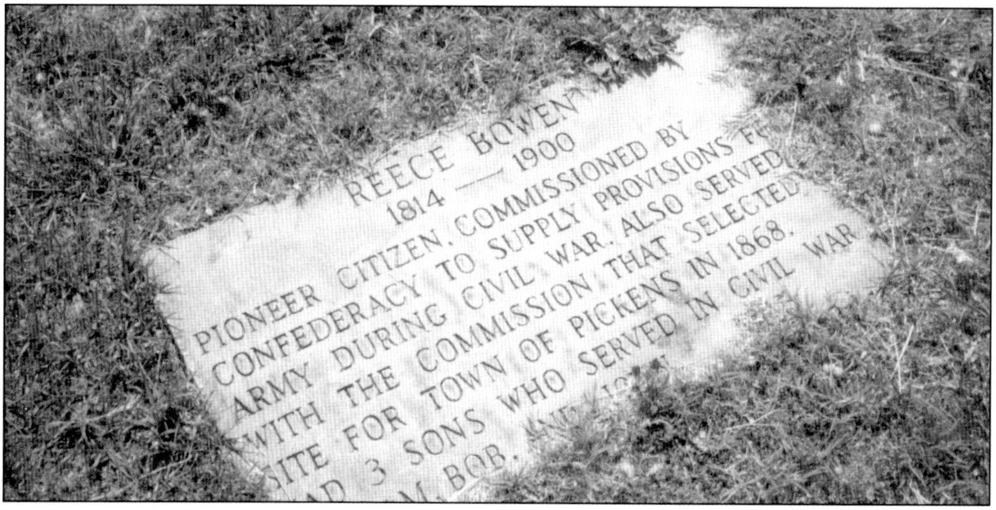

Reece Bowen Marker. Reece Bowen (1814–1900), a pioneer citizen commissioned by the Confederacy to supply provisions for troops during the Civil War, found his family, especially his three sons, in a conflict that would ultimately change Pickens County forever. In 1868 Bowen assisted the commissioners in relocating Pickens to its present site near the Bowen House on Ireland Road. Likewise, Robert A. Bowen (1843–1927) served in the Confederacy. He became Pickens County clerk of court in 1868. He was also the postmaster for the new town. (Photo by P.E. Peters.)

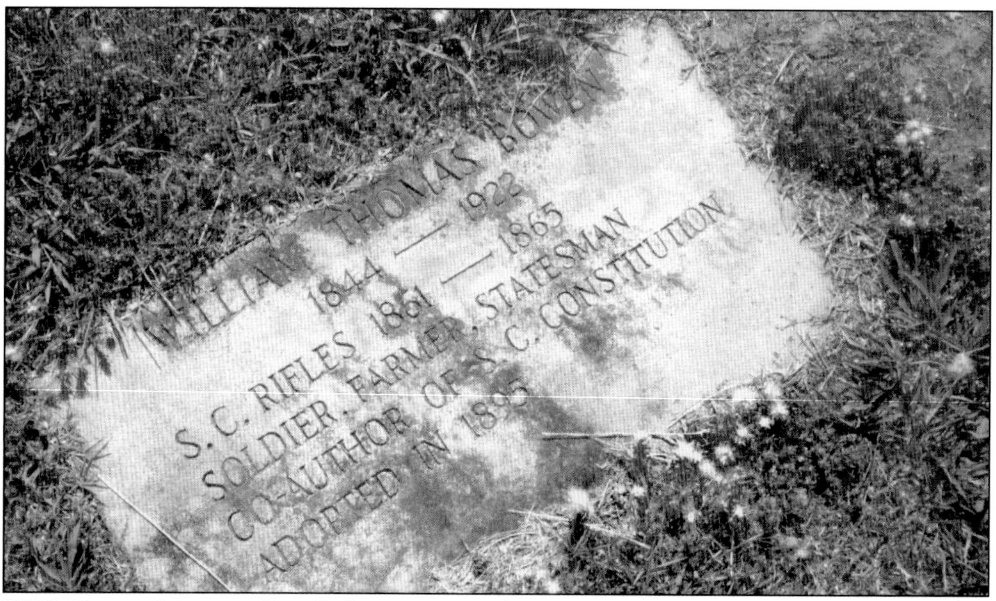

W.T. Bowen Marker. Ben Robertson's grandfather was W.T. Bowen (1844–1922). W.T. Bowen, a soldier, farmer, and statesmen, co-authored the South Carolina Constitution, which was adopted in 1895. Ben Robertson wrote in *Red Hills and Cotton*, "We are farmers, all Democrats and Baptists—a strange people, complicated and simple and proud and religious and family-loving, a divorceless, Bible-reading, murdersome lot of folks, all of us rich in ancestry and emotionally quick on the trigger." Robertson's manuscripts, letters, momentos, and photographs are a part of the special collections at the Strom Thurmond Institute in Clemson. (Photo by P.E. Peters.)

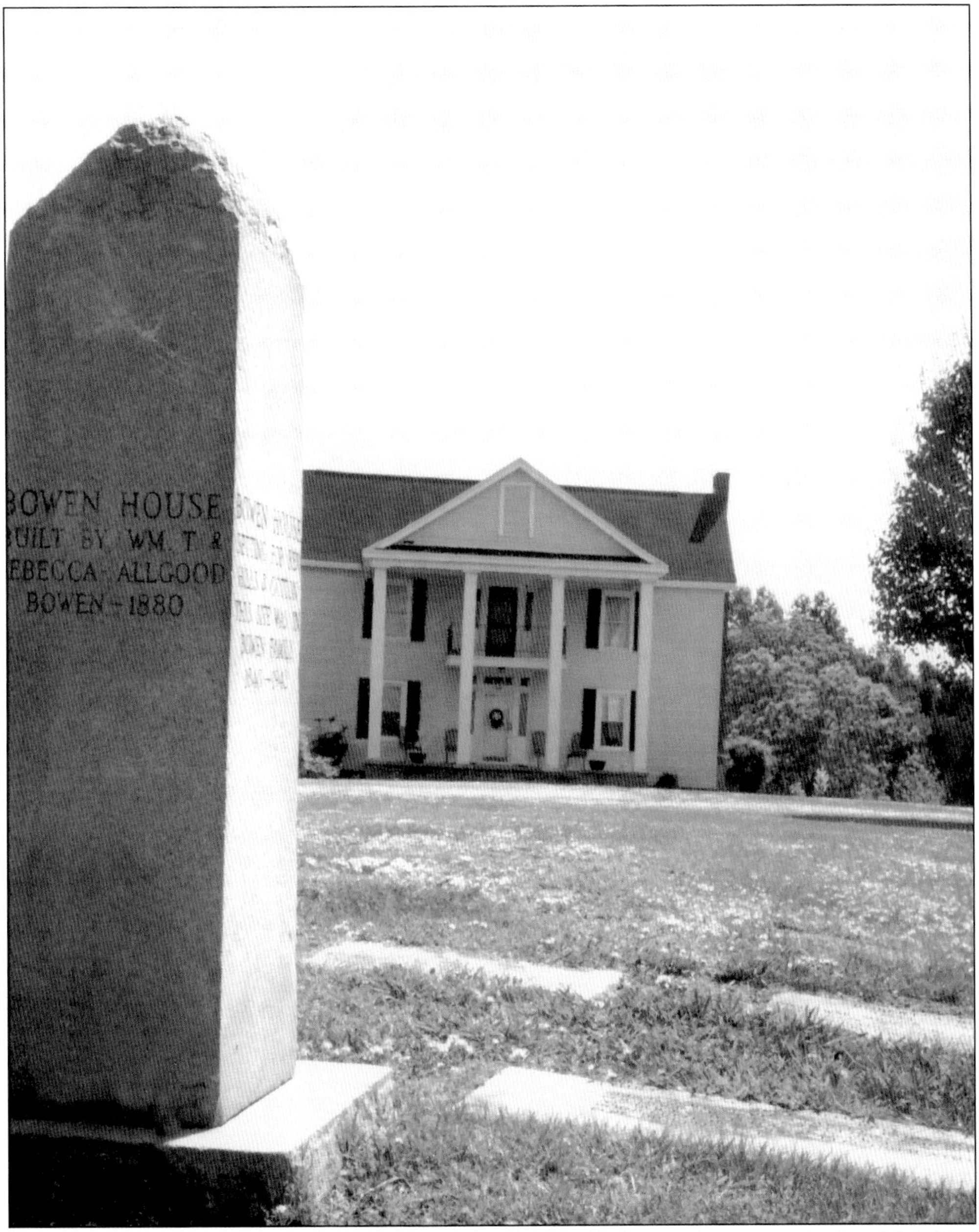

Bowen House on Ireland Street. After journalist Ben Robertson's mother died in 1910, Ben and his sister were placed in the home of Wade C. O'Dell (Uncle Wade and Aunty Betty), but it would be this rural estate, the Bowen House, that Ben would describe in his 1940s memoir *Red Hills and Cotton*. Located between the city of Pickens and Easley on Ireland Road, the Bowen Homestead, built by William Thomas and Rebecca Allgood Bowen, operates much like it did when it was constructed in the Tabor Community in the 1880s. The house remains a privately owned farm with a hilltop view of Table Rock and Glassy Mountains. On the site there are several markers that indicate the various contributions of the Bowen family to Pickens County. Many of the Bowens and the Robertsons are buried in the nearby town of Liberty. (Photo by P.E. Peters.)

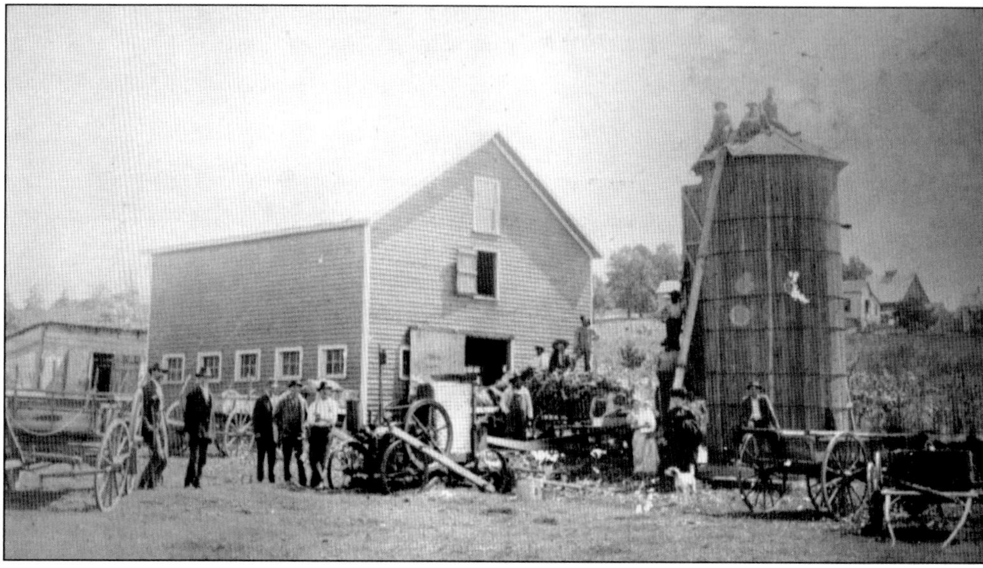

Palmetto Stock Farm. Cutting ensilage, or the process of preserving fodder in a silo, was a common sight at the beginning of the 20th century. T.B. Higgins, owner of the Palmetto Stock Farm in Easley, S.C., takes time to pose with his well-dressed family and his farm employees. (Photo courtesy of Pickens County Museum.)

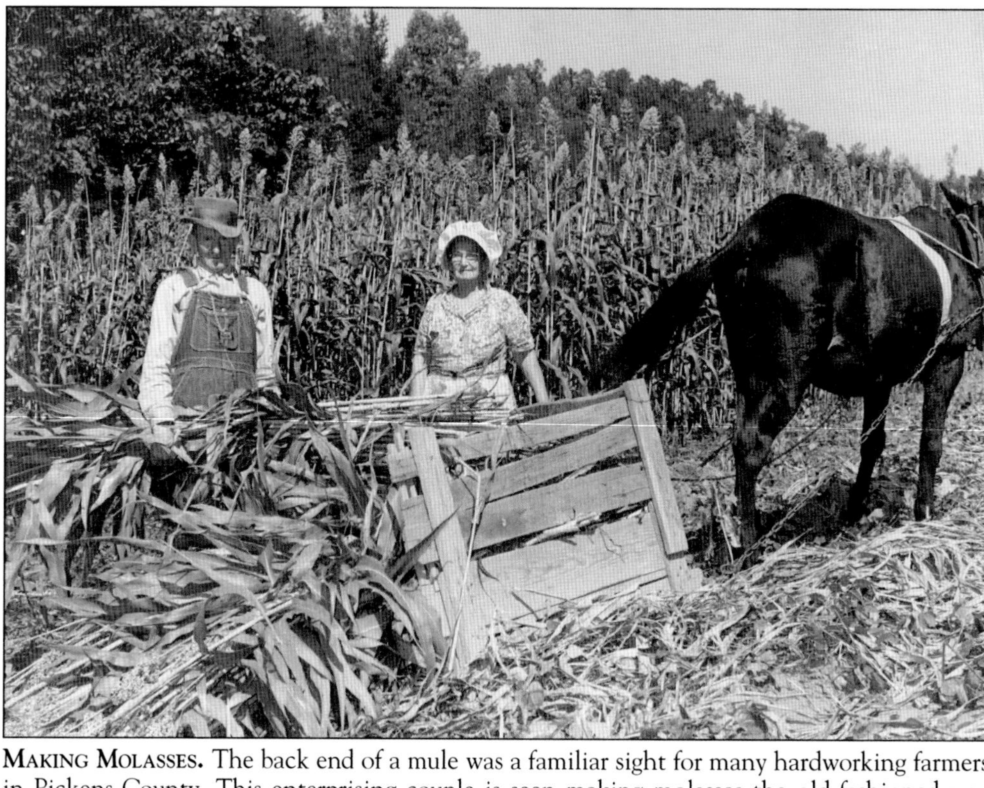

Making Molasses. The back end of a mule was a familiar sight for many hardworking farmers in Pickens County. This enterprising couple is seen making molasses the old-fashioned way during the 1960s. Farming in Pickens County might have been hard, but it was rewarding work. (Photo by William E. Payne.)

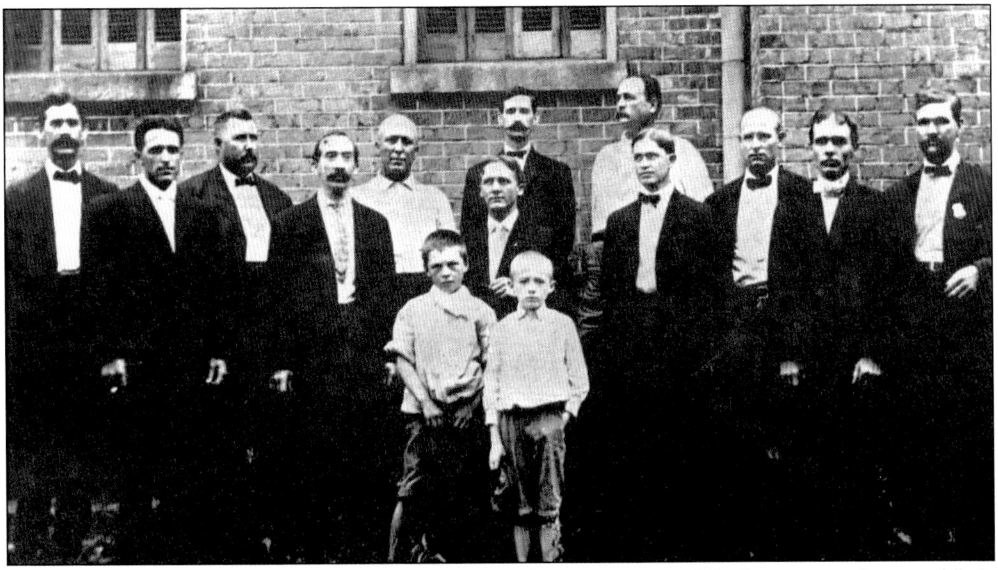

TOWN OFFICIALS. Founded as the county seat, the new town of Pickens was chartered July 27, 1868, according to town hall records. The courthouse and jail were built on land once owned by Elihu Griffin. By 1909, small businesses had set up shop in the new town and Old Pickens had been abandoned. Pictured here, from left to right, are the following city officials of 1909: J.A. Peek, Dr. J.L. Valley, Dr. F.S. Porter, B.F. Parsons, W.T. Jones, J.R. Ashmore, Mayor B.B. Laboon (in bowtie with mustache), J.F. Harris (in solid white shirt), L.F. Robinson, G.W. Corbin, J.N. Hallum, and H.A. Nealy, the chief of police. The children remain unidentified. (Photo courtesy of the Pickens County Library and *The Pickens Sentinel.*)

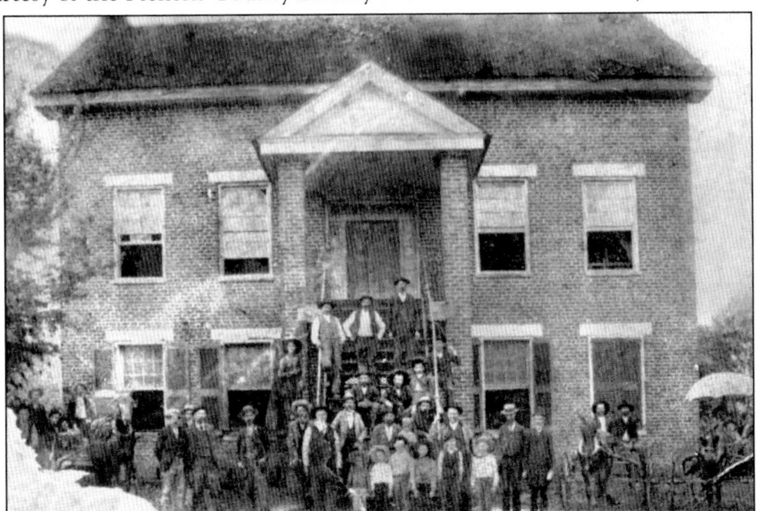

FIRST COURTHOUSE. The first county courthouse, erected between 1868 and 1869, was architecturally simplistic and functional in design. The courthouse, professionally photographed here in 1891 by A.D. Young of Easley, was a vital part of the new county's growth after the Civil War. Some documents and land grants issued prior to 1868 were, and continue to be, housed in Oconee County, despite legislative acts that have significantly redefined the upstate area and the counties of Oconee and Pickens. (Photo courtesy of the PDHRT and Jerry Alexander.)

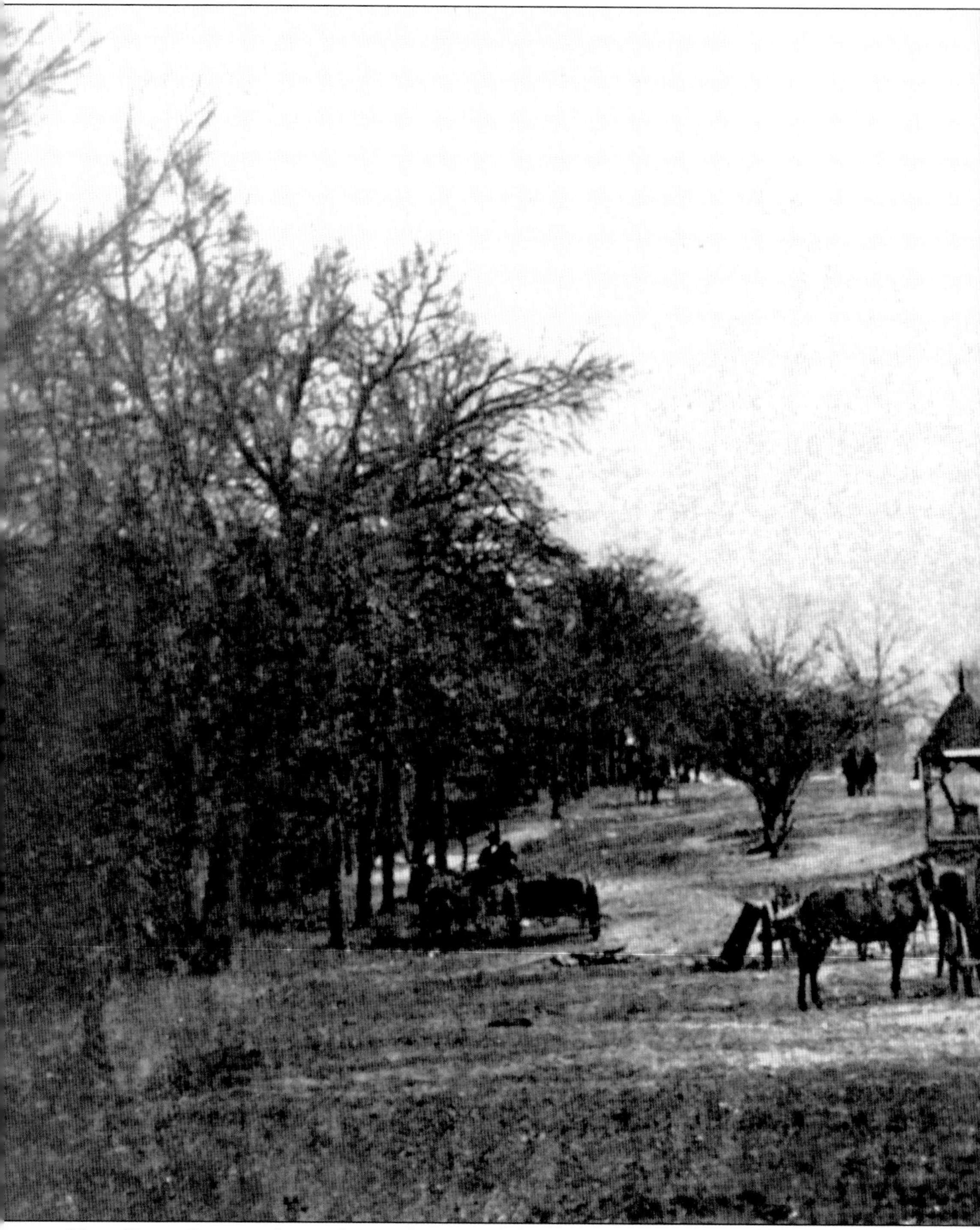

New Town Pickens. Located 14 miles east of the Keowee River, the new city of Pickens thrived near Town Creek as depicted in this 1907 view of Main Street facing east toward

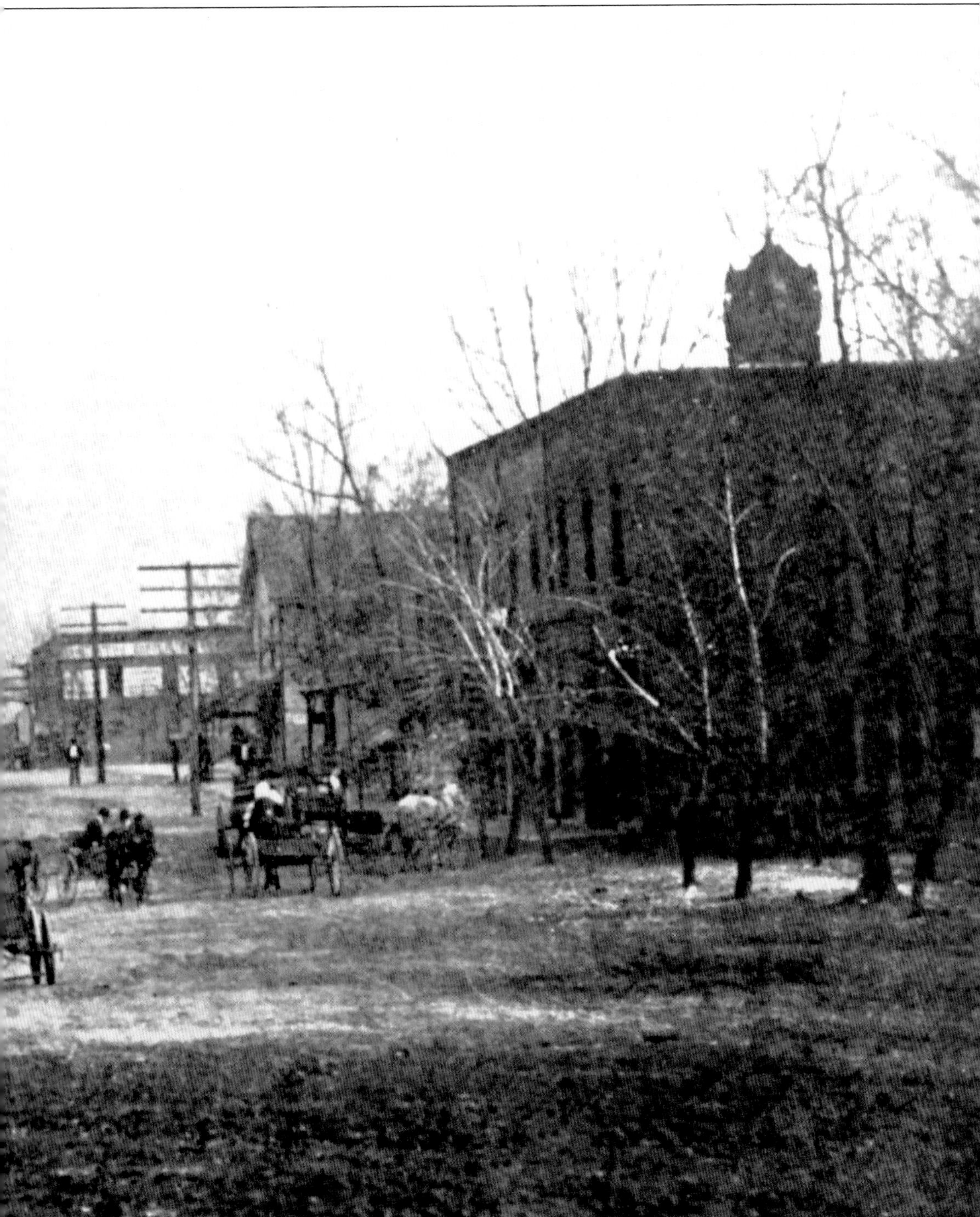

the city of Greenville, S.C.. At the right is the steeple of the second Pickens County Courthouse. (Photo courtesy of the South Caroliniana Library, USC, Columbia.)

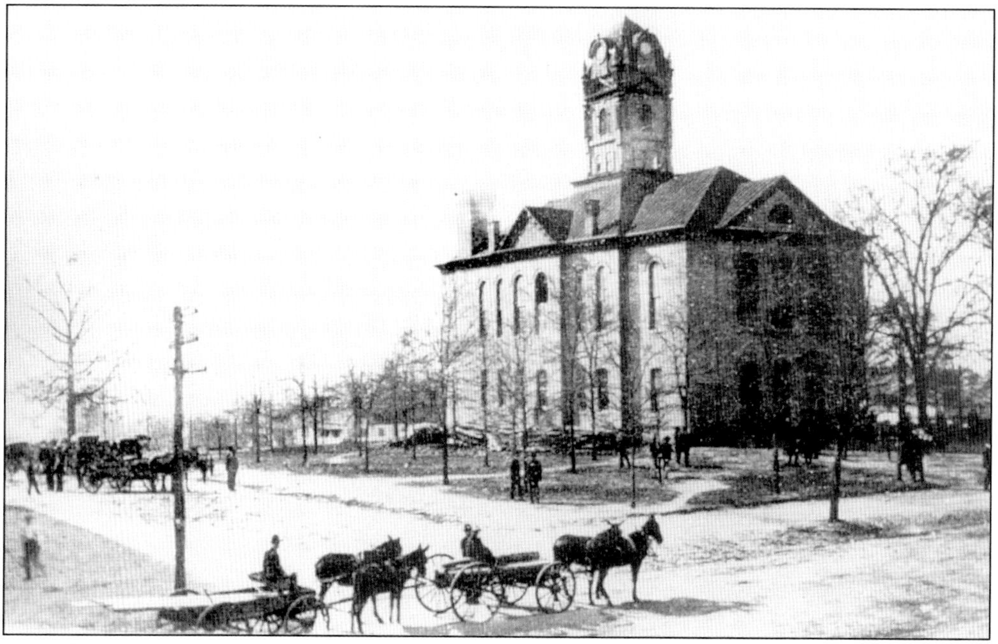

The Second Courthouse. Erected from 1891 to 1892, the second Pickens County Courthouse dominated the agricultural landscape until 1959. At the left is Court Street, which opened in 1893, and at the rear of the courthouse is the sheriff's cottage, which was built five years later. Horse and buggies, visible in the foreground, lumber along Main Street. (Photo courtesy of the PDHRT.)

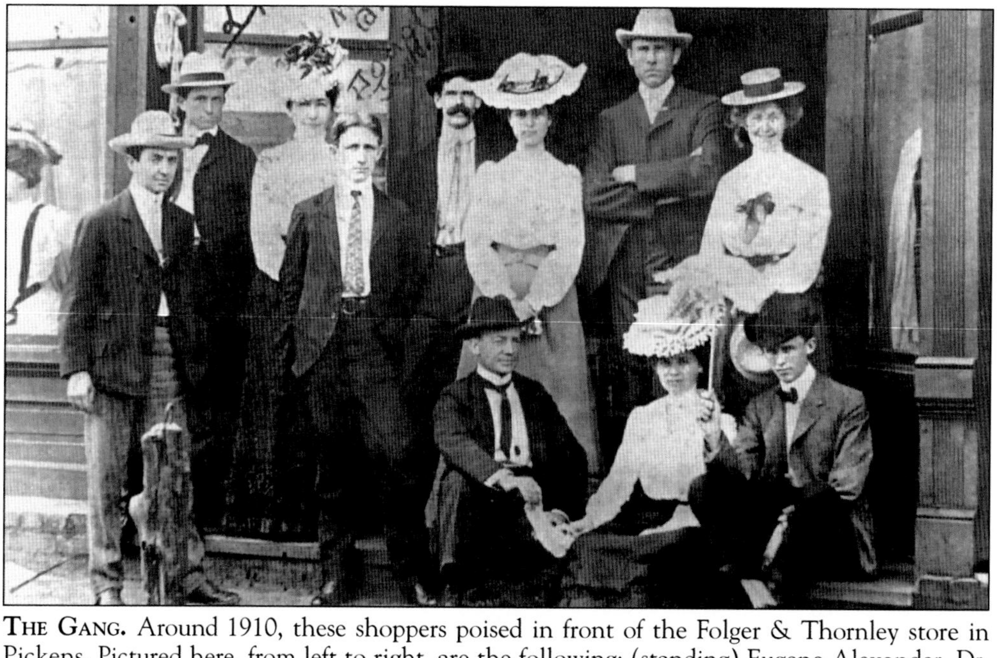

The Gang. Around 1910, these shoppers poised in front of the Folger & Thornley store in Pickens. Pictured here, from left to right, are the following: (standing) Eugene Alexander, Dr. Earle Russell, Miss Nita Ambler, Douglas Jenkins, Dr. A.B. Wardlaw, R.E. Bruce (Big Bruce), and Miss Clovie Griffin; (seated) Bill Ambler, an unidentified lady with her parasol, and Mr. Bertrand Thornley. (Photo courtesy of the Pickens County Library.)

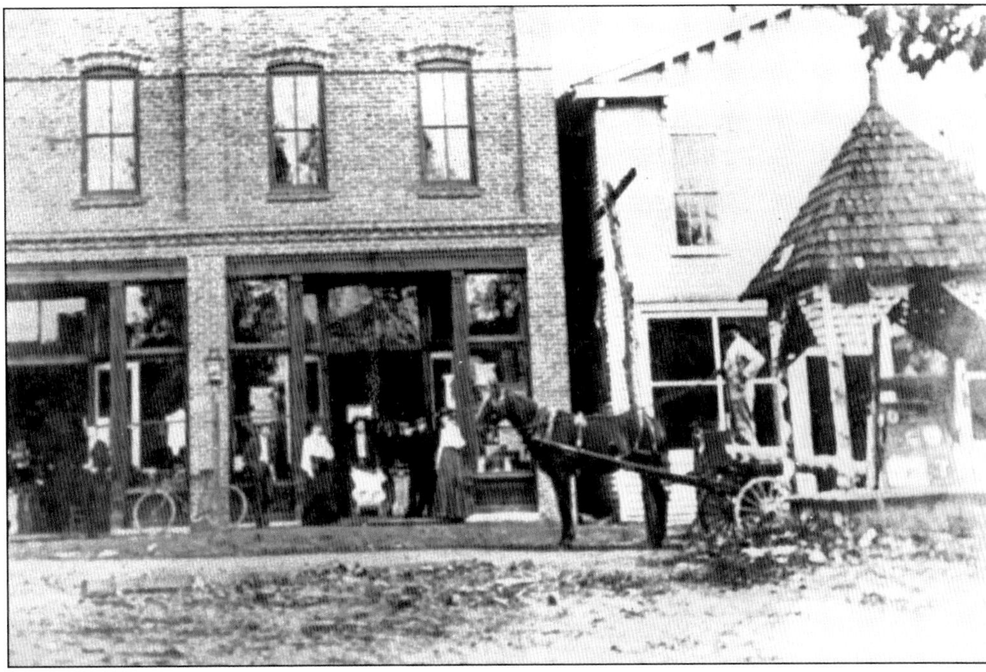

Horse in front of Store. This view features the popular Pickens mercantile firm of Folger & Thornley. At the right of the image is the white building that housed the firm of Hagood, Alexander and Company. It also housed Alexander and Folger. A well was dug in 1884 and sits in front of the white building with its 1890s shelter protecting the waters. The brick structure at the left was erected in 1903. (Photo courtesy of PDHRT.)

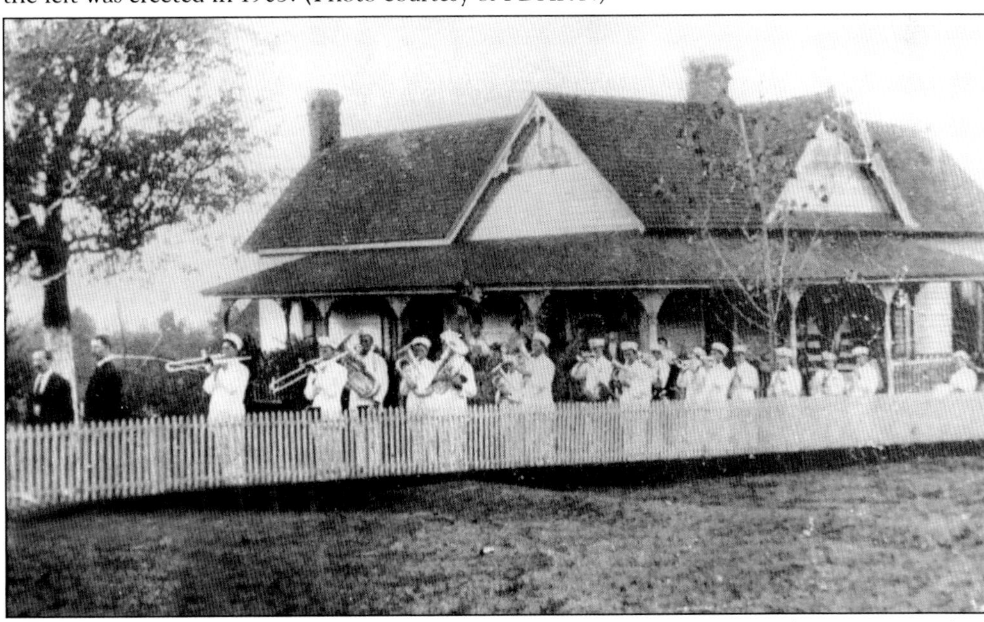

Band. At the beginning of the 20th century, the city of Pickens was a happy, noisy place, especially during the days of the fair. The Piedmont Band is shown playing at the residence of B.F. Parsons during the Pickens County Fair on September 22, 1909. (Photo courtesy of PDHRT.)

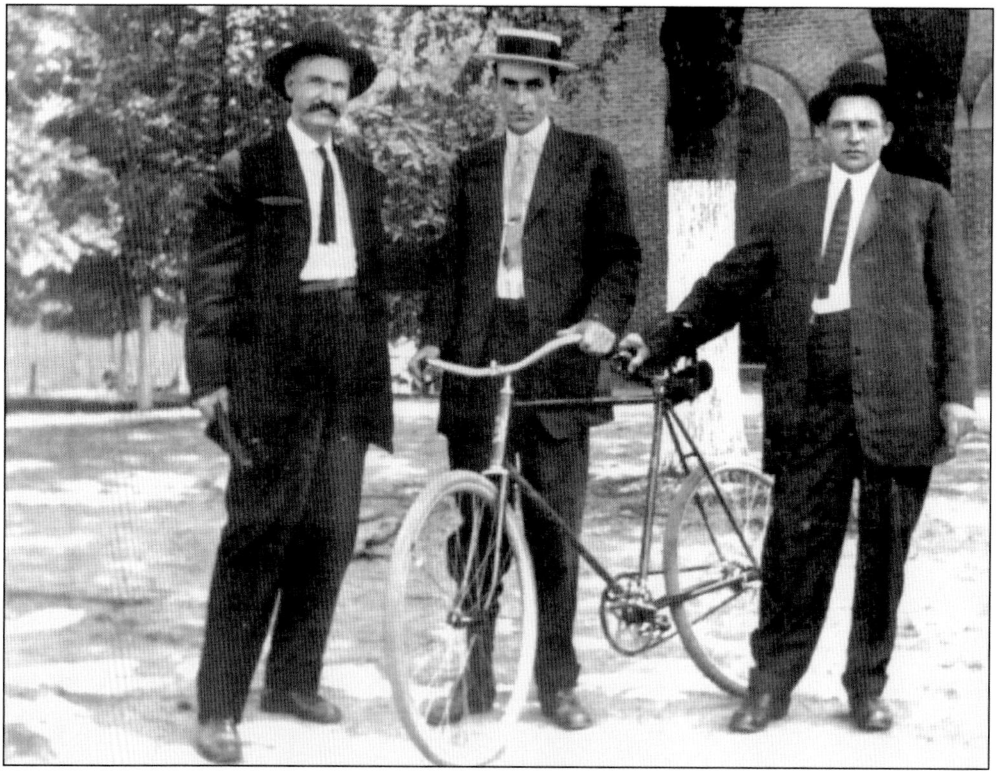

THREE MEN AND A BIKE. Chief H.A. Nealy, Edwin Earle, and J. Hovie Earle pose with a bike in front of the second Pickens County Courthouse. In the early 1900s, county residents utilized wagons, horses, and the short-line train (called the Pickens Doodle) as their primary mode of transportation. (Photo courtesy of Pickens County Library.)

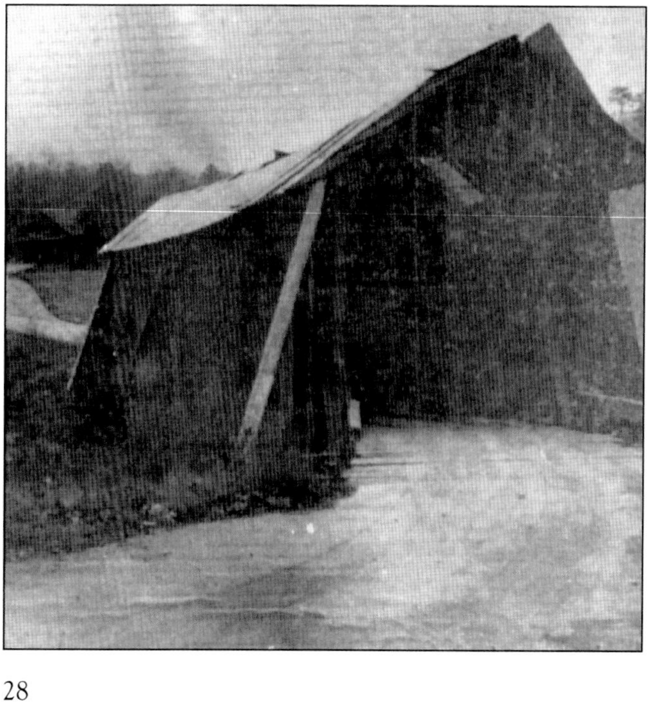

CATEECHEE COVERED BRIDGE. In 1895, the Cateechee Covered Bridge stretched across Twelve Mile River on Six Mile Road. By 1945, progress dictated its removal and the covered bridge was torn down. An iron bridge and a new road bypassing Cateechee replaced the covered bridge that evokes nostalgic memories for those romantics who remember Sunday afternoons here. (Photo courtesy of the Jerry Alexander.)

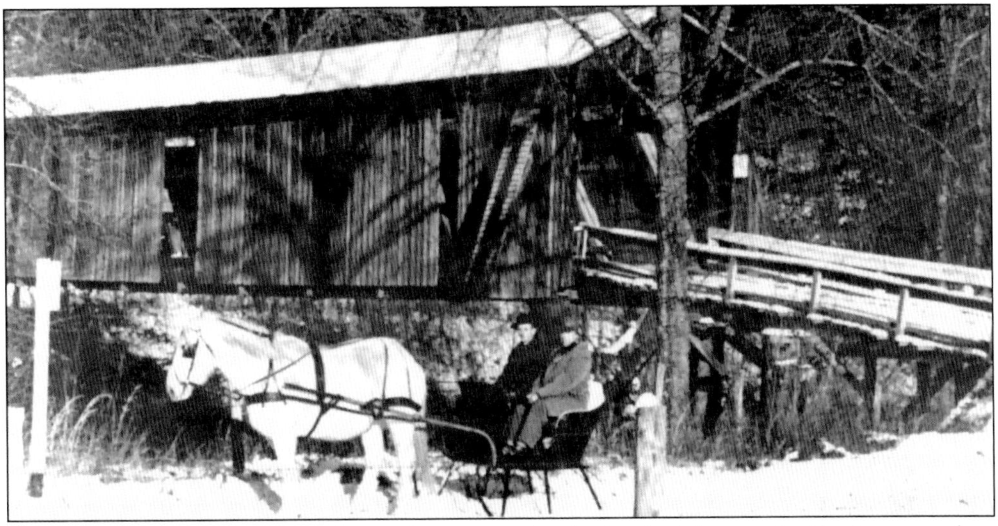

CHAPMAN COVERED BRIDGE IN SNOW. Pioneer settlers had to ford deep and wide rivers, so when a bridge was built, people considered it a monumental gift and appreciated the craftsmanship of the architects, who often worked with little money and few supplies. This is especially true of Chapman's Covered Bridge, which spanned the river Keowee between Oconee and Pickens County. The North Carolina Lake Toxaway Dam Burst of 1916 destroyed the first bridge, which was built in 1907. In the early 1920s, James B. Craig of Pickens contracted with Oconee and Pickens officials to rebuild the bridge. It was 14 feet wide, with a clearance of 12 feet, and rested on the metal foundations of the 1907 bridge until being relocated to the Keowee Toxaway State Park as a preservation effort. After the covered bridge was reassembled, it was vandalized and burned to the ground. Likewise, Chapman's Ford has disappeared, inundated as part of Duke Energy's Keowee-Toxaway. (Photo courtesy of the Pickens County Library.)

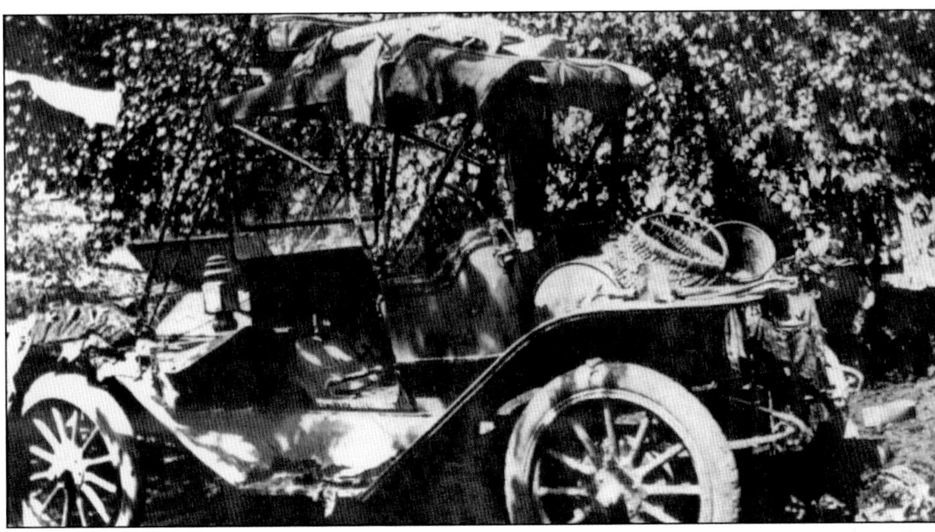

JALOPY. A North Carolina resort area lined the spine of the Blue Ridge Mountains along Route 64. It was called Toxaway or Lake Toxaway. The dam of Lake Toxaway burst on August 13, 1916, spilling floodwaters into the houses and businesses along various Pickens County waterways, rivulets, and creeks. Even the jalopies did not escape the cataclysm, which is well documented in family photos such as this one. (Photo courtesy of the Pickens County Library.)

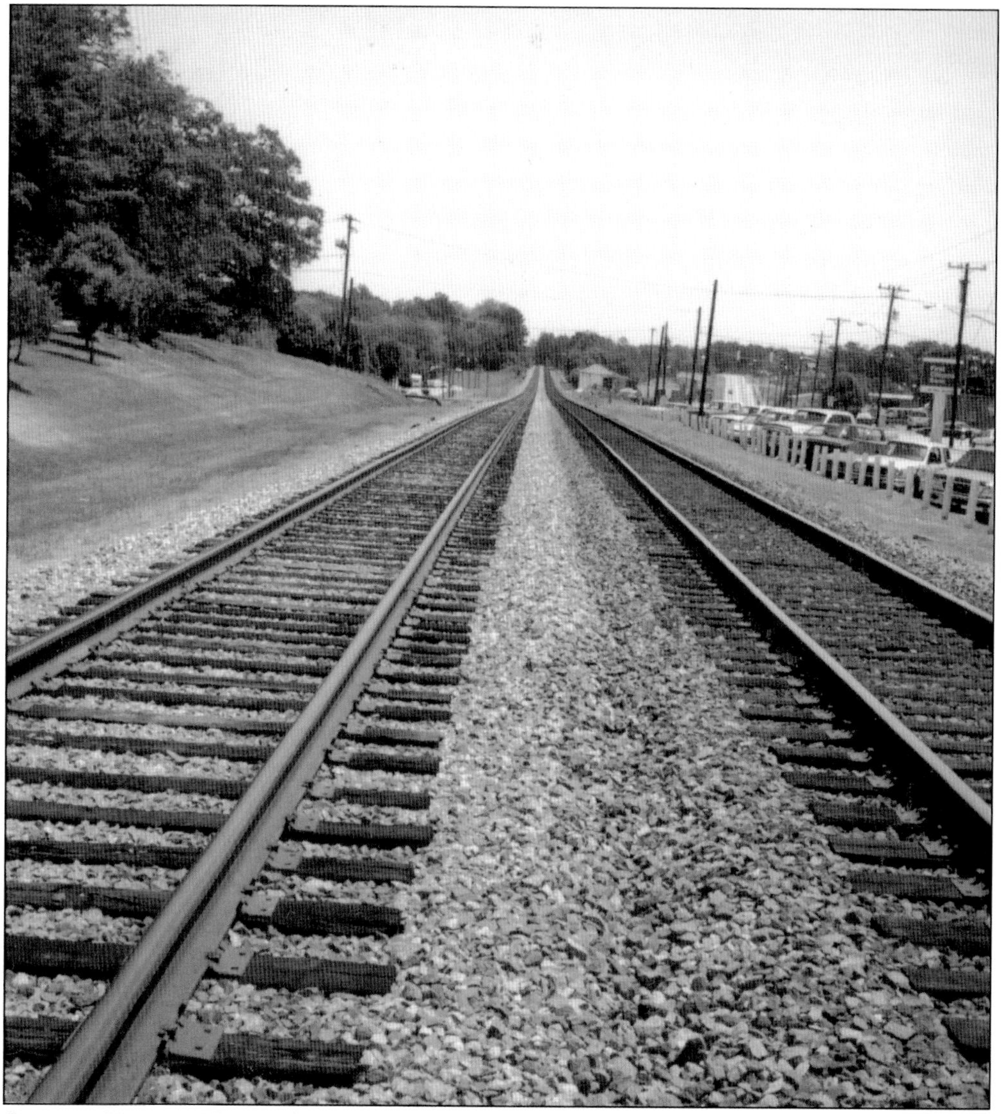

Central Tracks. Upstate farmers sent their crops, especially cotton, to Augusta in the 1830s. Once in Augusta, G.A., the products traveled down river to Savannah (Charleston's rival). To recover the market, Lowcountry investors created the successful 1833 "Best Friend" steam engine and the Charleston-Hamburg railroad. During the 1840s and 1850s, South Carolina legislators granted railroad charters, but few short lines were completed in the Upstate. The Civil War thwarted several developers' plans, and since each company had its own particular track gauge, an integrated Southern rail system did not truly exist until 1890. In the 1870s, the Atlanta and Charlotte Air Line Railroad (now the Southern Railway) began operating and the hamlets of Easley, Liberty, Central, Norris, and Calhoun (now Clemson) blossomed beside the railroad tracks. At the same time, the towns of Pickens, Six Mile, and Pumpkintown grew and by 1900 the county's population had reached 19,000. According to county records, Pickens County, largely an agrarian society at the beginning of the 20th century, could boast about a diversified economy with its 3 cotton mills, 2 railroads, 3 banks, 3 roller mills, 37 sawmills, 10 shingle mills, and 4 brickyards. (Photo by P.E. Peters.)

Two

Cities and Industries

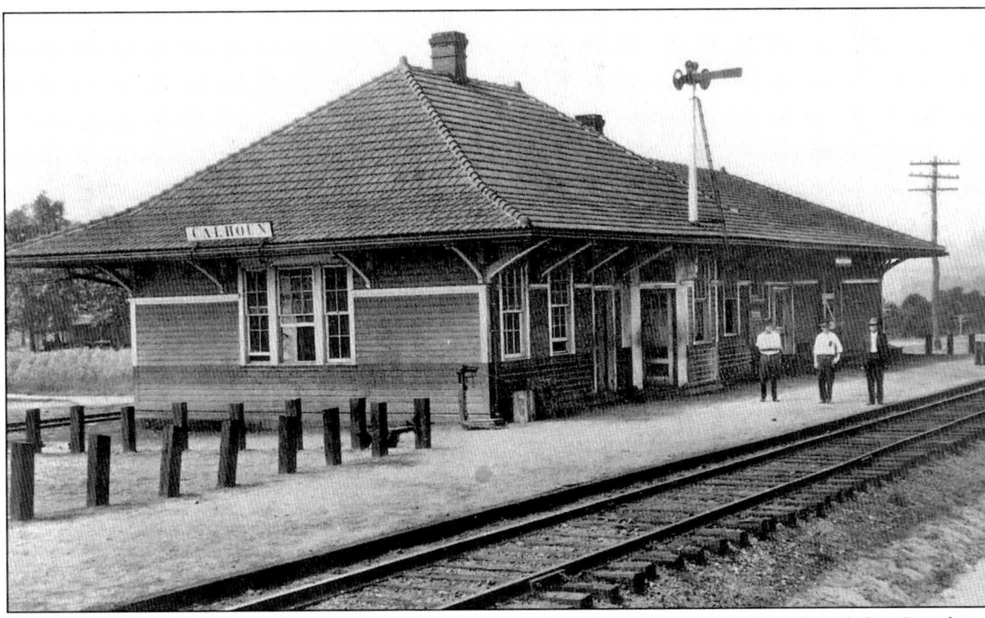

Calhoun Depot. The village of Calhoun started in 1872 on the north side of the Southern Railroad at a point about one mile east of the junction of the rivers Twelve Mile and Keowee. The town was chartered in 1892, but in 1943 its name was changed to the city of Clemson, which has grown in population and physical size along with the nearby university. (Photo courtesy of the South Caroliniana Library.)

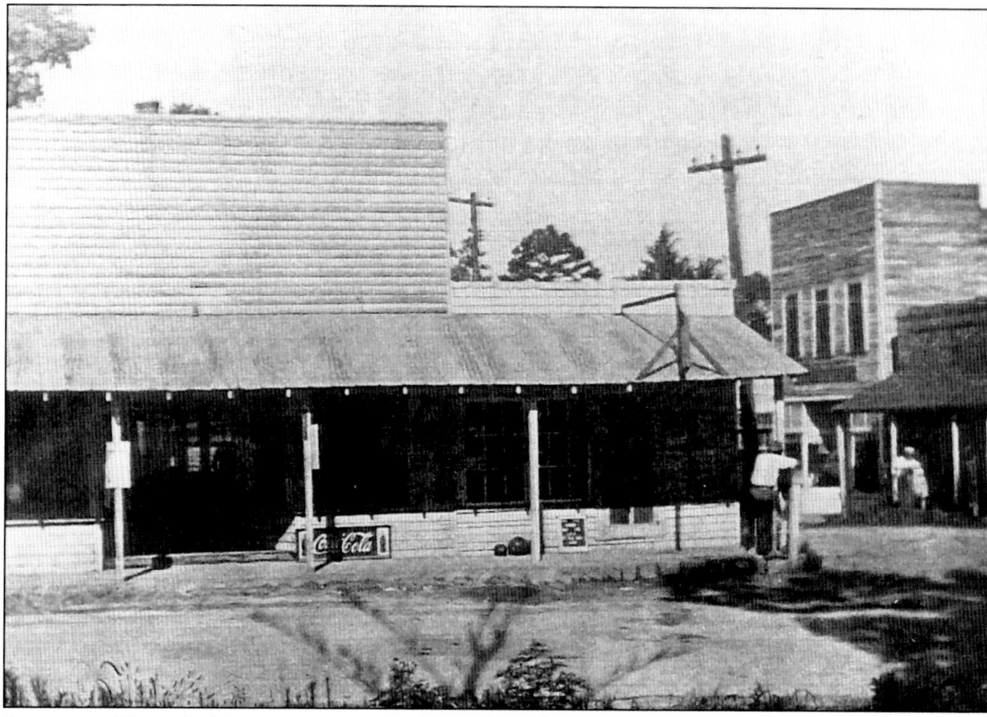

CALHOUN WAY. Calhoun was a quiet place when the all-male military school had no classes. Small shops served the cadets, but Clemson educators and their families generated the bulk of the retailer's sales. In time, the quaint business district would change as alumni and tourists visited the Upcountry. (Photo courtesy of the Pickens County Library.)

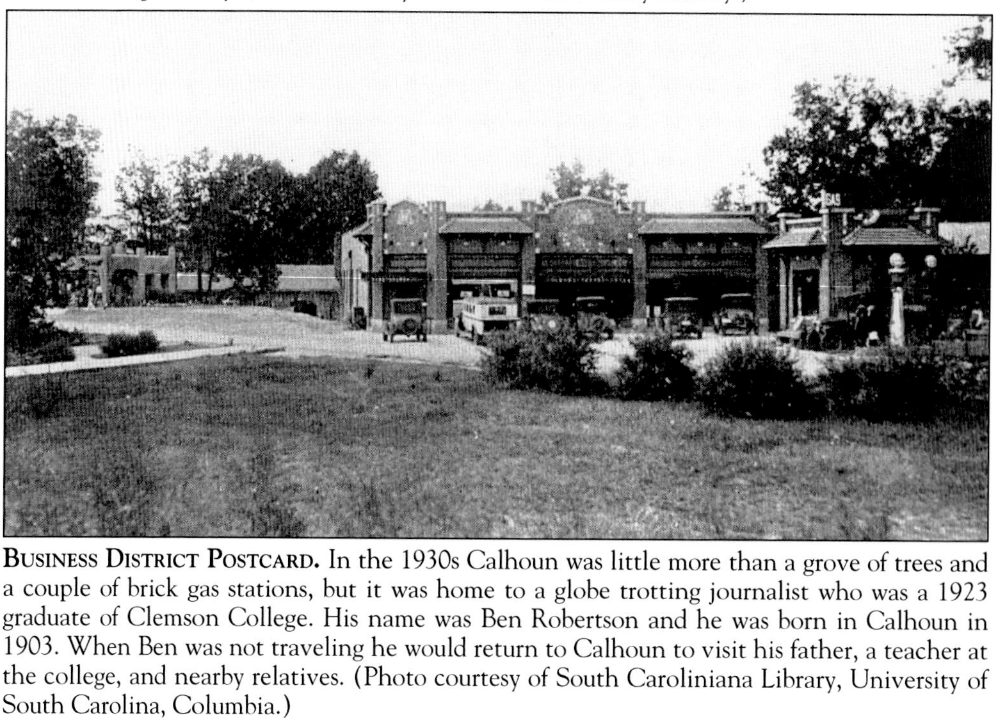

BUSINESS DISTRICT POSTCARD. In the 1930s Calhoun was little more than a grove of trees and a couple of brick gas stations, but it was home to a globe trotting journalist who was a 1923 graduate of Clemson College. His name was Ben Robertson and he was born in Calhoun in 1903. When Ben was not traveling he would return to Calhoun to visit his father, a teacher at the college, and nearby relatives. (Photo courtesy of South Caroliniana Library, University of South Carolina, Columbia.)

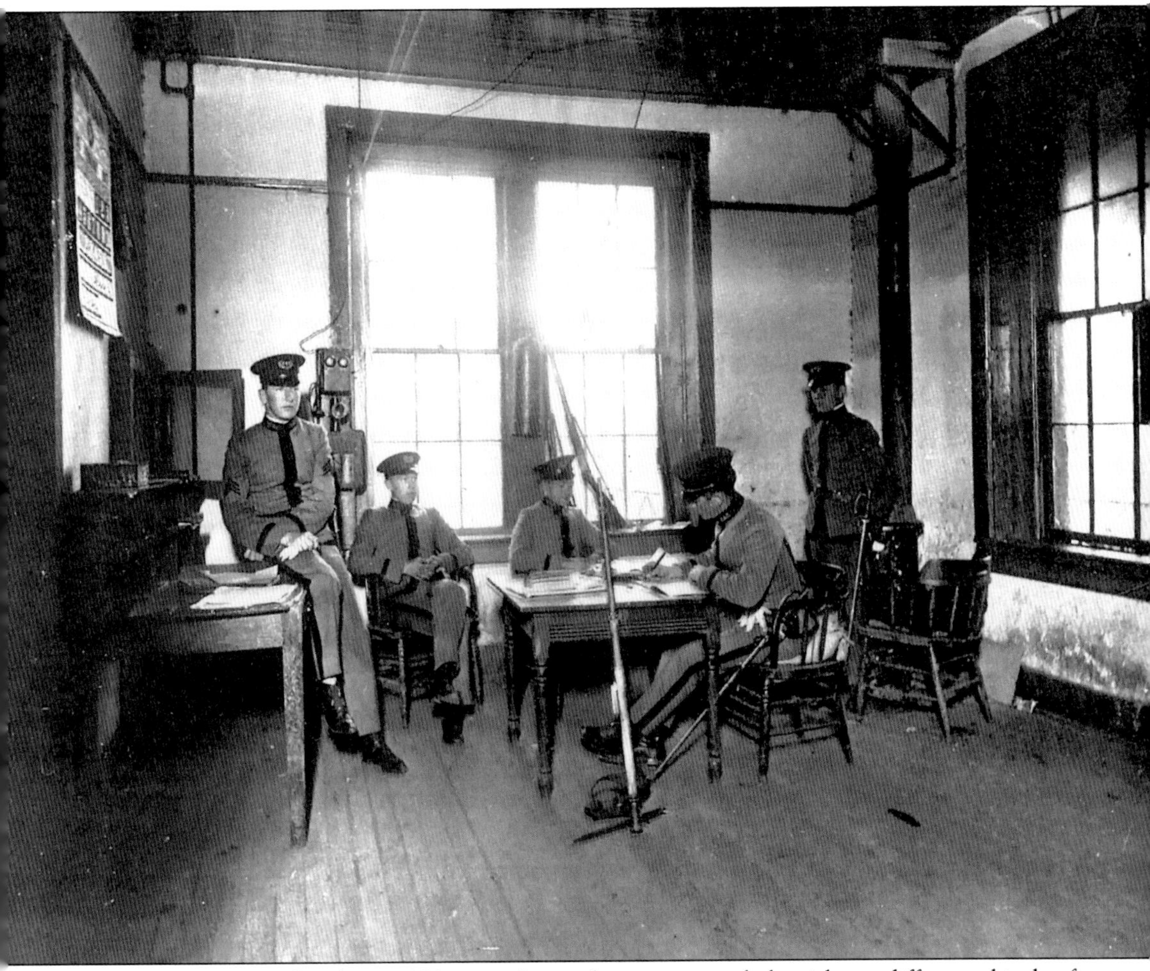

CADETS. During the late 1800s, southern farmers struggled with a different kind of slavery. Increasingly, they relied on a "crop-lien" system that financed much-needed supplies like fertilizers and seeds. Under this system, a farmer—whether a landowner or sharecropper—mortgaged an ungrown crop to a creditor for an indefinite amount. As a result, many farmers became "slaves" to banks or country stores. By the 1880s, two-thirds of Carolina croplands had been mortgaged. Thomas G. Clemson, a successful, highly educated farmer in his own right, believed scientific information would allow southern farmers to prosper. A tempestuous Gov. Benjamin R. Tillman, who had terms from 1890 to 1894, agreed. Like Clemson, Tillman was convinced that rural communities were significantly disabled without the latest technical and agricultural information. Tillman grumbled about The Citadel, a "dude school," and he severely criticized the pitiful agricultural programs at South Carolina College. He strongly supported the formation of Clemson Agricultural College, which opened in 1893 with an enrollment of over 400 men, the largest in the state at the time. Cadets, many from farming families, were taught the latest in agricultural techniques and inventions. They learned in an atmosphere that promoted discipline, then they graduated to return home to work in the fields, as well as in the factories. Pictured above are Clemson cadets (c. 1900s) in the guardroom of one of the barracks. (Photo courtesy of the Pickens County Library.)

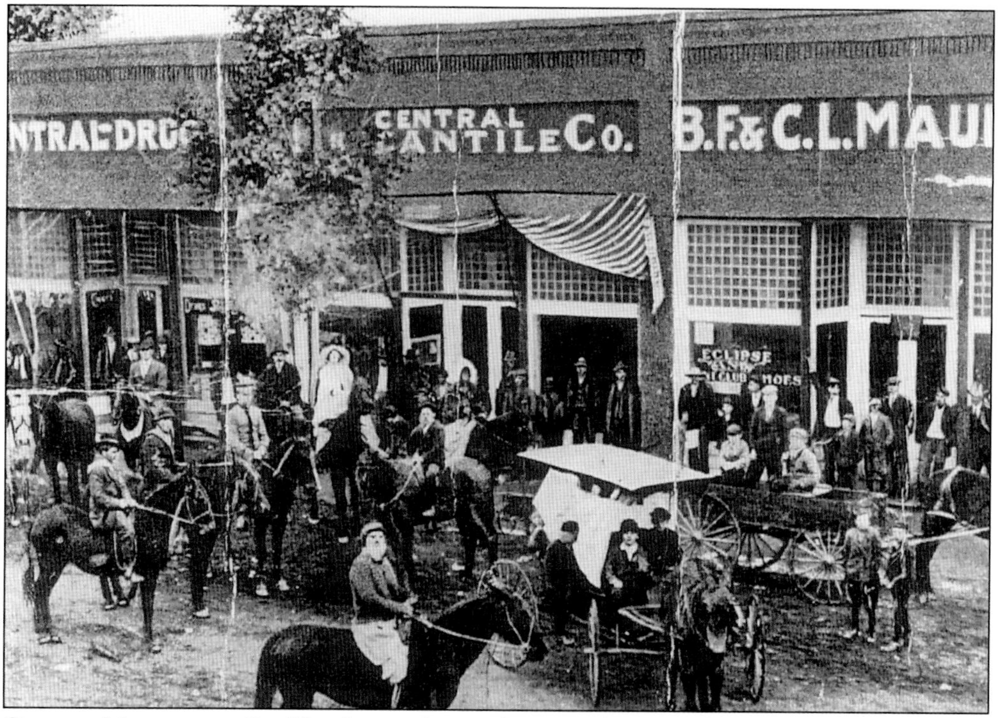

CENTRAL MERCANTILE CO. The first settlers in the area of present-day Central were Methodist ministers. In 1873 the first post office was established as Centre. Its exact location remains a mystery, but national postal records indicate that in 1875 a second postmaster, Mr. Ross Eaton, replaced the first, Mr. George W. Burroughs. By this time, the town was referred to as Central since it is midway between Atlanta and Charlotte, about 133 miles from each. (Photo courtesy of the Central Heritage Society.)

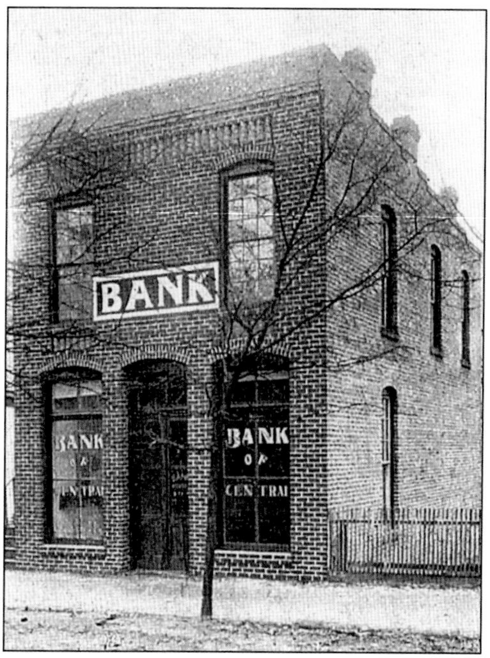

BANK. The Bank of Central was chartered in 1904 with J.N. Morgan as its president. The Farmers Bank, located on Gaines Street, opened later with capital stock at $25,000. The town of Central advanced, but not without adversity. These two banks crashed with Wall Street in 1929. (Photo courtesy of the Central Heritage Society.)

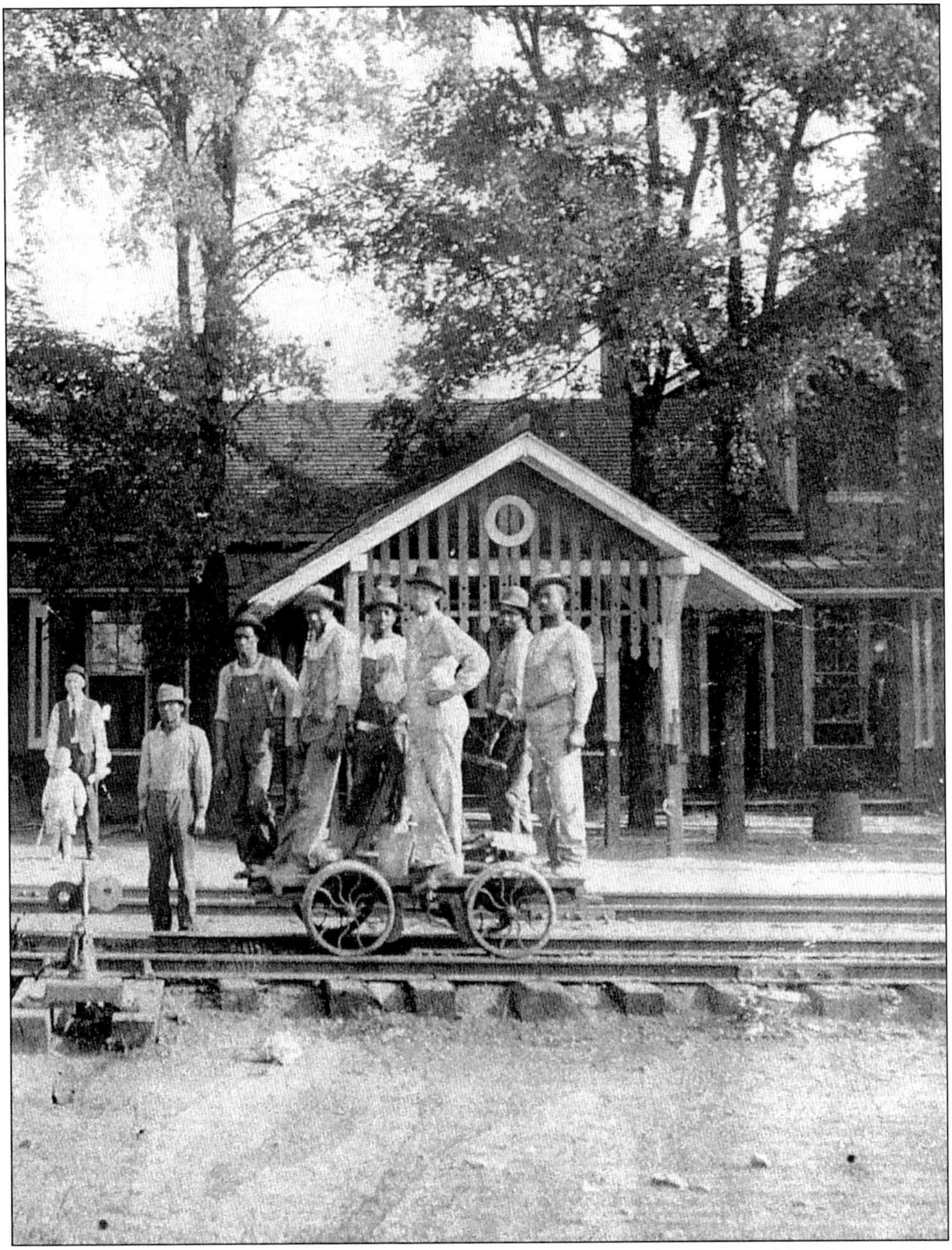

Railroad Workers on Wagon. According to historian and educator Mrs. Mattie Mae Morgan Allen and a memo from the Southern Railway Systems, the connecting link in the railroad line extending north from Atlanta and south from Charlotte was completed and open for operation on September 28, 1873. Several track assemblers were photographed in front of the Central Hotel to commemorate the occasion. Engineers, conductors, and telegraph operators, along with family members, relocated to Central and the town experienced a building boom as it was the hub of railroad activity. (Photo courtesy of the Central Heritage Society.)

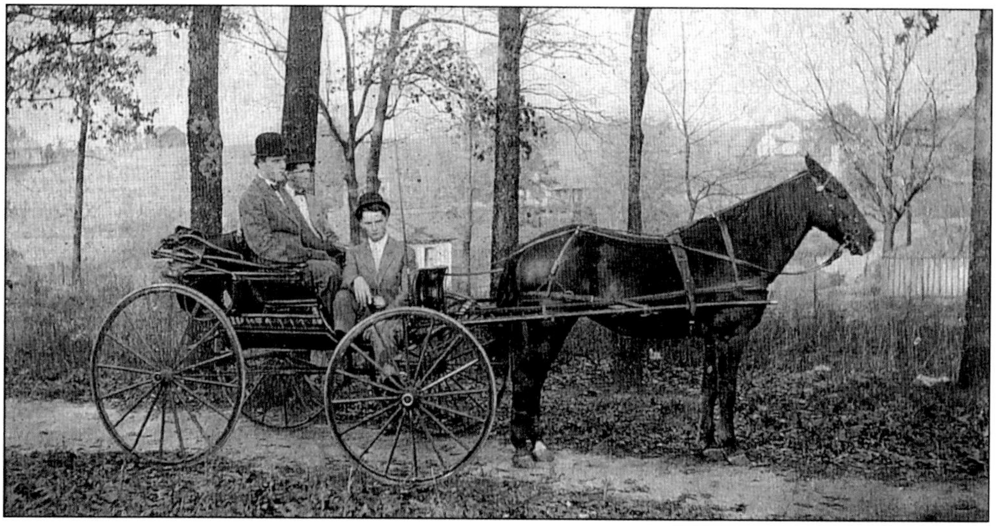

Issaqueena Village. Cotton was one of Pickens County's chief products and in 1903 local businessmen organized Issaqueena Mills. In this view, the Issaqueena Mill Village can be seen in the background. The men in the buggy include Charlie Gaines and Silas Clayton. The horse's name was Violet, and according to newspaper advertisements of the period, R.G. Gaines & Bro. sold horses and mules for $200 or less. (Photo courtesy of the Central Heritage Society.)

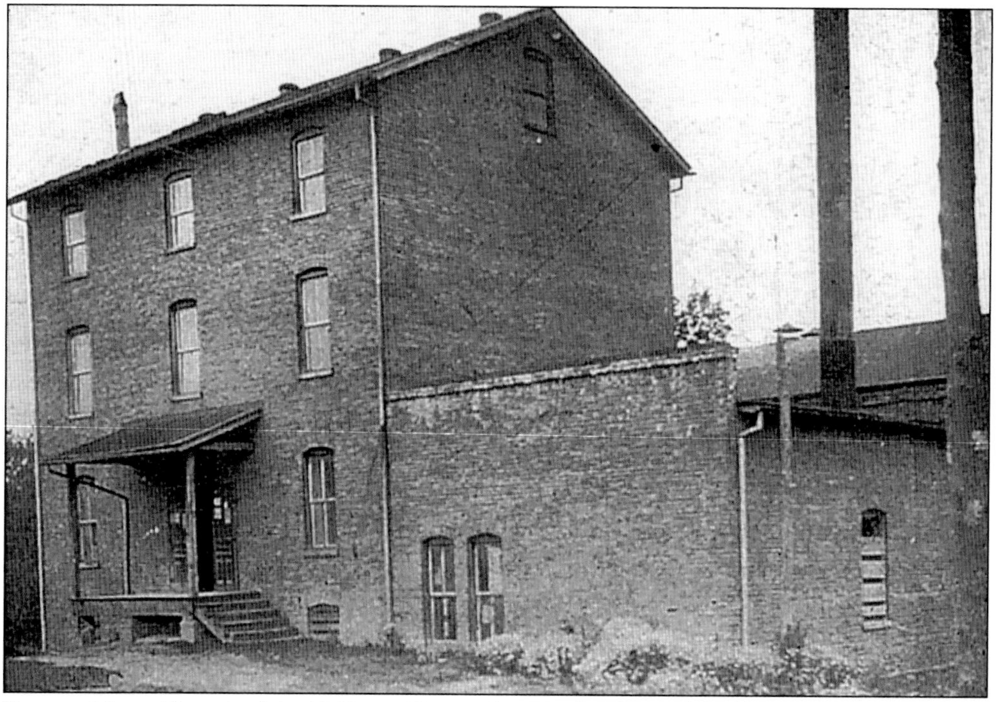

Roller Mill. Organized in 1902 on Gaines Street, the Central Roller Mill has served the community throughout the 20th century. Occasionally the mill becomes idle, but with its contemporary additions the mill can produce 100 barrels of flour, 5,000 pounds of corn meal, and 15 tons of mixed feed per day. It operated at this capacity until the 1970s. Presently, the roller mill functions as a retail and warehouse space for an antiques store. (Postcard courtesy of the Central Heritage Society.)

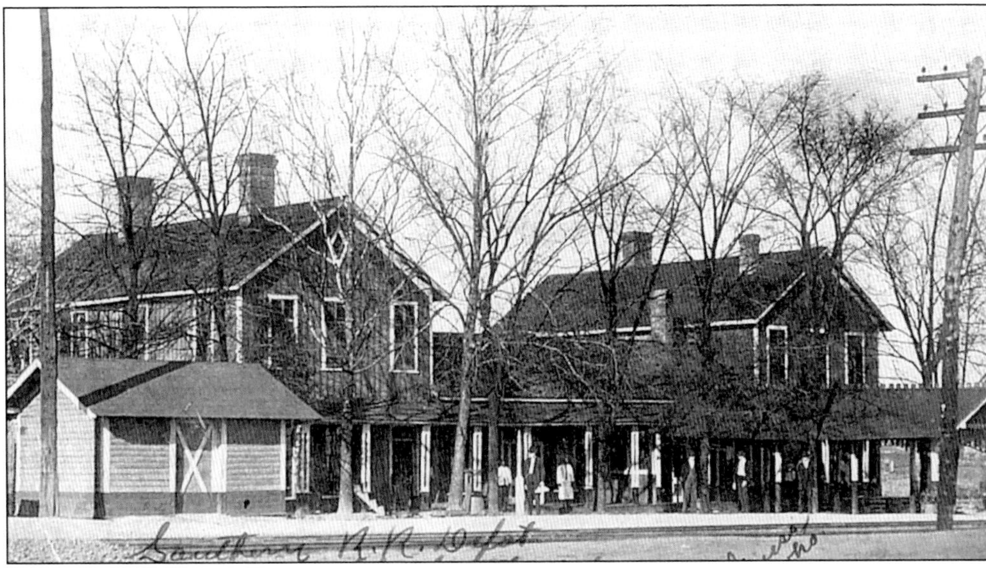

HOTEL. Railroad Hotel, or the Central Hotel, served as a restaurant for passengers of the northbound No. 12 and the southbound No. 39 since the trains stopped in Central at noon. The thriving hostel also provided offices for telegraph operators and Southern Railroad ticketmasters. Sample rooms allowed drummers and traveling salesmen to easily display their products for the inspection of local merchants. Unfortunately, the railroad company's terminal facilities moved to Greenville in 1897, adversely affecting the hotel. It closed and became the residence of John Simms, a freight agent. In 1936 the building burned and it was never rebuilt. (Photo courtesy of Southern Wesleyan University, Central, South Carolina.)

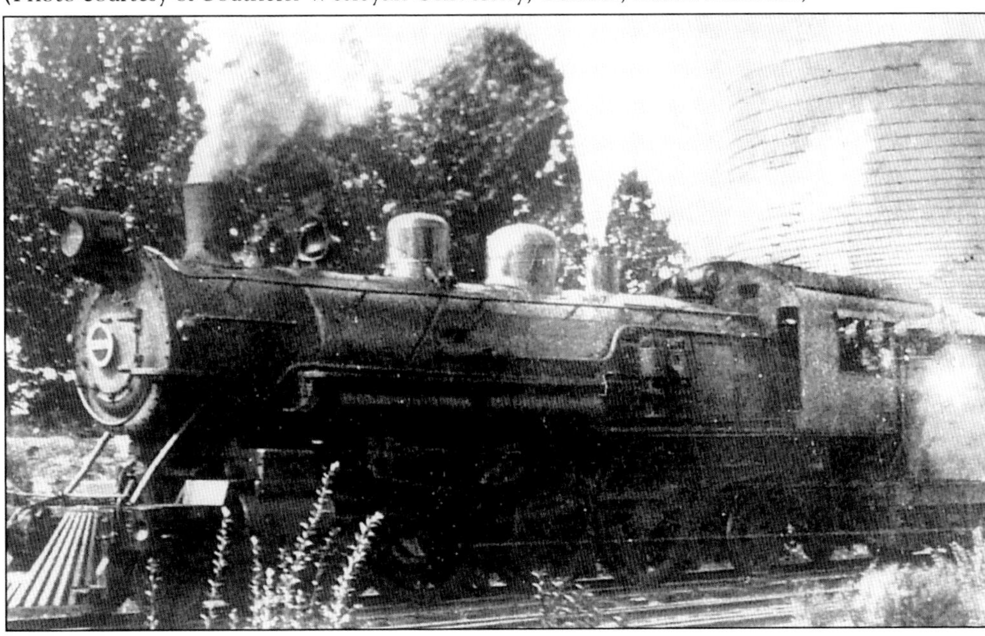

TRAIN. On Sunday, July 4, 1897, families associated with the railroad industry relocated to Greenville in order to keep their jobs. Trains still passed through the village, but Central's growth stalled until 1904, when the Issaqueena Cotton Mill began operations. (Photo courtesy of the Central Heritage Society; photo by Olive Maw Finch, 1923.)

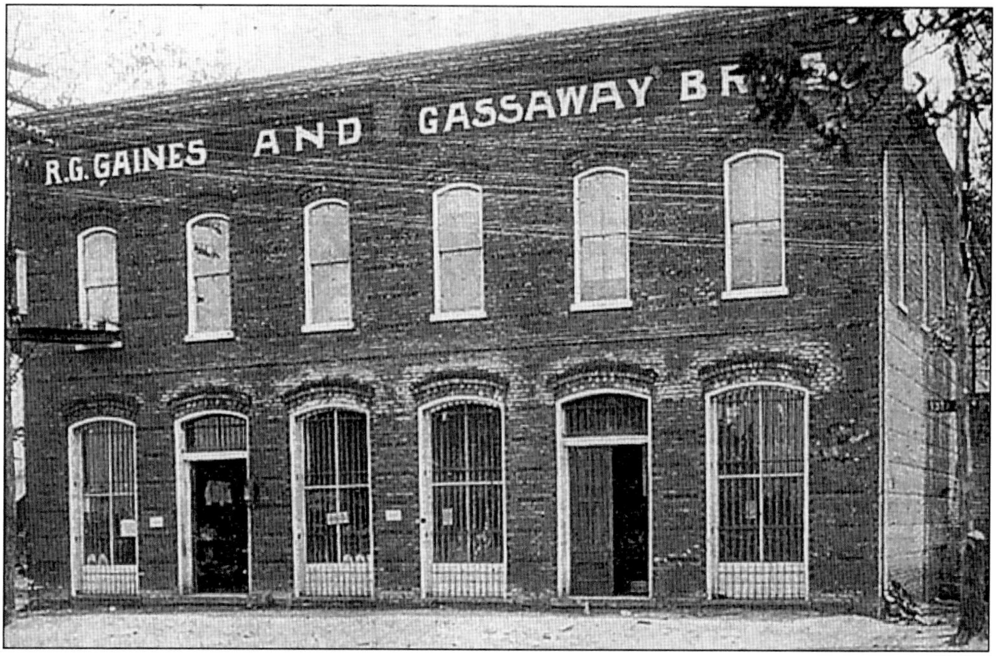

GAINES AND GASSAWAY STORE. When the railroad terminal moved to Greenville, a few stores in Central closed. R.G. Gaines and Gassaway on Gaines Street remained open and even expanded into a two-story brick store with an elevator. Gaines and Gassaway actively traded in general merchandise, farm livestock, and cotton bales. (Courtesy of the Central Heritage Society.)

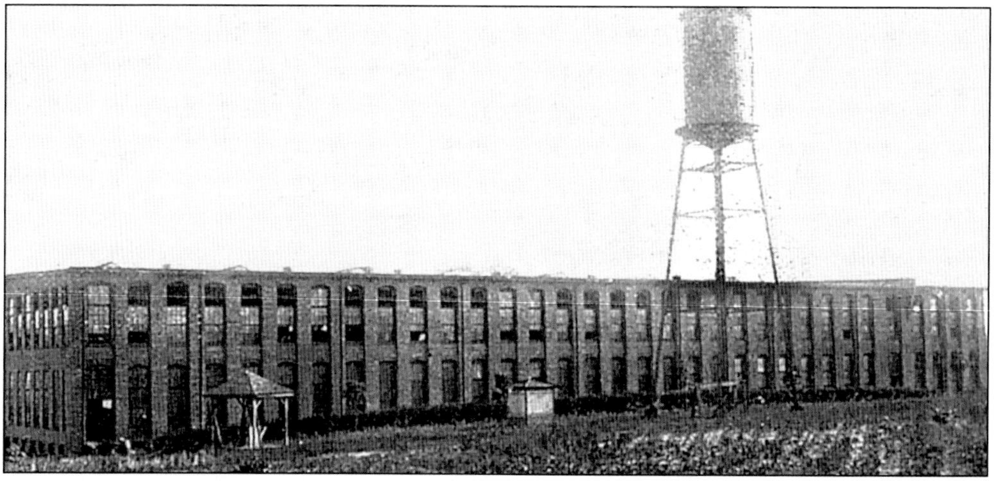

ISSAQUEENA MILL. D.K. Norris led fund-raising efforts to establish capital for the Issaqueena Mill. When the mill opened in 1904, kerosene lamps were used for lighting. Outhouses served as employee restrooms and the machinery was powered by steam engines and boilers, which were wood burners that were eventually replaced by coal burning units. In 1930 the mill went into receivership. During the Great Depression employees took a 15% cut in pay. The mill remained open under court order from 1930 until 1935, and by the 1950s Issaqueena Mill had become Plant No. 12 of the Cannon Mills Company. In 1970, the mill turned out 29 million yards of sheeting material. The plant employed about 345 people. (Photo courtesy of the Central Heritage Society.)

MORGAN MERCANTILE. One of the first mercantiles built in Central about 1895, the Morgan Store was a joint venture between two brothers. (Photo courtesy of the Central Heritage Society.)

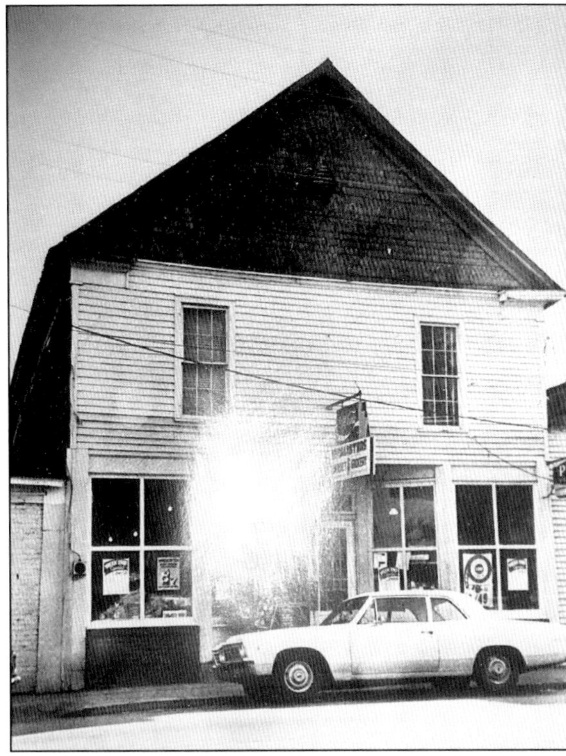

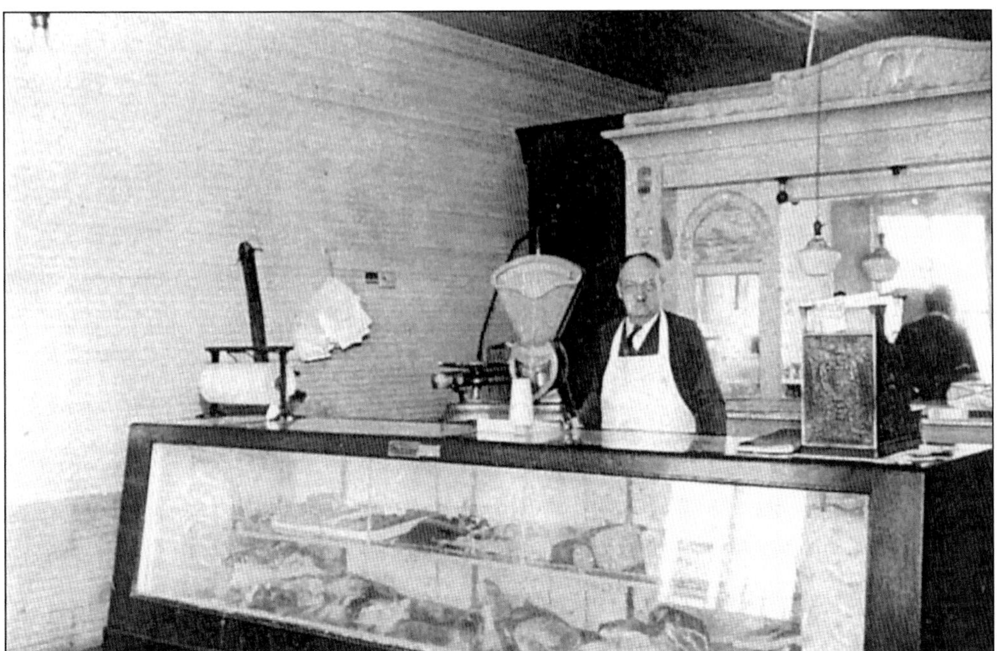

MEAT MARKET. In 1932 Horton's Meat Market on Main Street in Central served ham and beef from a refrigerated display case. Shown on the countertop, from left to right, are a butcher paper dispenser, a weight scale, and a mechanical cash register that operated efficiently without electricity. (Photo courtesy of the Central Heritage Society.)

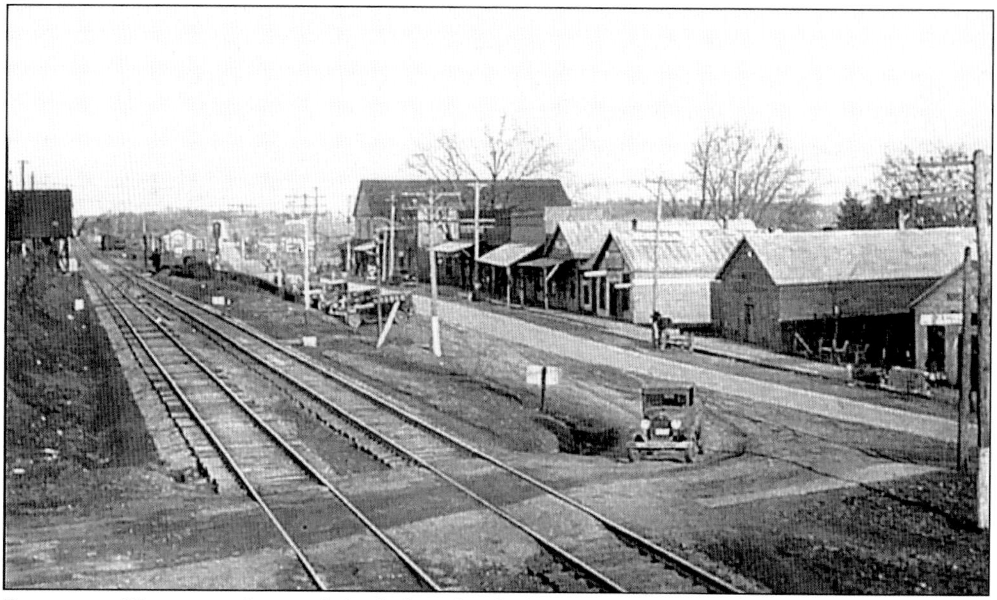

RAILS AND HIGHWAY. Automobiles led to the decline of railroad passenger services. Improved roads such as S.C. 93 increased mobility for a middle class eager to travel. From Clemson to Easley, Highway 93 parallels the railroad track. Pictured is Central and Highway 93 during the Depression era. The next whistle stop to the east would be the town of Norris. (Photo courtesy of the Central Heritage Society.)

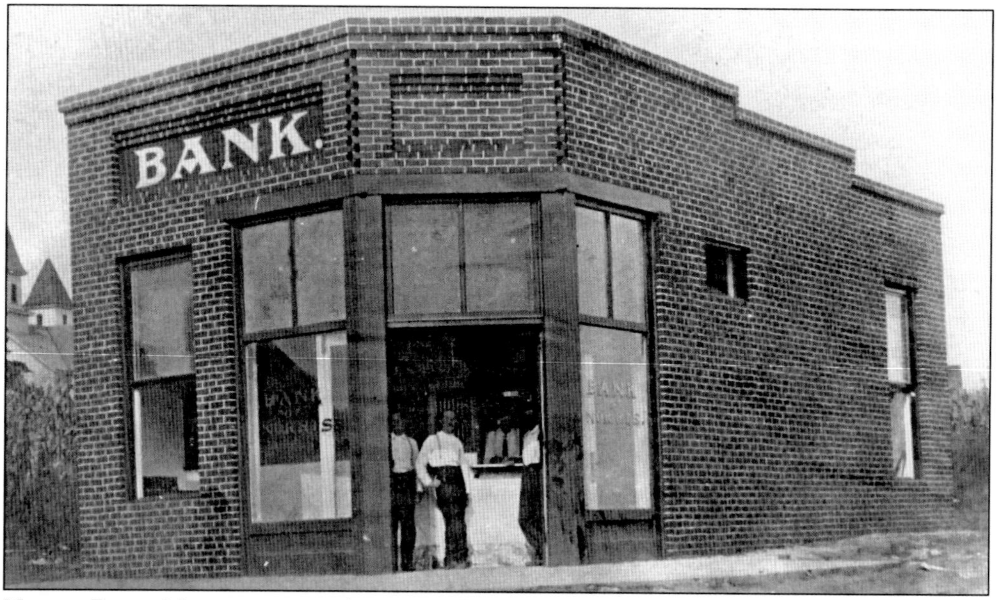

NORRIS BANK. Norris was once known as Bowen's Siding. During the 1890s, Henry Bowen of Easley relocated to the Norris area where he opened a sawmill. His logging operation employed 75 to 100 workers and gradually the community adopted the name Bowen's Siding. By act of a 1909 petition, the community chartered and renamed the town Norris in honor of local industrialist D.K. Norris. In 1968 Norris had a population of about 600 people. In 1990 the population had grown to more than 860. (Photo courtesy of South Caroliniana Library, University of South Carolina, Columbia.)

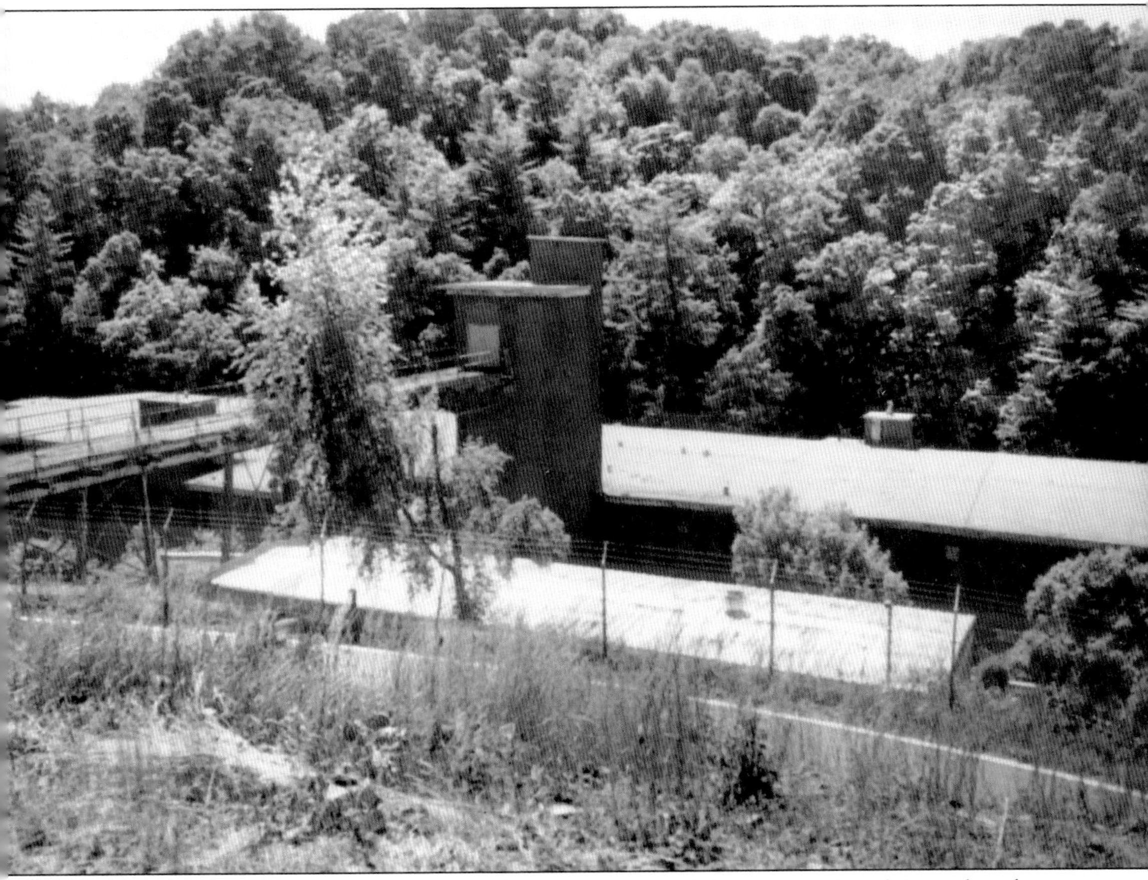

Norris Mill Entrance. About 2 miles from Norris is the hilly community of Cateechee, home of the first industrial cotton mill in Pickens County, constructed from 1895 to 1896. Owned by the Norris Brothers and run by D.K. Norris, a wealthy planter from Vance, S.C., the Norris Cotton Mill at Cateechee hugs Twelve Mile River in a steep river valley. Because of the rugged terrain, employees entered the mill from this tower. They were lowered into the four-story production facility constructed on a foundation of bedrock. According to author and historian Jerry Alexander, Norris Cotton Mill purchased raw cotton from nearby farmers. Finished cloth from the mill was hauled by mule and wagon to the railroad depot at the town of Norris. (Photo by P.E. Peters.)

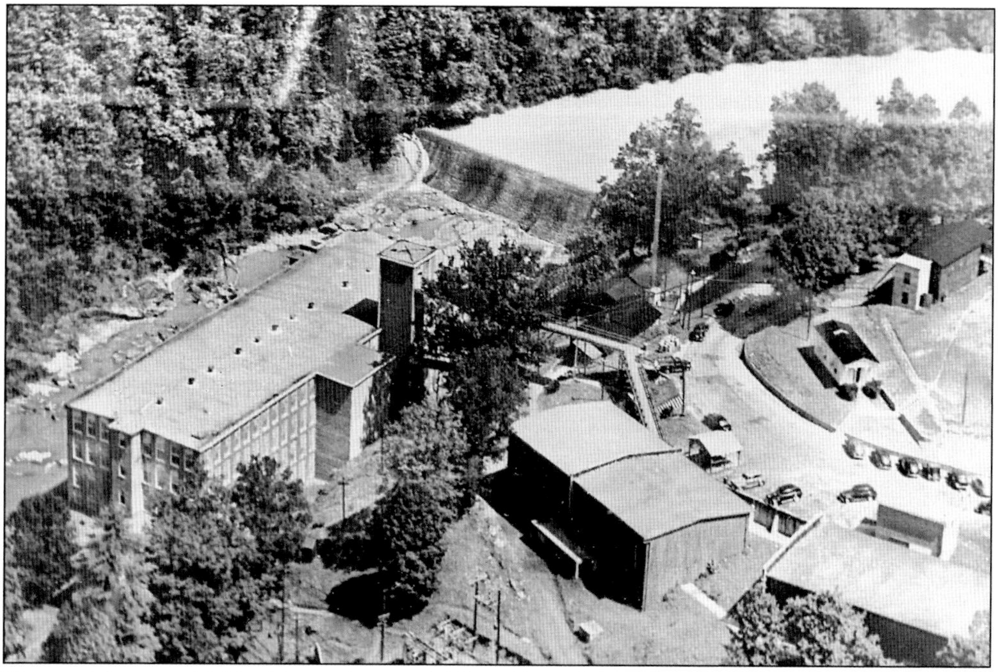

NORRIS MILL (C. 1950). Norris Cotton Mill at Cateechee, located near S.C. 93 between the towns of Liberty and Central, began operations in 1896. It was the first cotton mill in Pickens County. The mill stood four-stories tall with two footpaths bridging the mill's elevator shaft to the exterior terraces of the village. This 1950s aerial view depicts the mill prior to the plant's expansion on the northern end. The windows were not bricked up until air conditioning had been introduced to the structure during the latter half of the 20th century. (Photo courtesy of Jerry Alexander.)

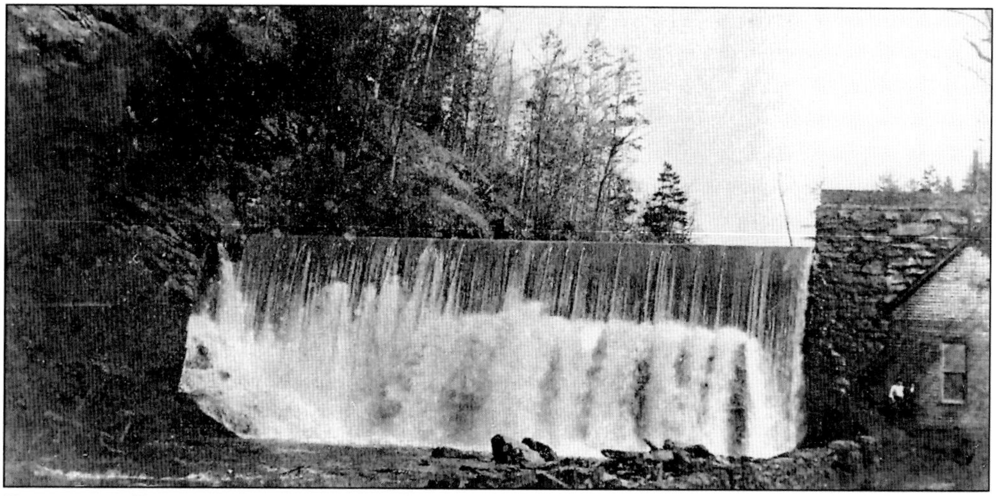

CATEECHEE POWERHOUSE. Norris Mill expanded, and by 1901, an electrical power plant functioned a mile downstream from the mill's location on Twelve Mile River. The dam for the power plant was constructed of rock and cement. On April 6, 1936, floodwaters destroyed the rock dam and damaged the weave room. Soon after a new dam of reinforced concrete was erected, and the Norris Mill functioned throughout most of the 20th century. (Photo courtesy of the South Caroliniana Library, USC, Columbia.)

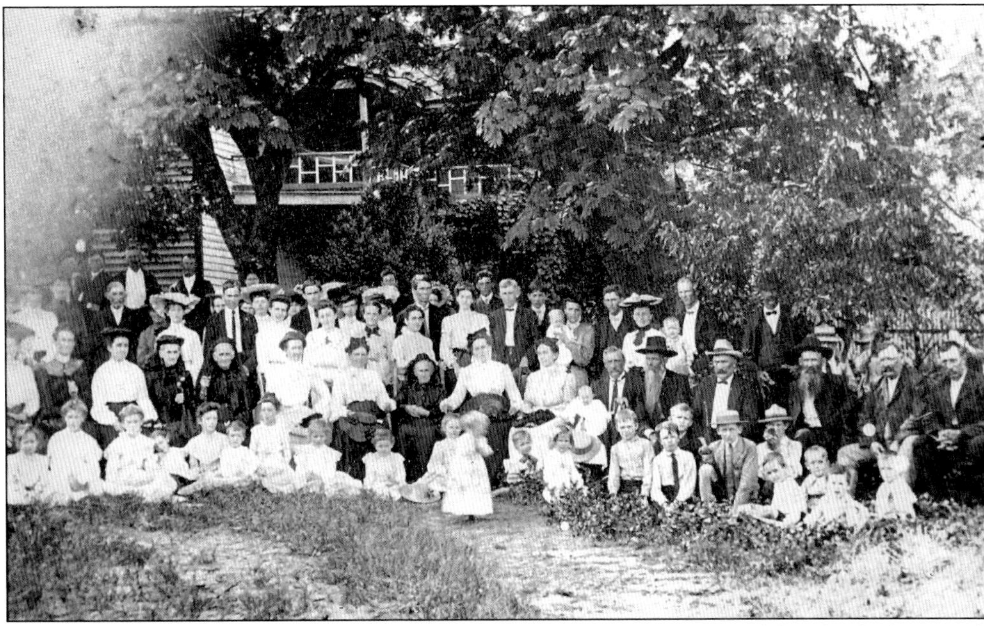

Boggs Reunion. By 1785, fewer than 23 families occupied the isolated farmlands that would eventually became Pickens, Oconee, and Anderson Counties. The Boggs family was one such group. They settled near Liberty Springs, which eventually became Liberty, S.C. Depicted here are members of the Boggs family at a reunion. In 1904, the house in the background was torn down and the First Baptist Church was built on the site. (Photo courtesy of PDHRT and Anne Sheriff.)

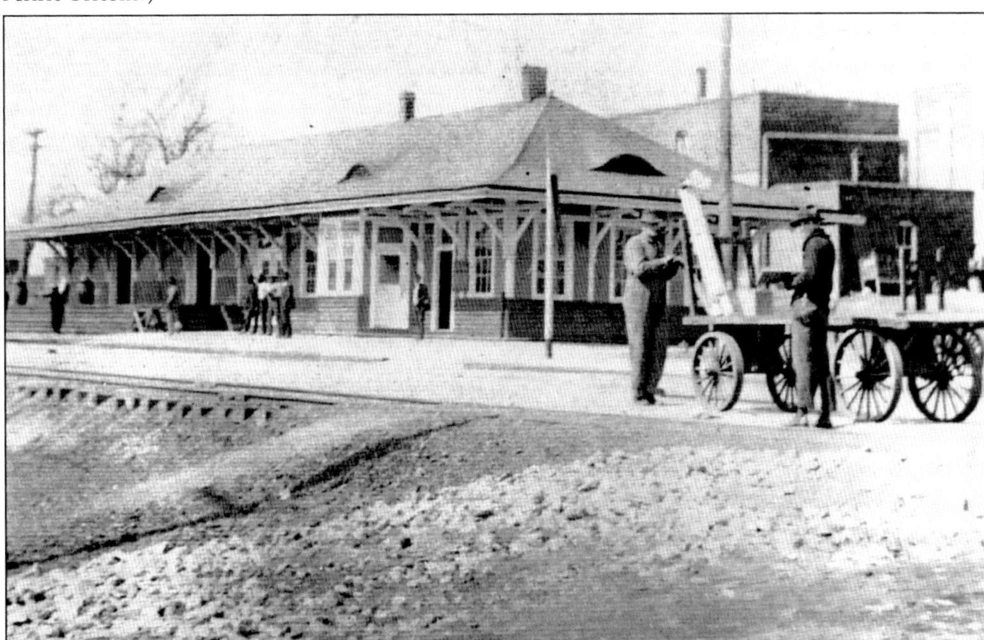

Liberty Depot. In the 1870s, railroad tracks were laid near the Boggs family house. Newspapers mention the first Liberty Depot in 1875 when Liberty was chartered as a town. The town's depot was torn down in 1974. (Photo courtesy of Anne Sheriff and Barbara Carter.)

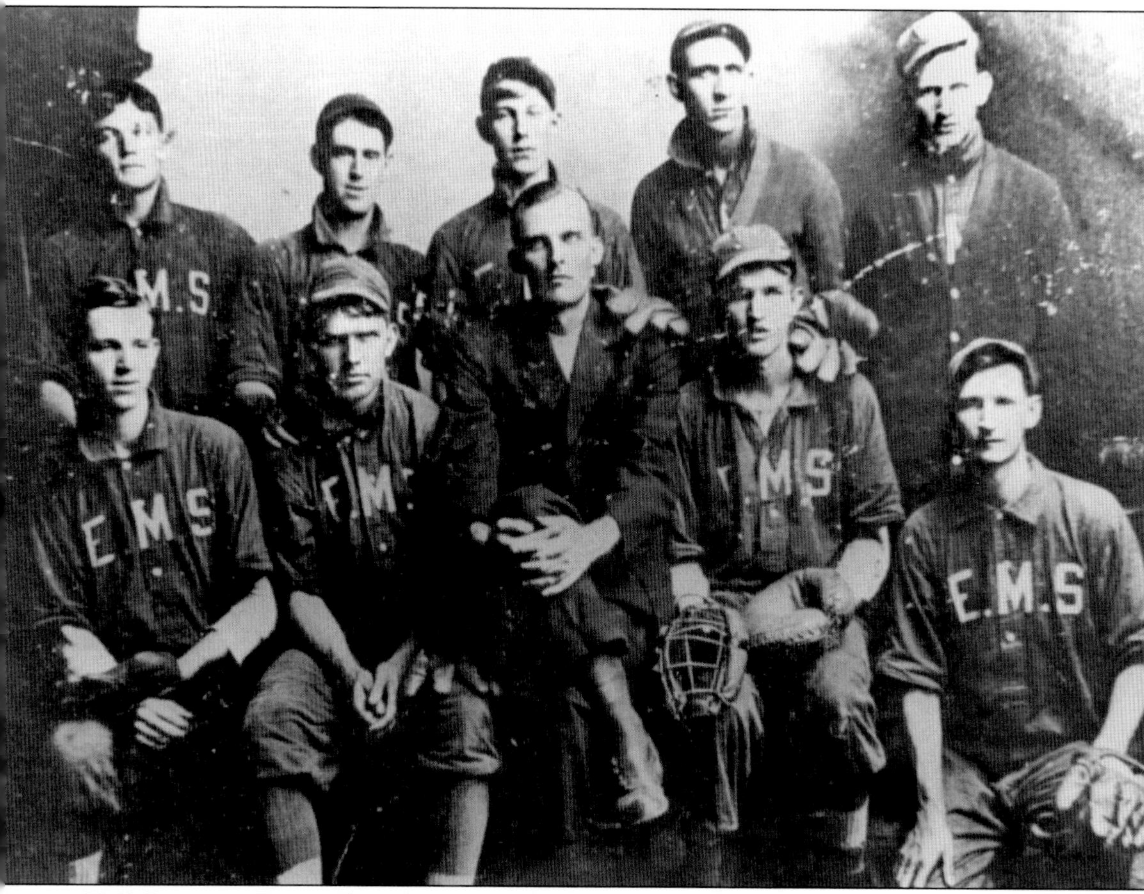

EMS Baseball Team. The Liberty Mill baseball team of 1900 included Jarrett Medlock, Peg Summey, Adie James, Bud Adams, Calum Asteen, Cliff Chambers, Charley Durham, Zig Hawkins (Manager), Barney Alanders, and Pearl Kay. Easley Cotton Mill purchased Liberty Mill and then transferred it to the Woodside Brothers. (Photo courtesy of the Pickens County Library and Zoy Medlock.)

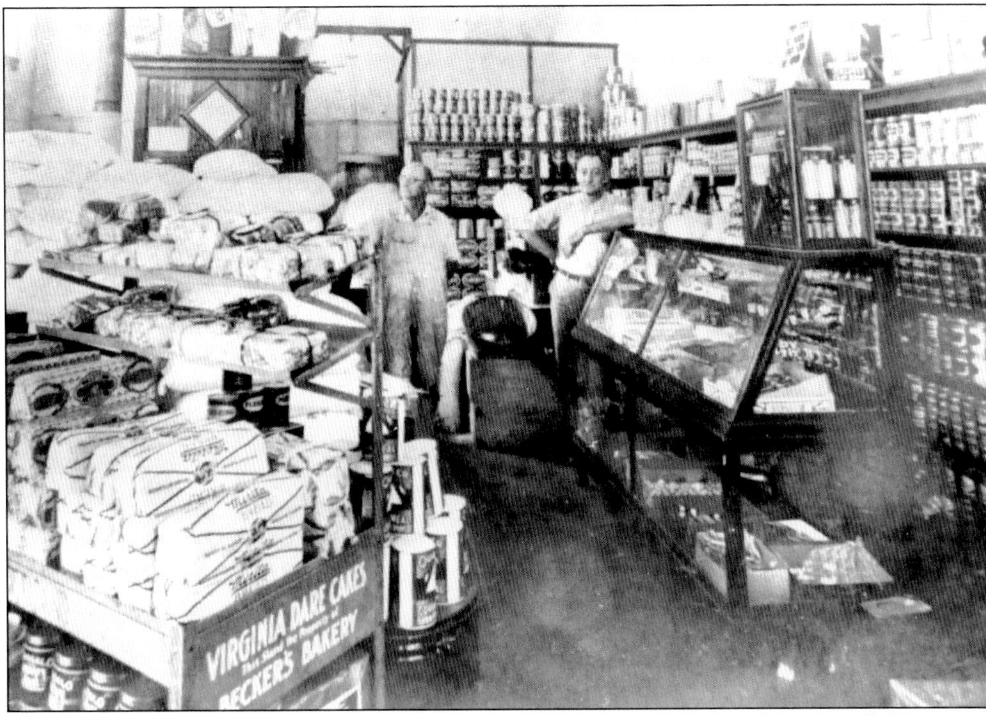

Interior Merchants/Campbell. Located on the northwest corner of Front and Commerce Streets in Liberty, George Campbell Grocery was small and convenient. The grocer existed at a time when franchises had not conquered Main Street and interstates had not scarred the landscape. (Photo courtesy of Eloise Campbell McMahan and Don Finley.)

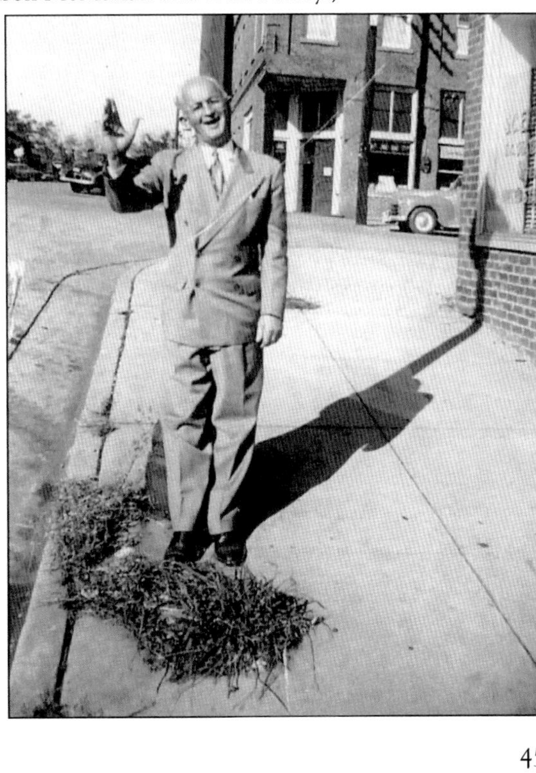

Commerce Street, Liberty. R.D. Boggs stands in front of the South Carolina Security Commission building on Commerce Street in Liberty and waves to his family and friends (c. 1950). In the background is a building that once housed the Masonic Hall. It has also served as a storefront for independent retailers. (Photo courtesy of Beverly Boggs Cureton and the Central Heritage Society.)

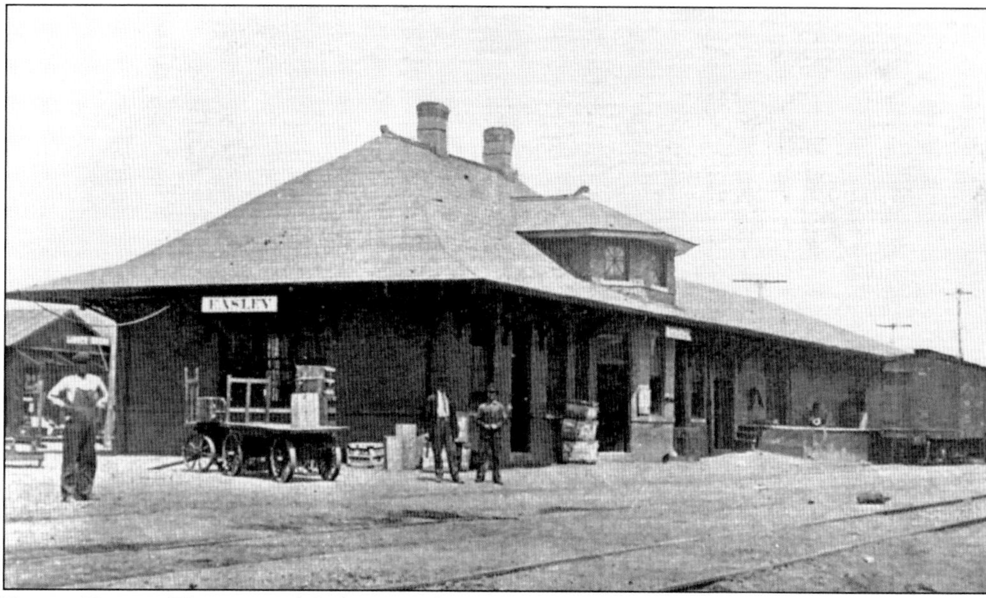

EASLEY DEPOT. The town of Easley was chartered in 1874 and is named for Confederate Gen. William King Easley. Born on a plantation near the Saluda River in Pickens County in 1825, Easley was an attorney for the Atlanta Airline (Southern Railway) and he persuaded officials to reroute the railroad through Pickens County. (Photo courtesy of the South Caroliniana Library, University of South Carolina, Columbia.)

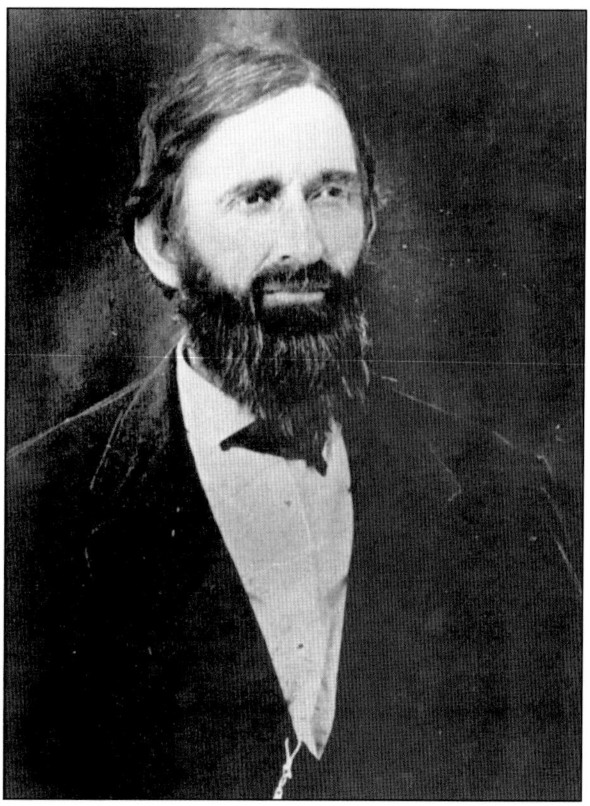

HOLCOMBE. Robert Elliott Holcombe, born in Pickensville in 1823, built a depot in 1874 near the site of the Old Market Square in downtown Easley. He did so in order to lure the railroads into this particular area where he owned land and stood to make a profit if the line succeeded. In 1863 and 1864 Holcombe represented Pickens County in the state legislature. During his lifetime he was a postmaster, magistrate, farmer, merchant, miller, and auctioneer. Holcombe was the father of nine children and the first mayor of Easley when the city was chartered in 1874. He died in 1893. (Photo courtesy of the Pickens County Library.)

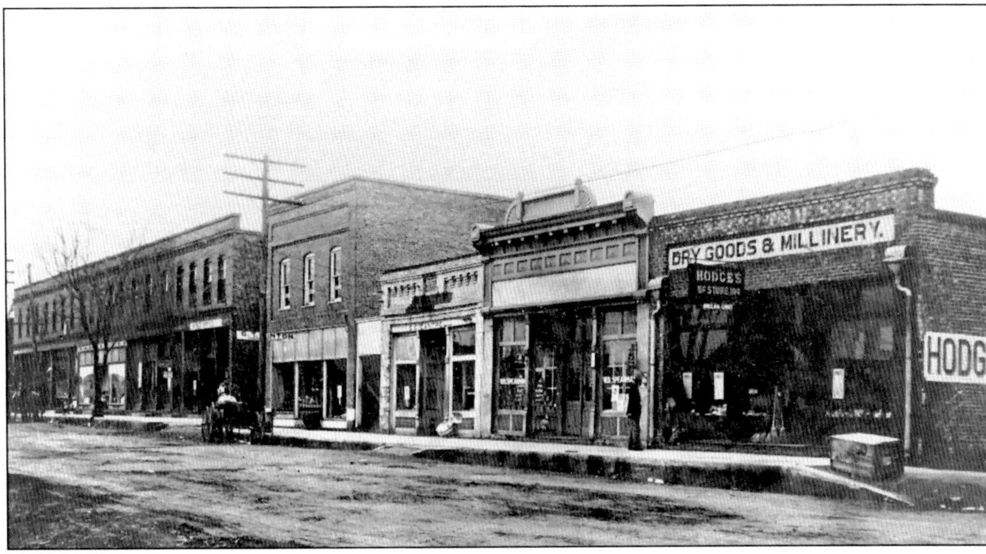

MAIN ST. LOOKING EAST. Prior to his death in 1872, W.K. Easley served as a delegate to the South Carolina Secession Convention and was a member of the South Carolina House from 1865 to 1866. According to Benjamin F. Perry, the provisional state governor of 1865 who was born in Oconee when it was still a part of Pickens County, W.K. Easley was an eccentric but good friend. Easley was instrumental in reorganizing the state's militia, and although his law offices were in Greenville, W.K. Easley practiced in the courts of Greenville, Anderson, and Pickens. Pictured here is Main Street Easley in the early 1900s. Many of these buildings still stand. (Photo courtesy of the South Caroliniana Library, University of South Carolina, Columbia.)

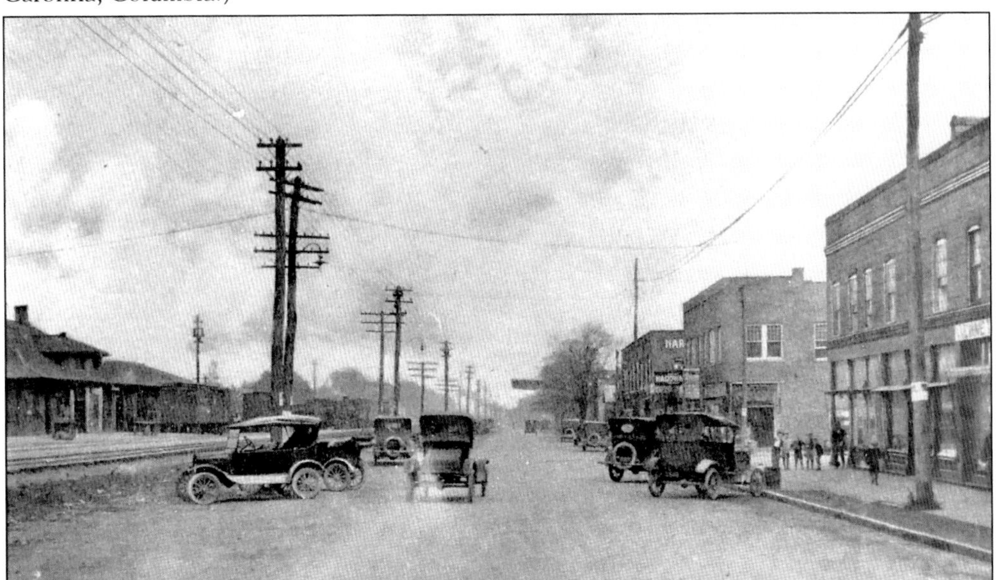

MAIN STREET, 1920s. The largest population concentration in Pickens County is in Easley, although Main Street looks about the same as it did in this view in the 1920s. At the far left of the image is the Southern (Mainline) Depot. (Photo courtesy of the South Caroliniana Library, University of South Carolina, Columbia.)

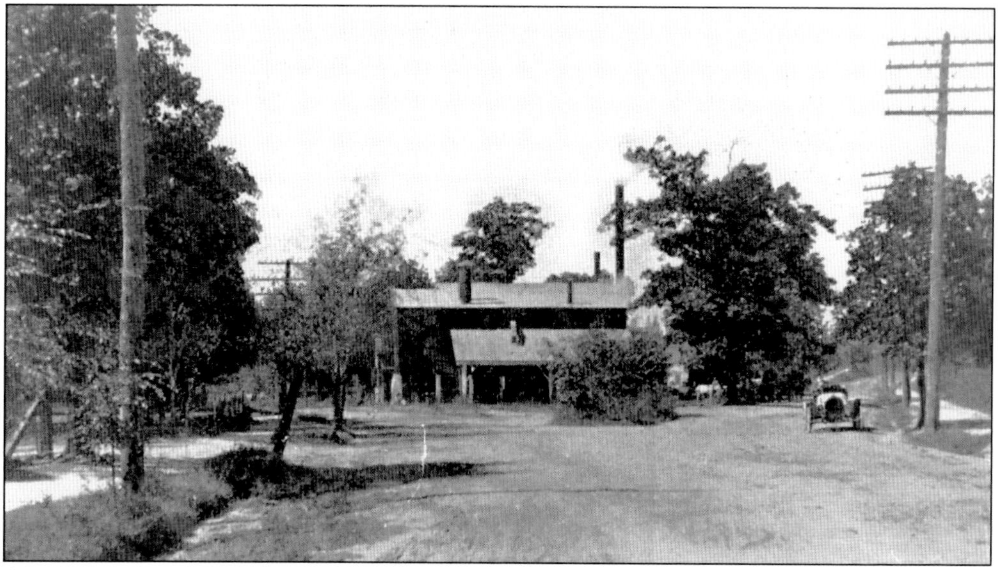

Ginnery and Oil Mill. The Ginnery and Oil Mill in Easley was organized from 1889 to 1890. D.F. Bradley, a collector of Internal Revenue during President Cleveland's administration, was elected president of the mill by the board of directors. (Photo courtesy of the South Caroliniana Library, University of South Carolina, Columbia.)

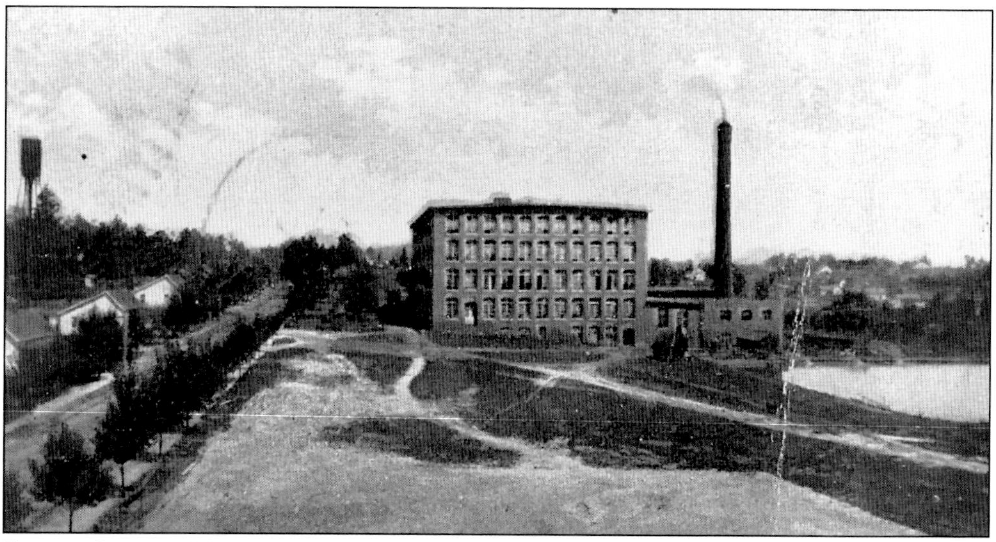

Easley Cotton Mills. Cotton prices were 5¢ per pound when John M. Geer, a cotton purchaser for Piedmont Mills, decided the town of Easley, a place where cotton was cheap, needed a mill. With capital stock of $200,000, Geer built Easley Cotton Mill, the first in the town. Easley Cotton Mill later purchased two plants in Liberty, the Liberty Mill and the Calumet Mill (Maple Croft Mill), both built around the turn of the 20th century. In the 1920s, the three factories became known as Woodside when the Woodside Brothers of Greenville—E.F. Woodside, president, J.D. Woodside, vice-president/treasurer, and John T. Woodside, vice-president/secretary—took over operations. Dan River Mills of Danville, V.A., acquired controlling interest in Woodside in 1956. By the 1970s the factories operated as the Woodside Division of Dan River. (Photo courtesy of the South Caroliniana Library, University of South Carolina, Columbia.)

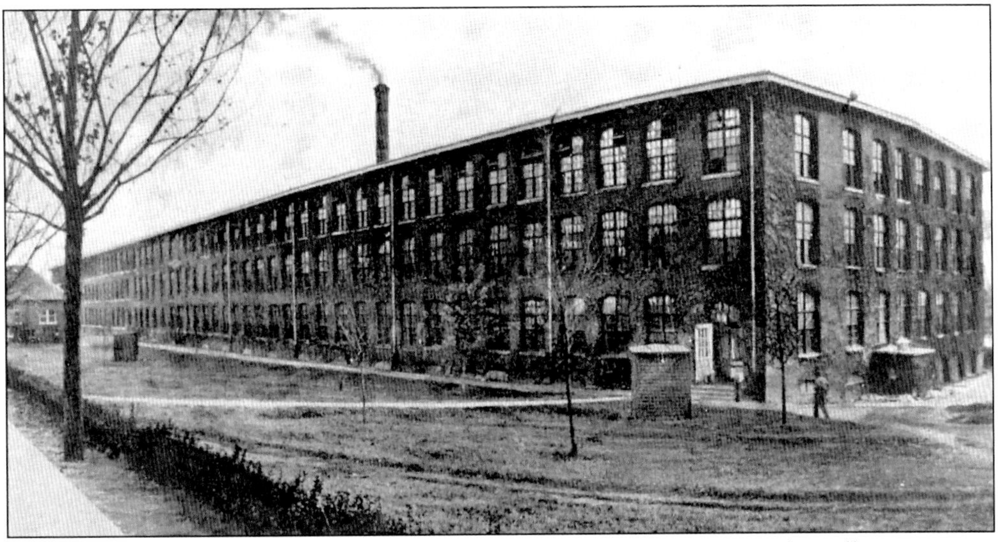

GLENWOOD COTTON MILLS. To the citizens of Easley, a productive textile mill was a pretty picture despite black smoke puffing from the chimneys. Glenwood Cotton Mills, chartered in 1902, was the second cotton mill built in Easley. Both the Easley and the Glenwood mills made print cloths and sheetings at the beginning of the 20th century. (Photo courtesy of the South Caroliniana Library, University of South Carolina, Columbia.)

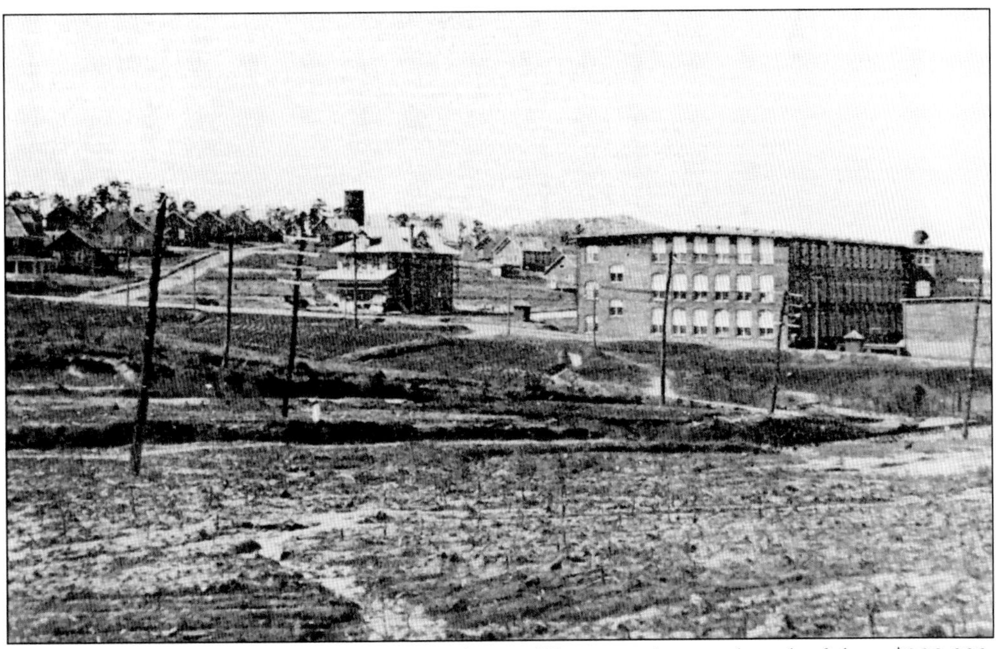

ALICE COTTON MILLS. Organized in 1910, Alice Mill began with capital stock of about $200,000. In 1923, her capital stock had increased to $500,000. The mill changed hands several times, and in 1927 it enlarged, adding residences to its village and machinery to the facilities. (Photo courtesy of the South Caroliniana Library, University of South Carolina, Columbia.)

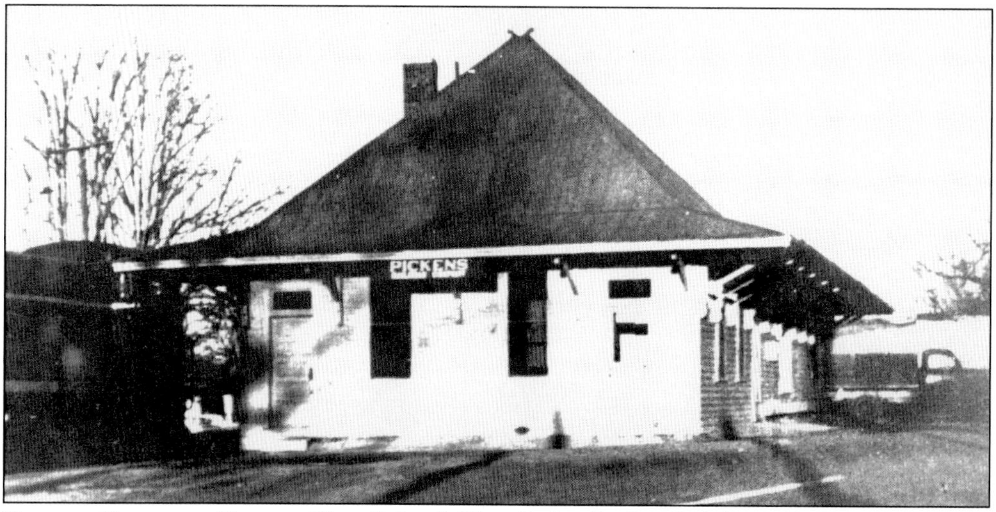

PICKENS RAILROAD DEPOT. The ill-fated Blue Ridge Railroad did not discourage Pickens stockholders from completing a short railroad line between Pickens and Easley. Even after the Pickens "Doodle" train jumped its tracks, stockholders remained firm in their commitment to keep the Pickens Railroad Company available for freight delivery and passenger service. While the Doodle never gained national awards, it is recognized as one of the few railroads in the country managed by women. Jane Gillespie was president. Prior to her leadership, Ethel A. Cannon (Ethel Weber) served as comptroller and general manager (1939–1958). Though the Doodle engine has been sidetracked, Pickens Railroad Company still provides services to its clients and to the railroad industry. The 1950s Pickens depot existed for passengers of the Doodle, not the engines of the Southern Railway. (Photo courtesy of the Pickens County Library.)

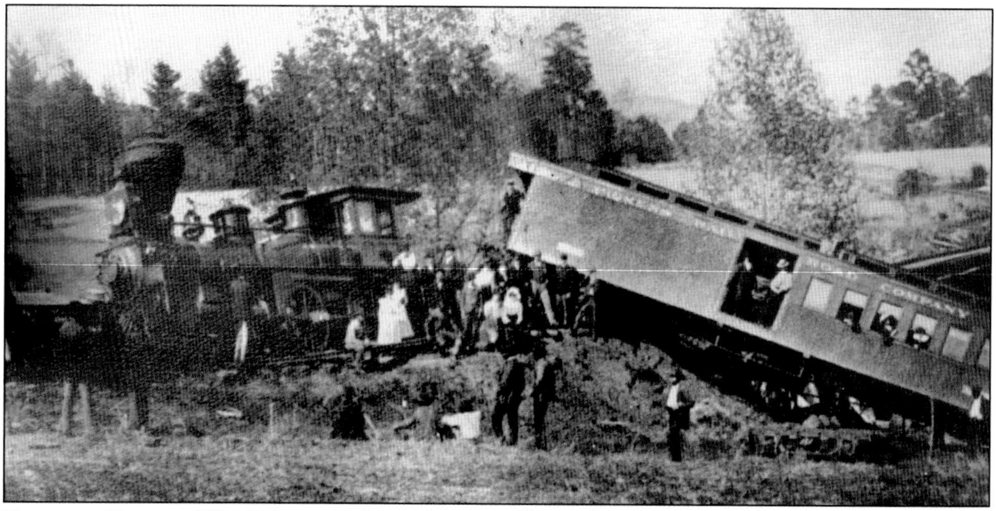

DOODLE TRAIN. J.T. "Troupe" Partridge, unofficial historian of the Doodle, retired in 1954 after working as conductor and superintendent. Troupe said that the majority of the railroad's 1898-to-1905 passengers were thirsty folk headed to the state dispensaries in Pickens. Troupe was a popular engineer with children. He threw chewing gum to them when they watched the train chug up and down the tracks. Pictured is the Doodle near the Arial Mill where it derailed in 1898. Troupe was a water boy for the Pickens Railroad at the time. (Photo courtesy of PDHRT.)

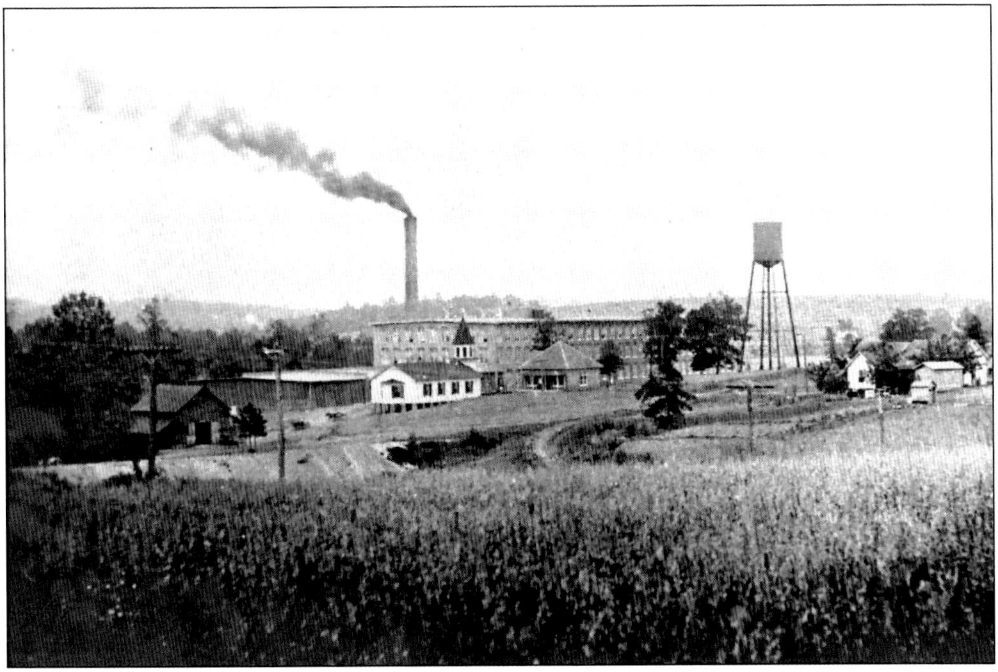

Pickens Cotton Mill. Chartered on May 4, 1906, by W.M. Hagood Sr., a native of Pickens County, the Pickens Cotton Mill was developed near the railroad, since there were no freight trucks at the time. Mayfair Mills acquired the factory in 1964. (Photo courtesy of the South Caroliniana Library, University of South Carolina, Columbia.)

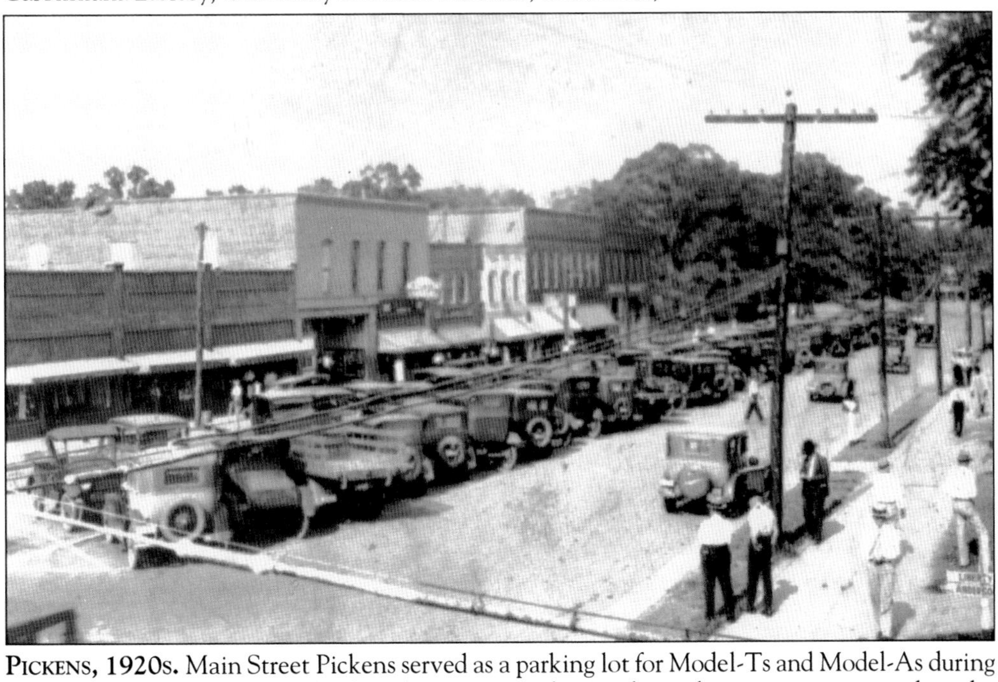

Pickens, 1920s. Main Street Pickens served as a parking lot for Model-Ts and Model-As during court days or holidays. Town life has always centered around courthouse events, even when the town was first located on the Keowee River, 14 miles west on Highway 183 near the Oconee Nuclear Station. (Photo courtesy of PDHRT.)

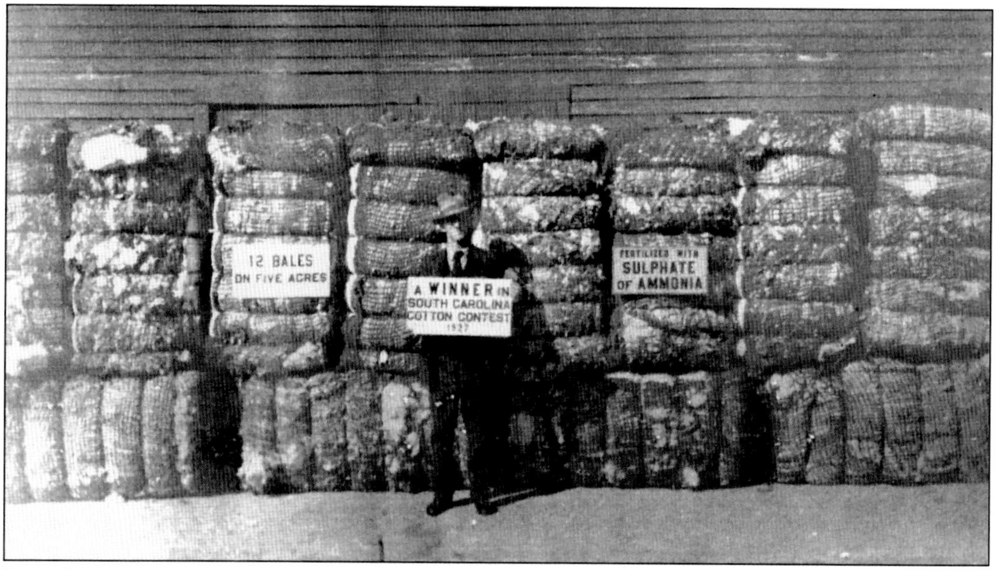

Jim Hendricks. On May 08, 1914, the Smith-Lever Act introduced in the House of Representatives by member Asbury F. Lever (1875–1940) was signed into law. It provided for cooperative agricultural extension services to be administered by land-grant colleges such as Clemson. Lever is buried at Cemetery Hill at Clemson University. His act allowed Clemson to assist a multitude of Pickens farmers in creating the best products. Pictured here is Jim Hendricks with his 1927 cotton crop. (Photo courtesy of Pickens County Library.)

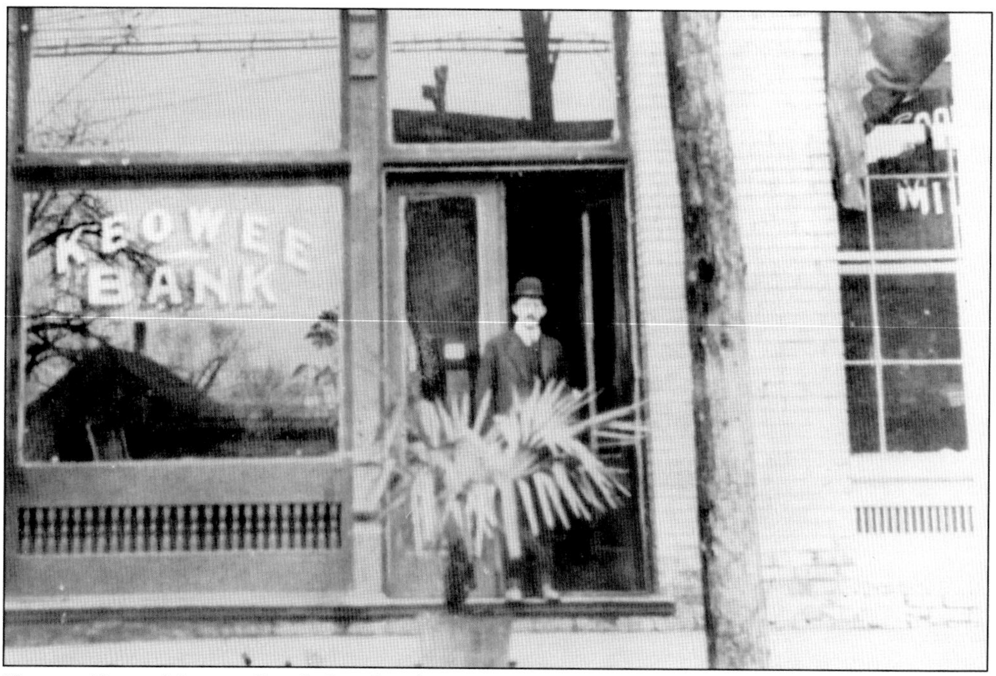

Keowee Bank. Monroe Smith, head cashier, opens Keowee Bank on Main Street Pickens. The building still stands as Garren's café. Keowee Bank closed during the Great Depression. (Photo courtesy of the PDHRT.)

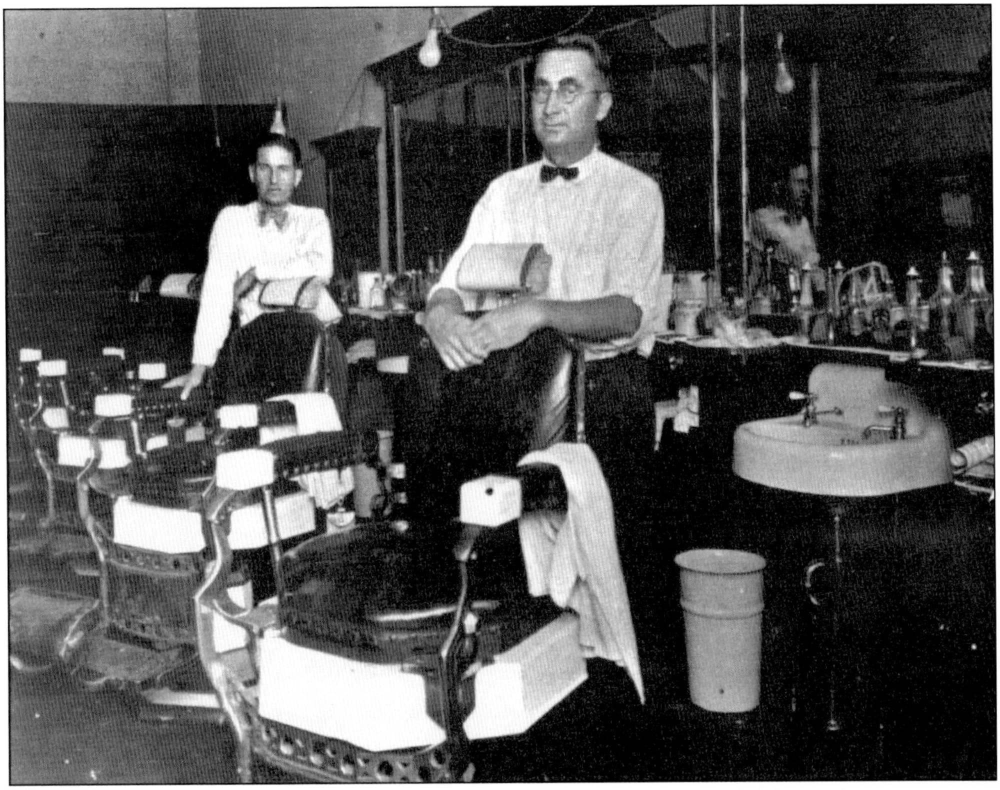

BARBER SHOP. By the 1940s timber farms had replaced cotton fields. Pickens' economy diversified and small service oriented businesses like J.M. Reece's Barber Shop flourished. (Postcard courtesy of Pickens County Library.)

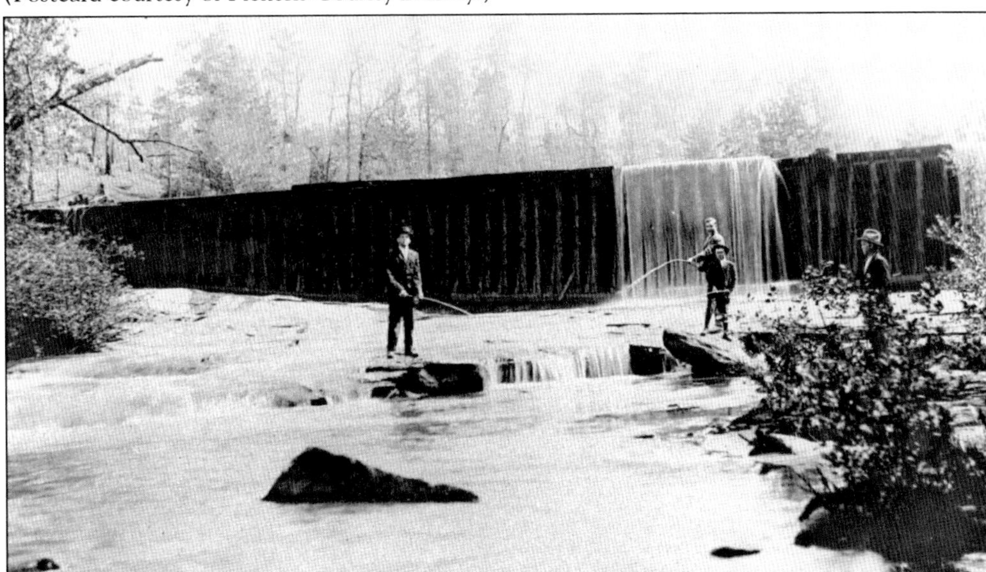

TOWN CREEK. In 1910, fishing was a favorite past time on Town Creek, but tourism activities would not dramatically effect Pickens until the latter half of the 20th century. (Photo courtesy of the South Caroliniana Library, University of South Carolina, Columbia.)

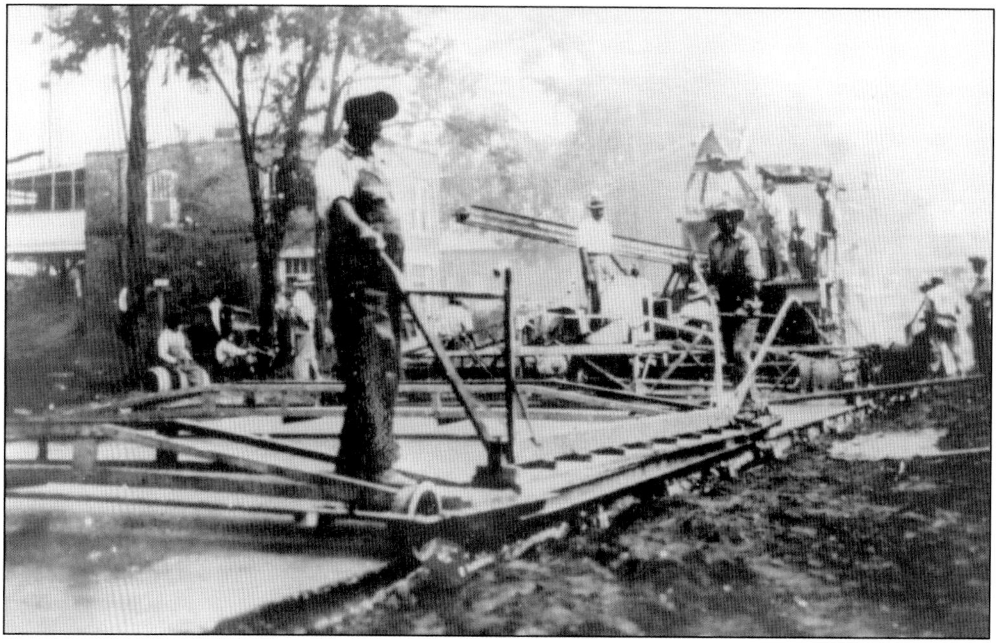

Paving Roads. In the 1930s, paving roads in town or in the rural communities amounted to a lot of sweat. (Photo courtesy of PDHRT and the Pickens County Library.)

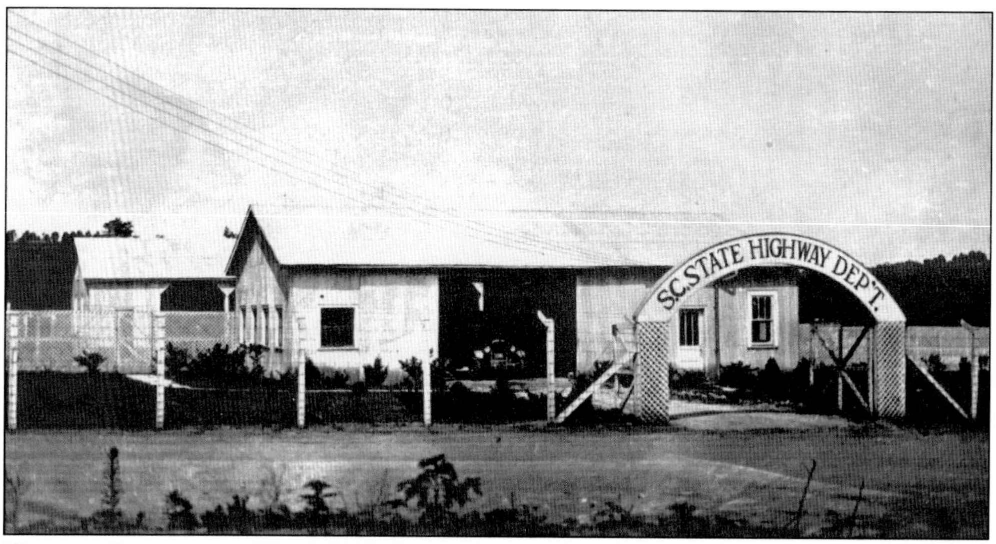

Highway Department. The S.C. Highway Department in Pickens during the 1940s offered few services to motorists, but it was a sign of the times. After World War II, a Sunday drive to the hills became a family event. Tourists from nearby counties began to regularly visit Table Rock, Sassafrass, Glassy, and other mountains. (Photo courtesy of the Pickens County Library.)

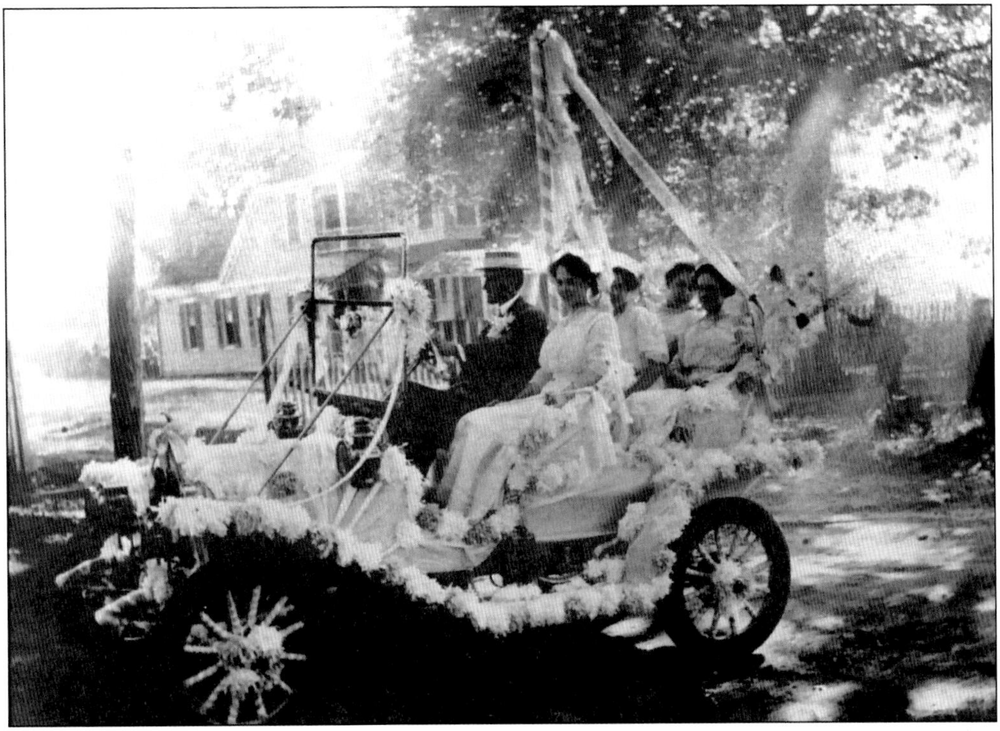

Decorated Car. This touring vehicle became a float for the Pickens County Fair in 1910, but 40 years later cars dominated the landscape as enthusiastic vacationers discovered the land that the Cherokee cherished. (Photo courtesy of the Pickens County Library.)

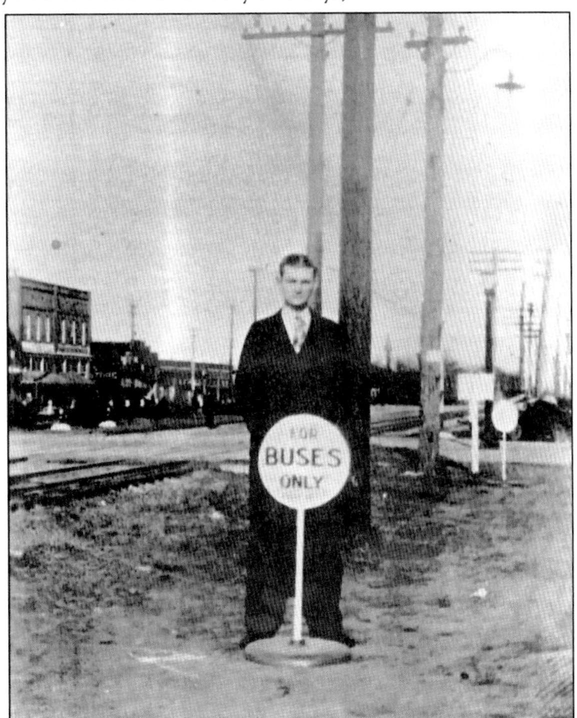

Bus Stop. Buses or trains transported folks who did not own cars. Mr. Charlie Welborn waits at the bus stop beside the railroad tracks on Main Street in Easley. Passenger service aboard trains like the Pickens Doodle gradually faded out of existence due to a disinterested public. (Photo courtesy of the Pickens County Library.)

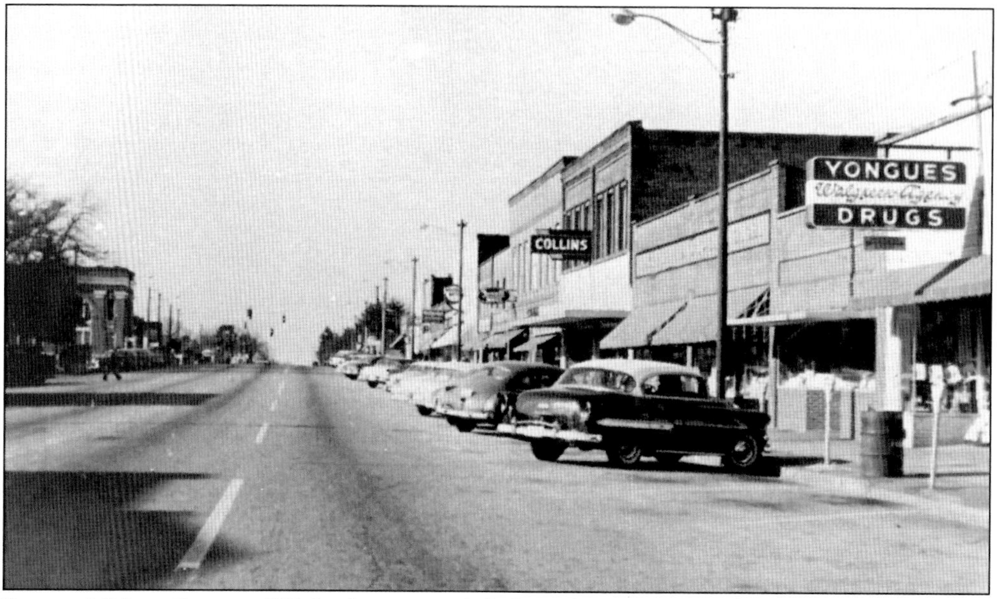

PICKENS' MAIN STREET. While the automobile brought tourists, it also brought traffic jams, traffic lights, and parking meters. Pickens witnessed a population boom after World War II. In this 1950s image, the photographer points his camera west toward Oconee. The Pickens Bank, erected in 1910, is in the background on the left. (Photo courtesy of the South Caroliniana Library, University of South Carolina, Columbia.)

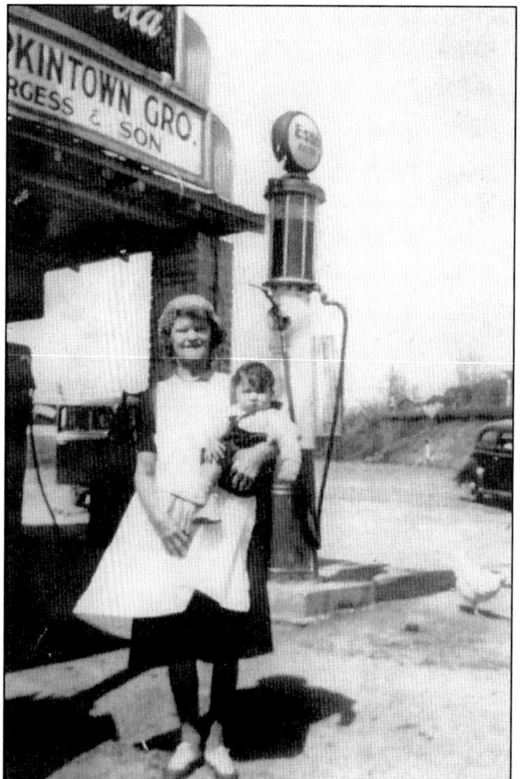

BECKY AND BABY. S.C. 8 leads from picturesque Pickens to Pumpkintown. Becky Reeves and baby Jimmy Holcombe are shown here in Pumpkintown in 1943. Little has changed at the junction. The store still stands. (Photo courtesy of Danny Cummings.)

Three

Education and Institutions

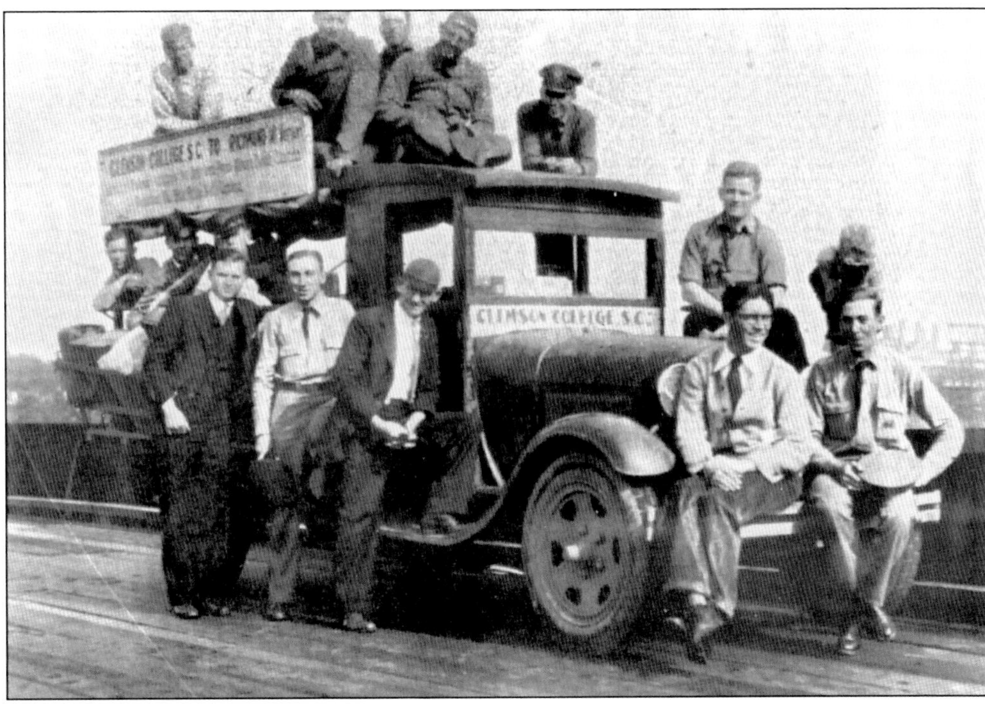

Clemson Boys and Bus. More than 400 men enrolled in Clemson Agricultural College when it opened in 1893. At the same time, the connectional missionary secretary of the Wesleyan Methodist Church, Rev. Eber Teter, began to scout out a site for a training school. Teter found a location further down the road beyond the town of Calhoun and near the city limits of Central. (Photo courtesy of the Pickens County Library.)

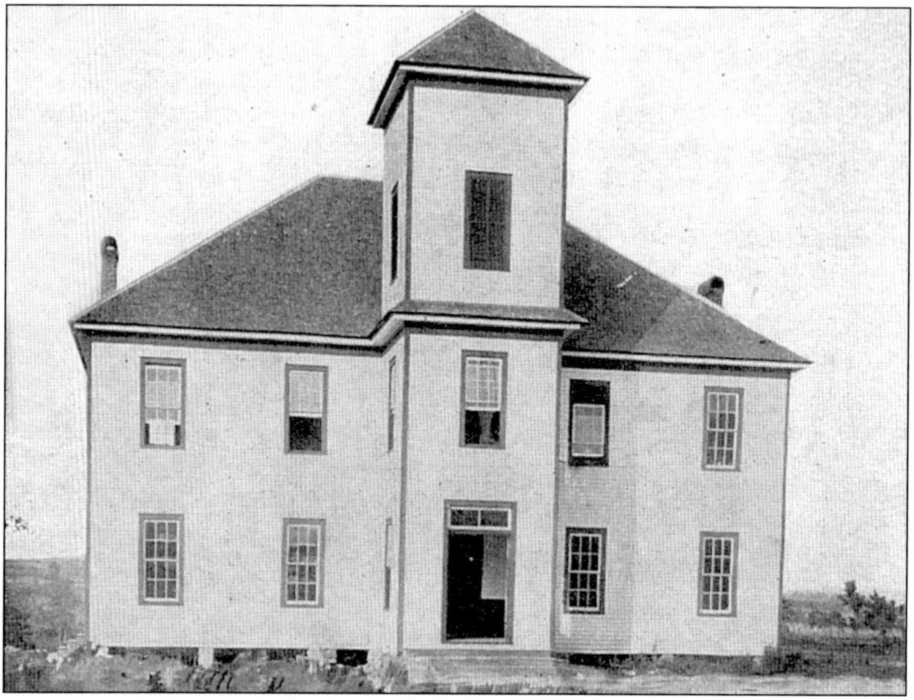

SMITH HALL. At the annual conference of 1901 a committee agreed to build a school. In 1903, Rev. Eber Teter called a meeting of the presidents of the Wesleyan Methodist Southern Conference to be held in Central, S.C. The site was affirmed at this meeting. With a gift from Charles B. Smith, Smith Hall (the administration building) was erected on College Hill in 1906. (Photo courtesy of Southern Wesleyan University and the Central Heritage Society.)

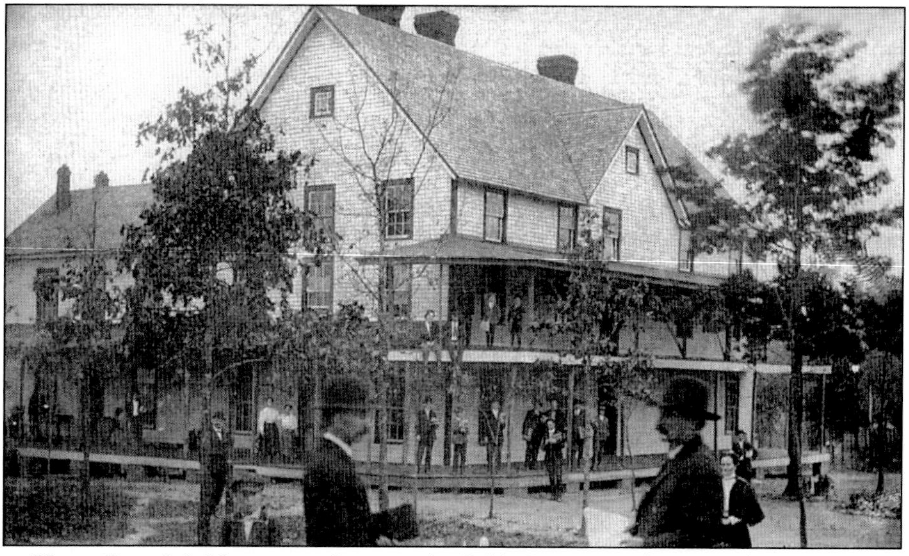

TETER HALL. Rev. L.J. Harrington became the Bible Institute's first president. He and three teachers opened the school on October 15, 1906. In 1907, Rev. A.C. Dunwoody and his wife managed a girls' dormitory, Dunwoody Hall. Teter Hall for boys opened in 1908. As seen here in this view from 1912, Teter Hall, named for Rev. Eber Teter, housed the dining hall for the school. (Photo courtesy of Southern Wesleyan University.)

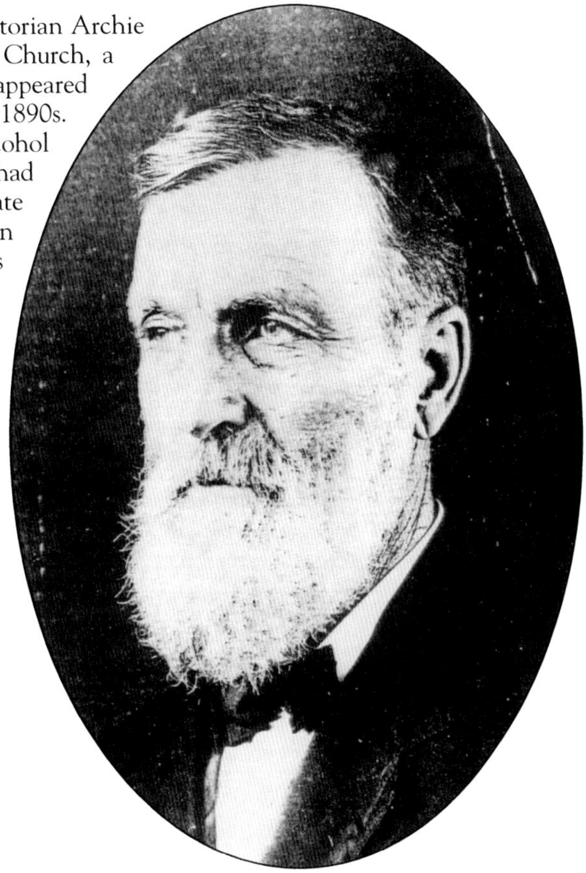

Portrait of Teter. According to historian Archie V. Huff Jr., the Wesleyan Methodist Church, a part of the Pentecostal Movement, appeared in the Upcountry around the late 1890s. Wesleyans renounced tobacco and alcohol consumption, and by 1900 they had established 25 churches in the state with 1,131 members. The Wesleyan Methodist Church needed ministers and the task befell Rev. Eber Teter to create a quality school to educate pastors. Teter found a soft hill in the woodlands of Central and the Wesleyan Methodist Bible Institute was soon under construction. (Photo courtesy of the Pickens County Library.)

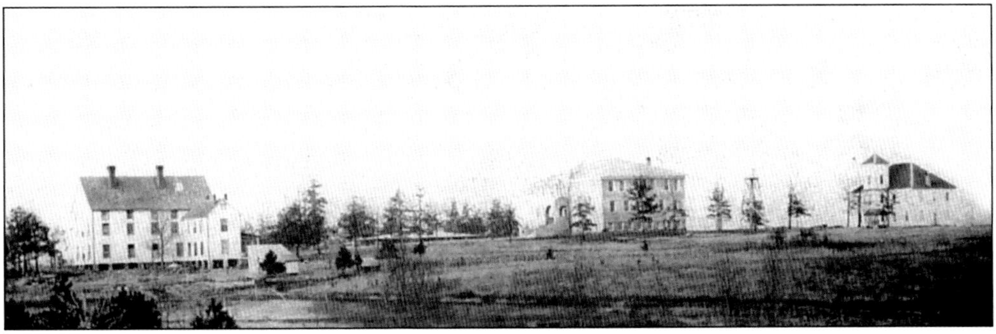

College Hill. Postcards of the Wesleyan Methodist Bible Institute are rare. This postcard depicts College Hill at the beginning of the 20th century. The structures shown here, from left to right, are Teter Hall, Grimes Hall, the water tank, and Smith Hall. At the time, the school offered classes from the first grade through the three-year college-level theological course, but in 1909 the school reorganized. Its 1909 charter renamed the institute. It became the Wesleyan Methodist College with degrees including Bachelor of Arts, Bachelor of Science, and a Bachelor of Divinity. (Postcard courtesy of Southern Wesleyan University.)

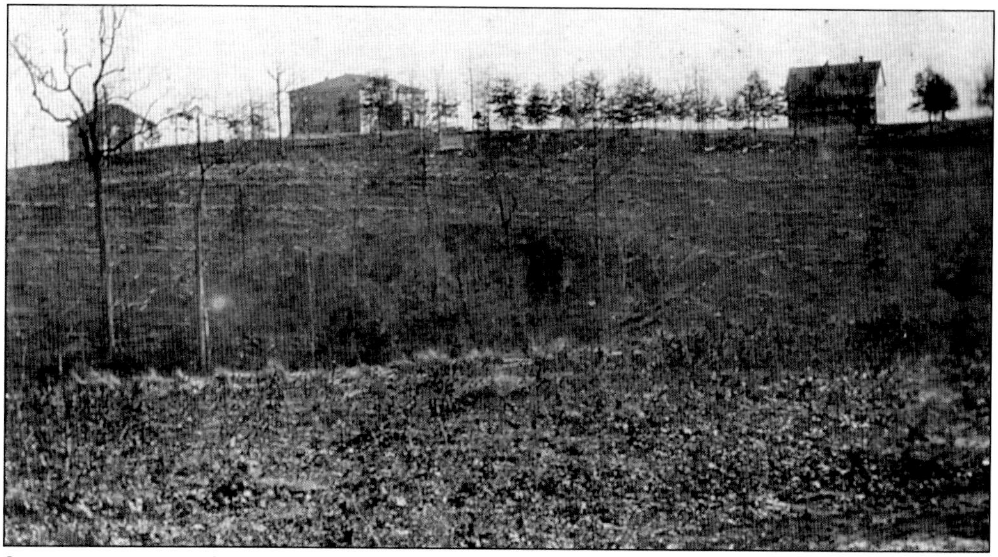

SKYLINE 1918. Wesleyan Methodist College is featured in this 1918 postcard image of College Hill. The structures, from left to right, are Dunwoody Hall, Grimes Hall, and Teter Hall. This view was photographed from a dirt road that would become S.C. 93. In 1928, Wesleyan Methodist College was reduced to junior college status by a meeting of the local board of managers and special representatives of the denominational board. With the exception of a four-year course in theological work leading to the Bachelor of Divinity, the college discontinued its degree programs. In 1931 the junior college was approved for teacher training. In 1953 the Southern Association of Colleges and Secondary Schools accredited both the high school and the junior college, yet the administration chose to phase out the high school. (Postcard courtesy of Southern Wesleyan University.)

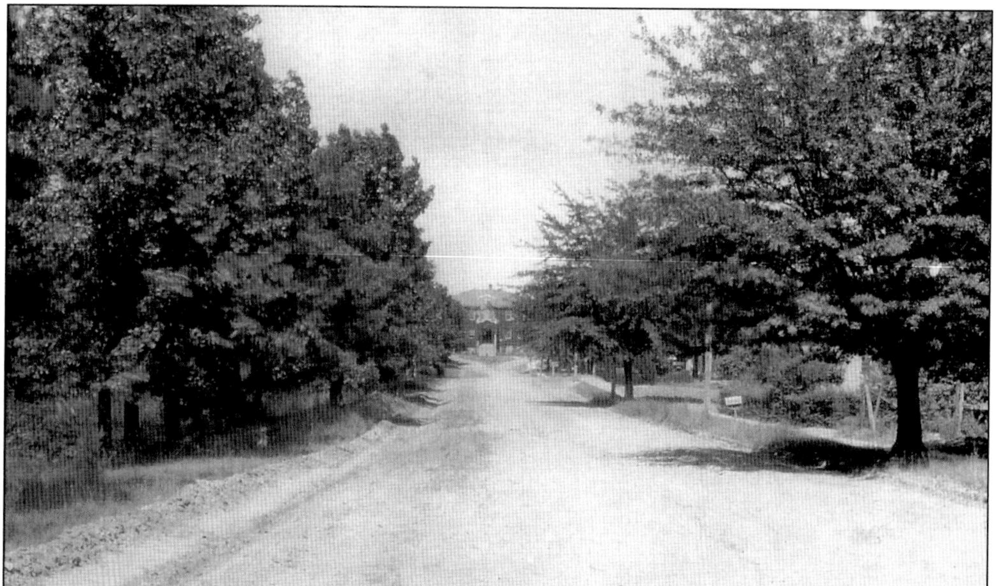

GRIMES HALL, 1918. The Claude R. Rickman Library stands on the site of Grimes Hall. This is College Hill before the avenue was paved. Grimes Hall was built directly in front of Smith Hall. (Photo courtesy of Southern Wesleyan University.)

SKULL. H.H. Atkinson poses with roommate Lawrence Garvin Clayton M.D. (at the right) for an 1877 photograph taken at the University of Virginia. Dr. Clayton (1854–1935) is one of the founders of Southern Wesleyan University. The feisty Clayton was considered by his peers to be a superior physician, quail hunter, and Blue Tick hound breeder. Dr. Clayton, born in Slabtown, Anderson County, and educated at its Thalian Academy, returned to South Carolina after completing his residency at the University of Maryland and the Baltimore Infirmary. In time, he set up practice in Central, where he made house calls on horseback. He married and raised 12 children. He was the president of the Pickens County Medical Society, and a gifted obstetrician. (Photo courtesy of Southern Wesleyan University.)

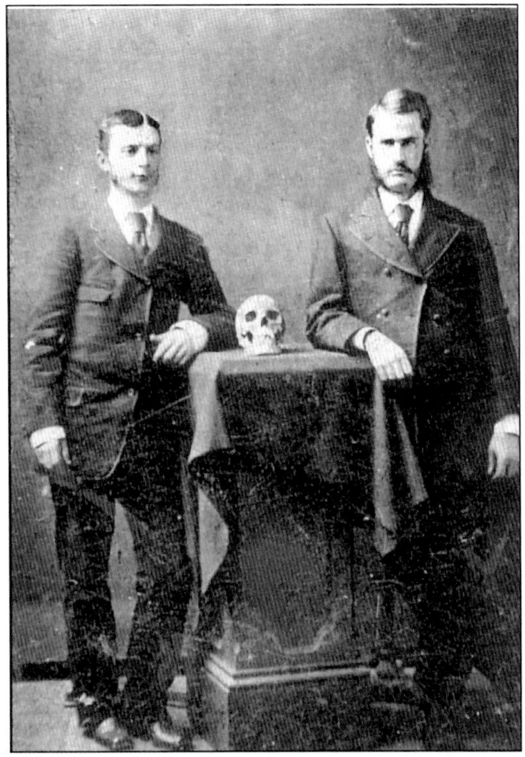

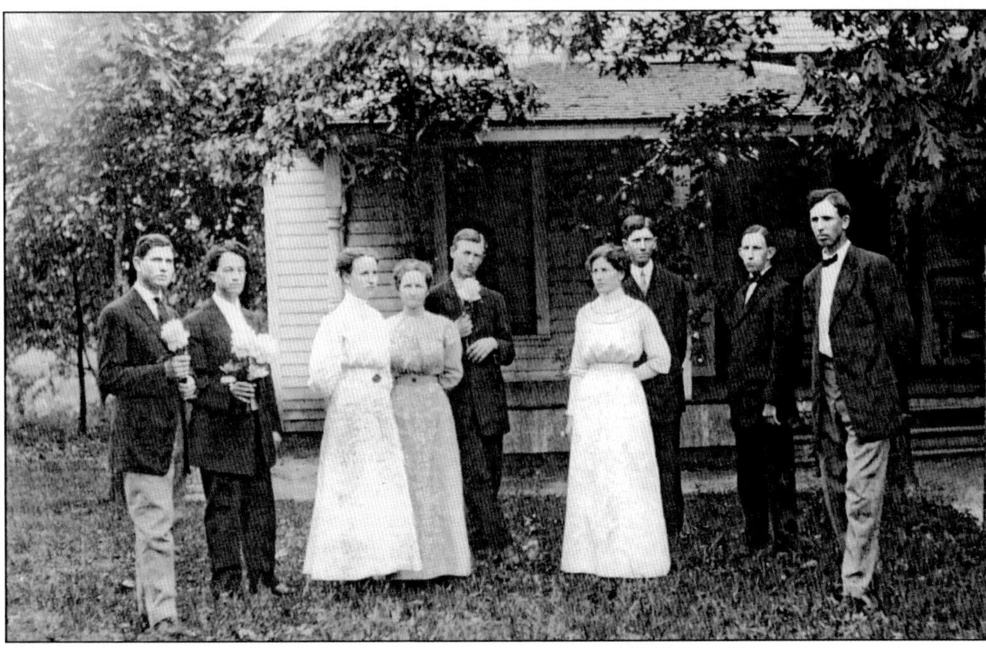

SPRING 1911. Some of the 1911 graduates of Southern Wesleyan University stand in front of the Tegan House, which still stands today. Shown here, from left to right, are Marvin Lawrence, Hammond R. Gunby, Fannie Correll, Rosa Lawrence, Bob Joe Correll, Corrie Lawrence, Tom Lawrence, John Frank Childs, and W.D. Correll. (Photo courtesy of Southern Wesleyan University.)

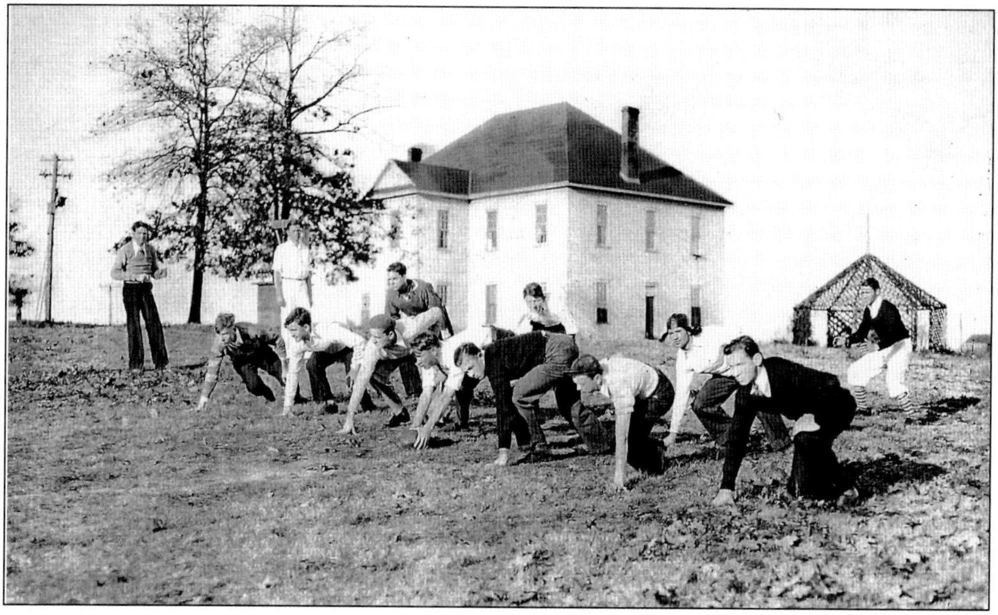

Football in front of Smith Hall. Unlike Clemson, Southern Wesleyan University admitted girls into its academic programs, but there were no cheerleaders at Smith Hall. Periodically, Southern Wesleyan musters up a football team. In this 1900s image, the team had no name. The guys just called themselves the Boys Athletic Association. (Photo courtesy of Southern Wesleyan University.)

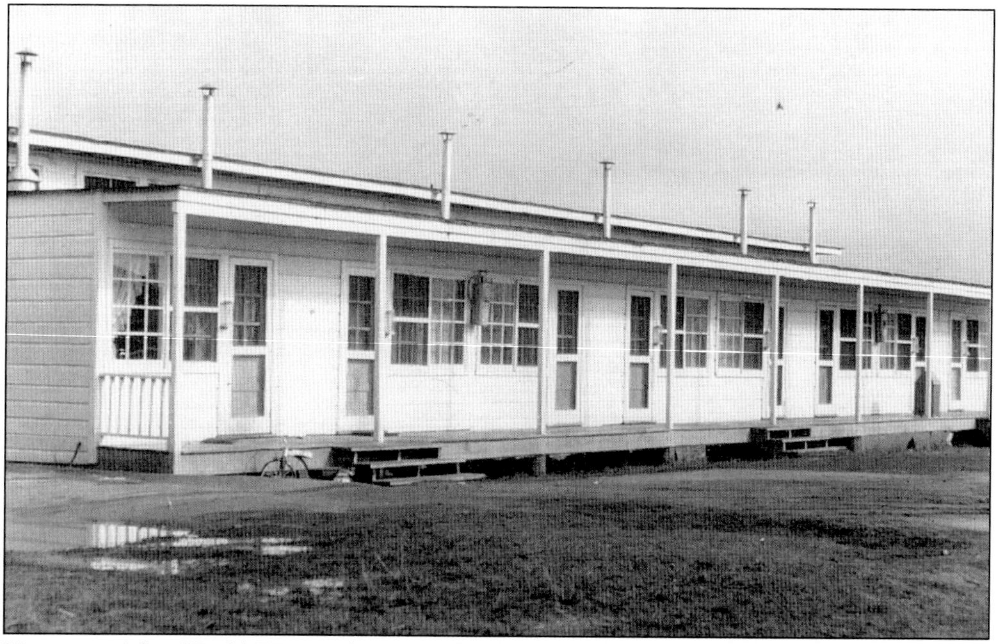

Vetville. After World War II, the G.I. Bill allowed men to pursue a college education. Due to the popularity of the G.I. Bill and ballooning enrollment, Southern Wesleyan utilized government surplus housing. The housing was called Vetville and was located near Grimes Hall. It was quickly constructed in 1946 for war veterans and their families. This unit no longer exists. (Photo courtesy of Southern Wesleyan University.)

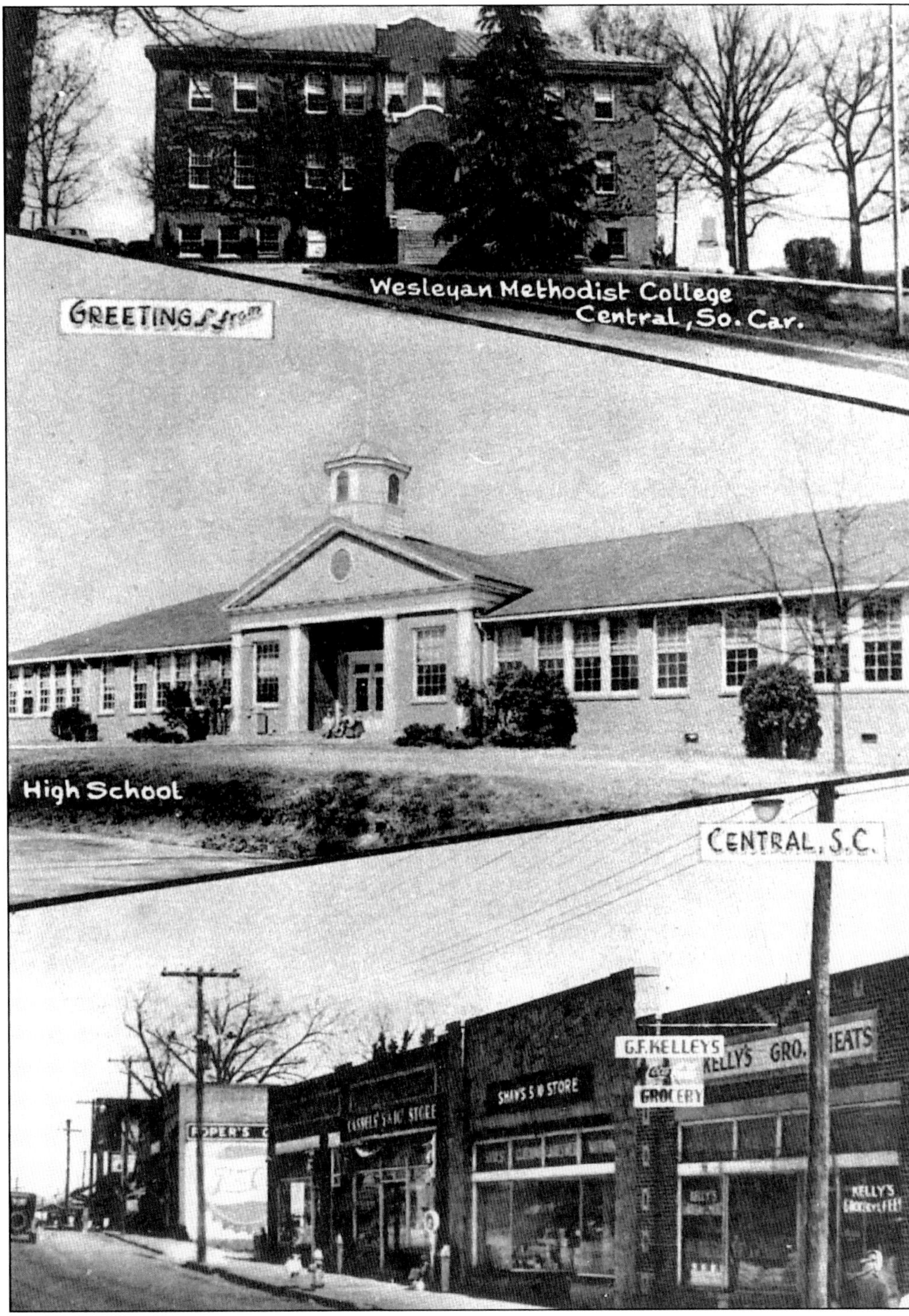

POSTCARD OF CENTRAL. A postcard from Central depicts Grimes Hall (top), razed in 1974. The high school building, closed in 1955, serves as an apartment complex, and quaint Main Street looks much like did in the 1940s. (Photo courtesy of the South Caroliniana Library, University of South Carolina, Columbia.)

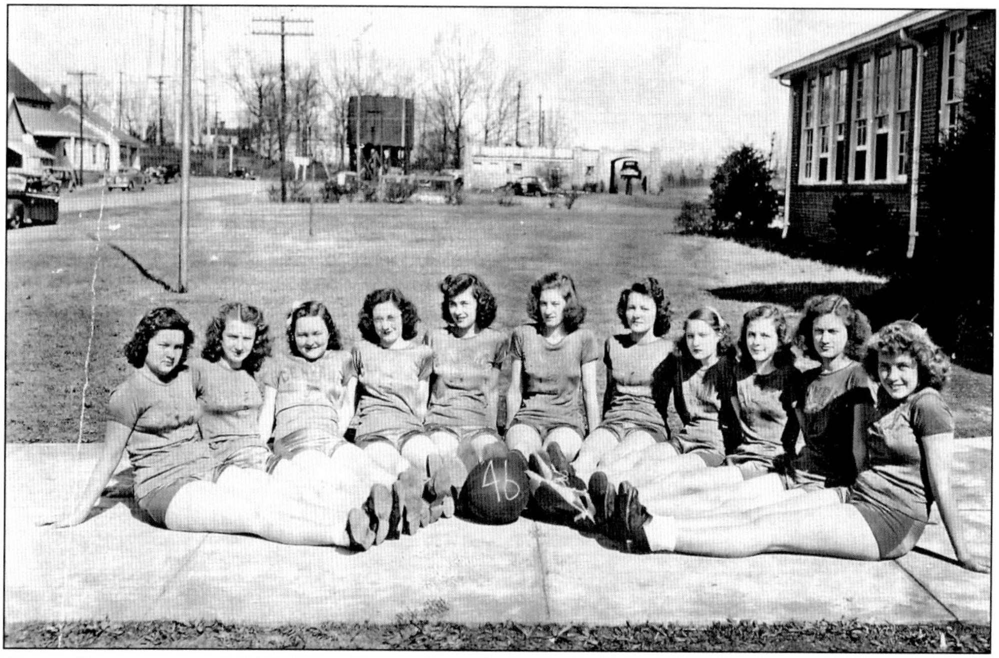

GIRLS BASKETBALL, 1946. The Central's girls basketball team poses for a picture in 1946. Shown here, from left to right, are Betty Horton, Mickey Newton, Frankie Sue Elliott, Carlene Burroughs, Mary Eugenia Dudley, Odessa Elrod, Pansy Dunn, Martha Sue Gaines, and Betty Ann Coker (Blanche Tinsley is not pictured). At the extreme right is the high school. Main Street (S.C. 93) and the railroad water tower are in the background. You would turn right to go to Central Wesleyan and left to go to Clemson. Notice the grey-stone garage complete with an automobile in the service bay. (Photo courtesy of Mary Eugenia Dudley Stone and the Central Heritage Society.)

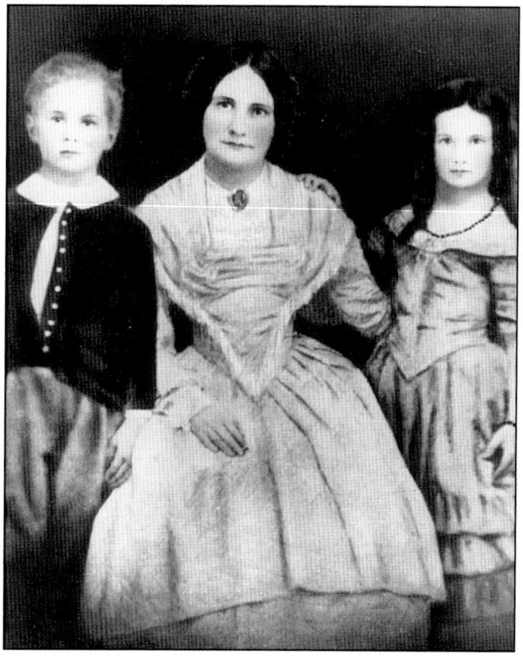

CLEMSON'S FAMILY. Southwest of Central is Clemson, a college born out of T.G. Clemson's sympathies and tragedies. Little John Calhoun Clemson (left) with his mother, Anna Maria Calhoun Clemson, and sister, Floride Clemson (Mrs. Gideon Lee), pose together in this portrait. John died near Seneca and with no heirs to the John C. Calhoun estate, Clemson bequeathed a cash fortune and over 800 acres for the establishment of the Clemson Agricultural College of South Carolina. Clemson died April 6, 1888, and did not witness the formation of the school. He would not realize that his actions initiated a new era in higher education in South Carolina. (Photo courtesy of the Strom Thurmond Institute.)

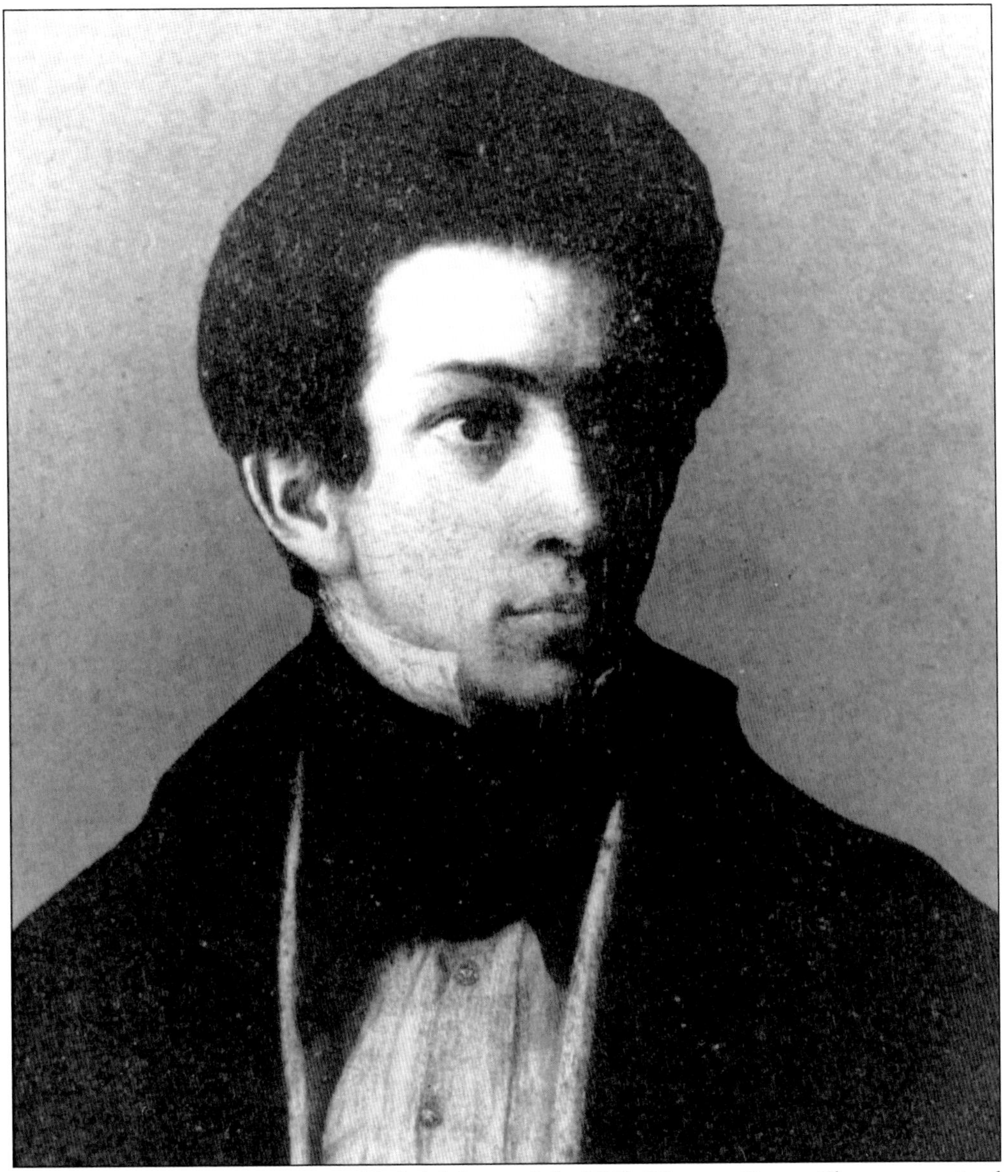

YOUNG T.G. CLEMSON. Born in Philadelphia in July 1807, Thomas Green Clemson received his formal education in the States and in Europe. He enjoyed science and agricultural studies. He married John C. Calhoun's daughter, Anna Maria, in 1838. In the post–Civil War days of 1865, Clemson remarked about the economically ruined South that "this country is in wretched condition, no money and nothing to sell. Everyone is ruined, and those that can are leaving." When Thomas Clemson died on April 6, 1888, he left most of his estate "to be used to establish a college that would teach scientific agriculture and the mechanical arts to the young people of South Carolina." He stated in his will that the school should be "modeled after the Agricultural College of Mississippi as far as practicable." In November 1889, Governor Richardson signed the bill accepting Thomas Clemson's gift that established the Clemson Agricultural College, with its trustees becoming custodians of Morrill Act and Hatch Act funds made available for agricultural education and research purposes by federal legislative acts. (Photo courtesy of the Strom Thurmond Institute.)

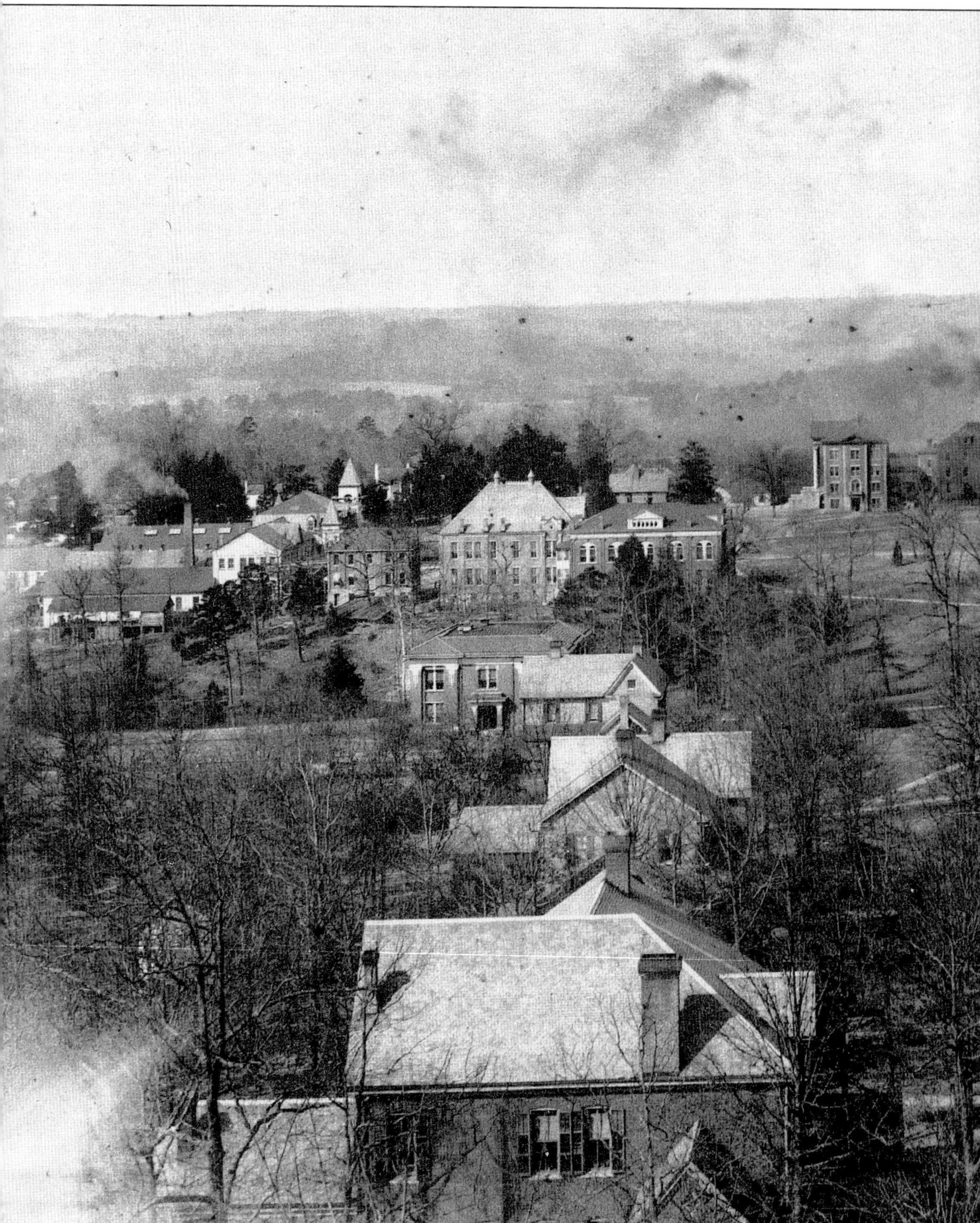

Clemson College. In 1883 Thomas Clemson remarked in his Last Will and Testament, "Feeling a great sympathy for the farmers of this State, and the difficulties with which they had to contend in their efforts to establish the business of agriculture upon a prosperous basis, and believing that there can be no permanent improvement in agriculture without a knowledge of those sciences

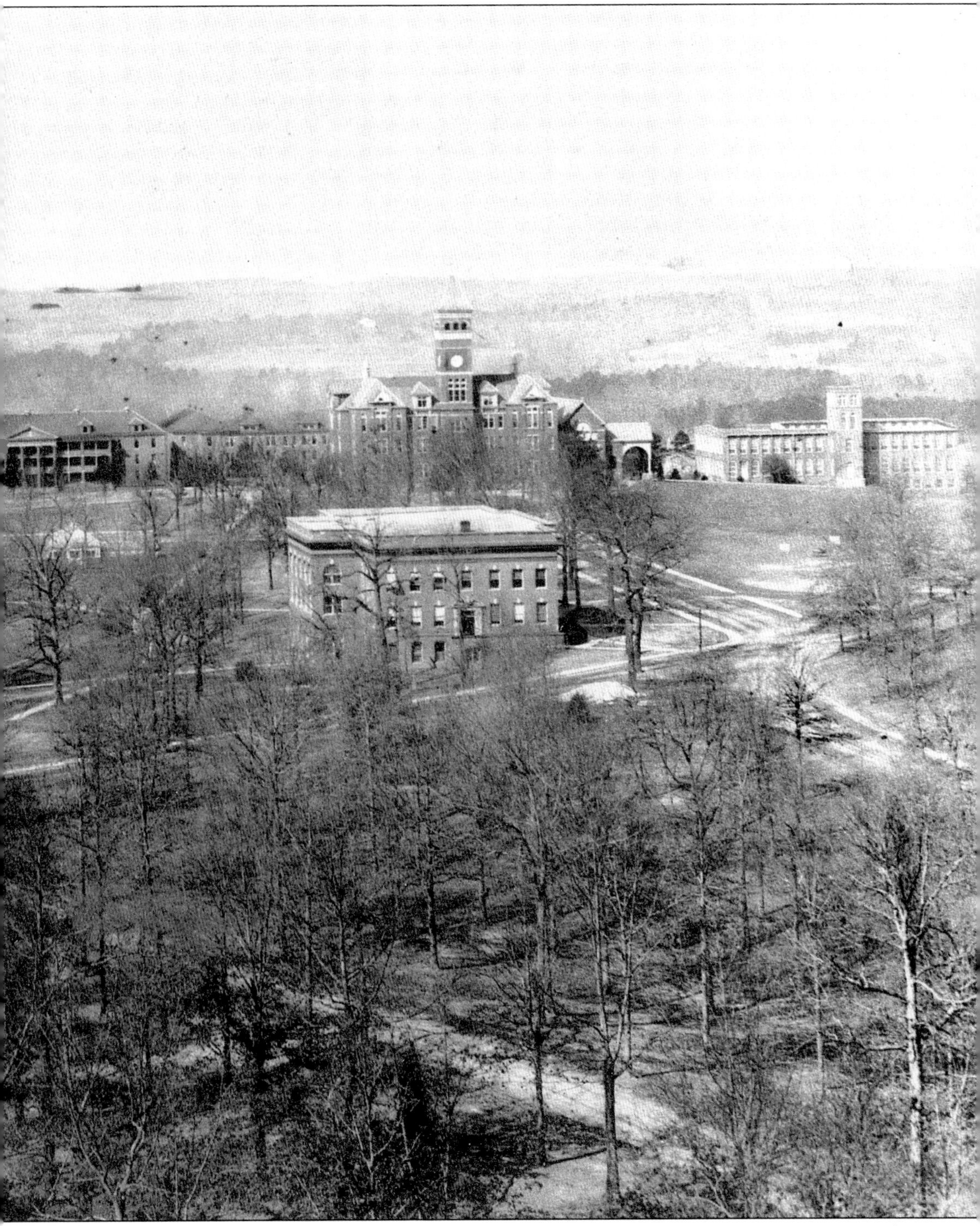

which pertain particularly thereto, I have determined to devote the bulk of my property to the establishment of an agricultural college upon the Fort Hill place." Clemson College formally opened in July 1893. From the beginning, the college was an all-male military school, and it remained this way until 1955. (Photo courtesy of the Strom Thurmond Institute.)

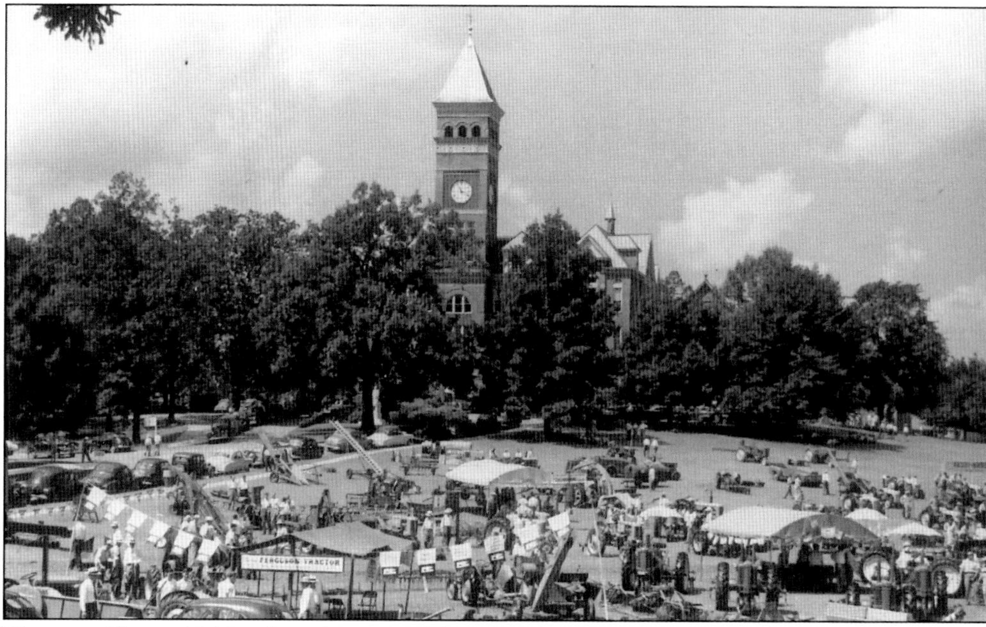

TILLMAN HALL, 1940s. An advocate of farmers, Gov. Benjamin R. Tillman (1890 to 1894) strongly supported the formation of Clemson College, where T. Clemson's dream had become a reality. Farmers and their families toured displays of new inventions and attended free lectures about scientific techniques that would improve their lives. This yearly event, called Clemson's Farm and Home Week, was sponsored by Clemson's Cooperative Extension Staff. (Photo courtesy of the Strom Thurmond Institute.)

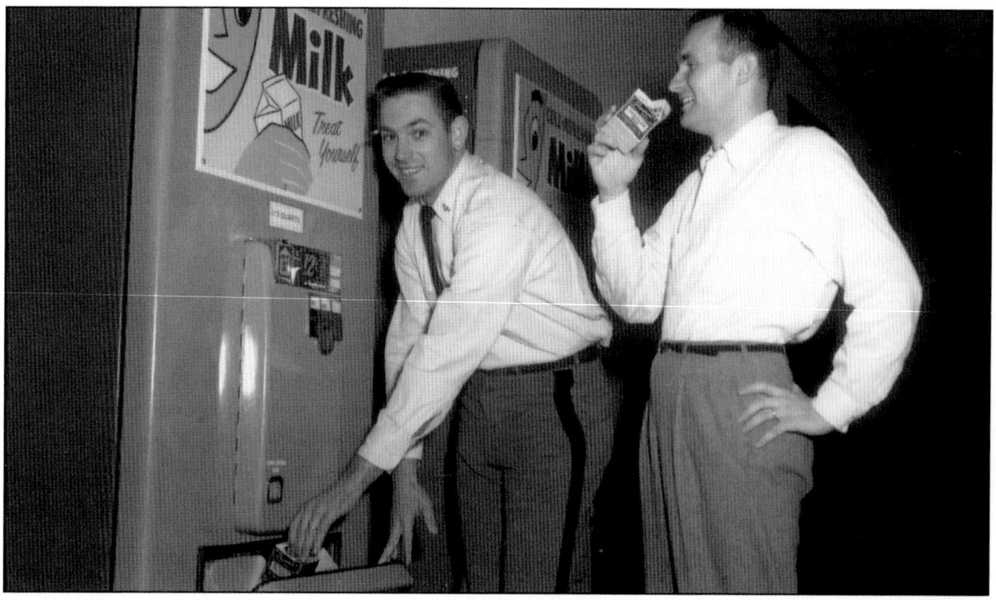

GOT MILK? Milk from a 1950s vending machine cost 12¢. For more than 25 years, Clemson Agricultural College researched and experimented in order to improve methods of producing, processing, refrigerating, and delivering vitamin fortified milk to the masses. Dairies small and large dotted the South, and Clemson was an essential player in the successful and profitable operation of these farms. (Photo courtesy of the Strom Thurmond Institute.)

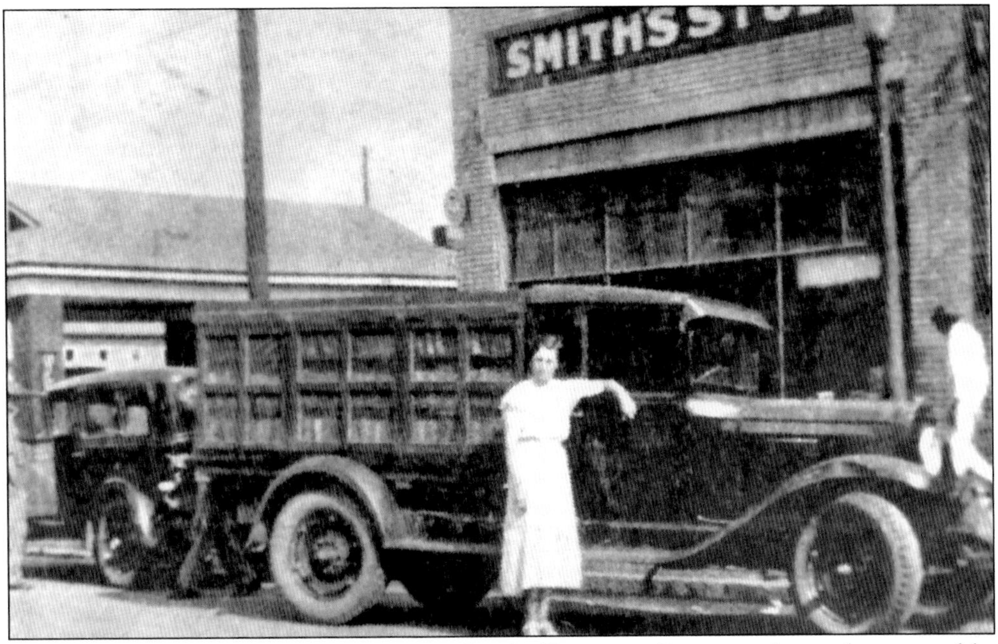

LIBRARY TRUCK. Financed as a project under the Economic Recovery Act and sponsored by the county and state boards of education, the Pickens County Library Association organized between 1929 and 1935 with the assistance of the Works Project Administration. The Easley branch library began in 1929 and the Pickens branch began in 1935 in an effort to provide free books to the people. Trucks were used to bring books to the people until suitable buildings were donated or sold to the library association. (Photo courtesy of Pickens County Library.)

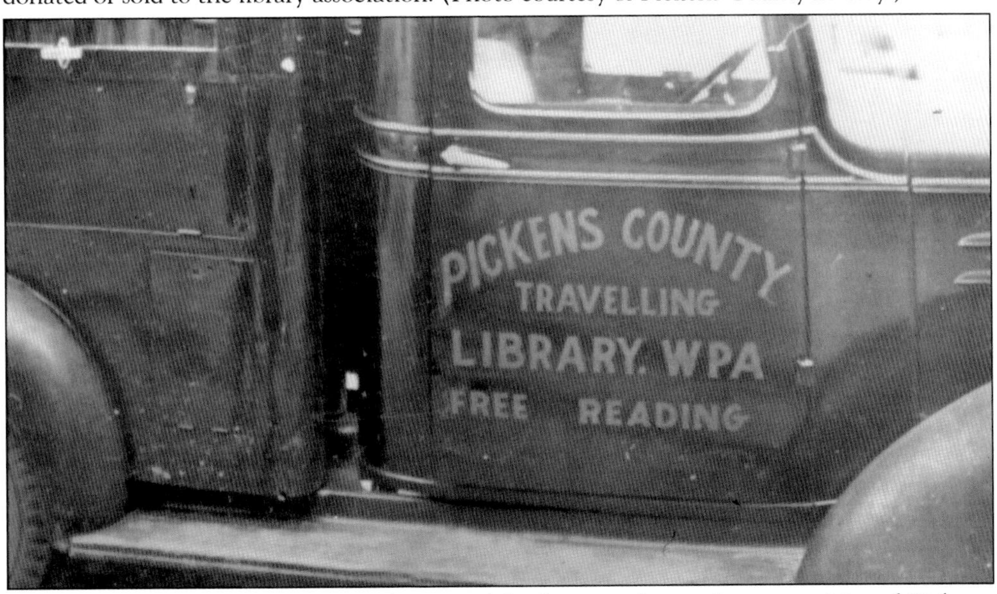

WPA FREE READING TRUCK. Trucks carried books into the rural communities of Pickens, but the George Washington Carver Library, a modest structure near the Pickens County Training School (c. 1940s), offered no such services to the African-American neighborhoods. Eventually, the Carver Library was incorporated into the training school. (Photo courtesy of Pickens County Library.)

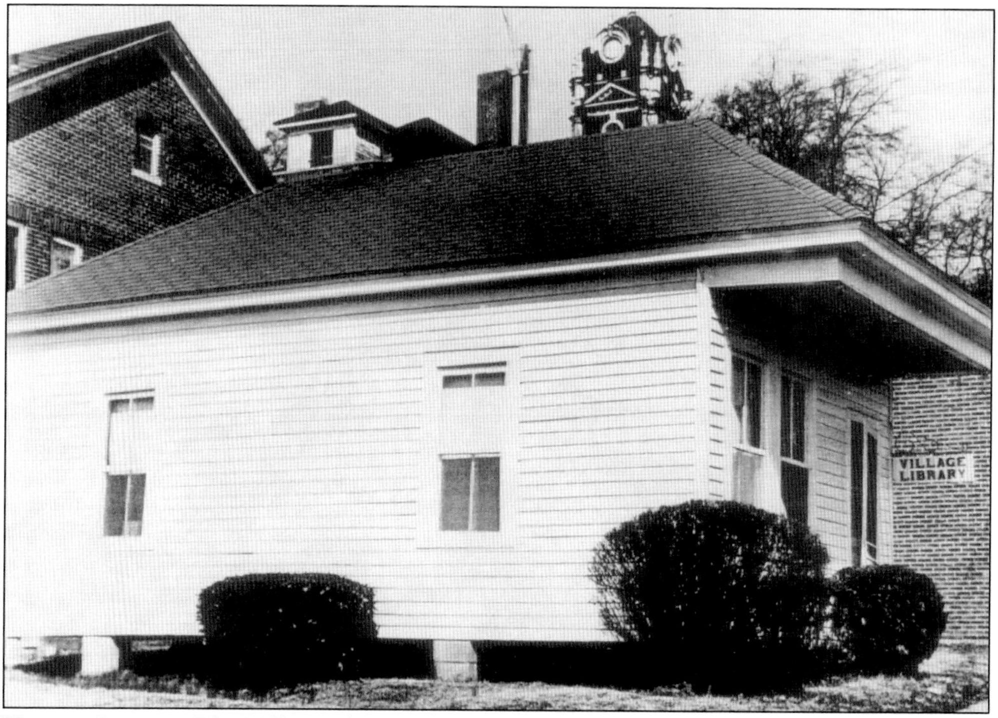

VILLAGE LIBRARY. The Village Library in Pickens was a modest wooden structure in 1959. Miss Margaret Wright was the librarian at the time. Note that the steeple is actually the top of the Pickens Courthouse erected in the late 1800s. (Photo courtesy of Pickens County Library.)

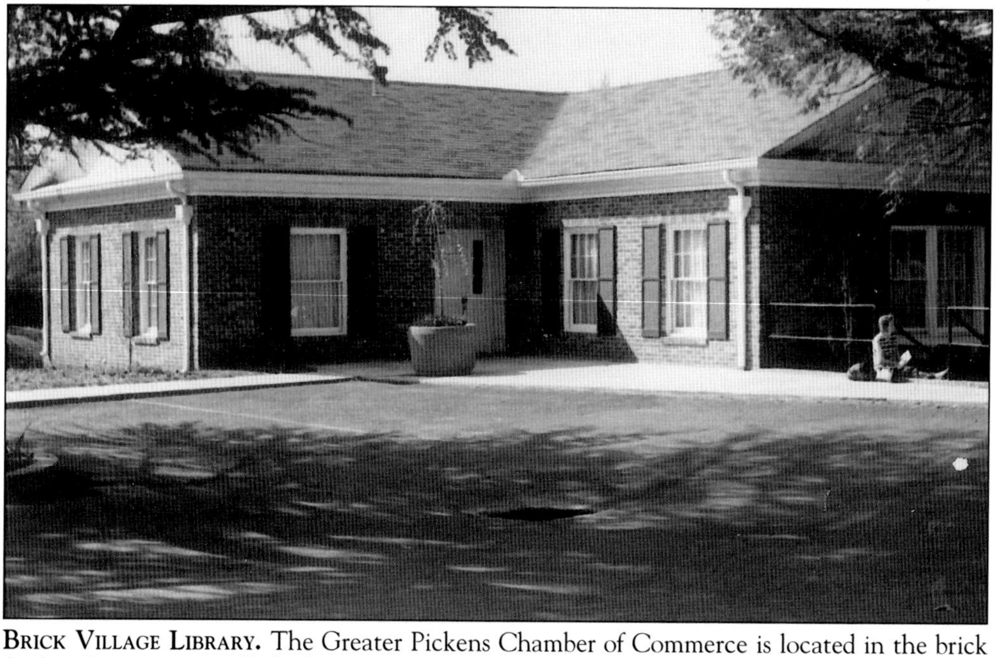

BRICK VILLAGE LIBRARY. The Greater Pickens Chamber of Commerce is located in the brick facility that was originally built in 1974 for the Village Library. The Village Library expanded in 1994 and relocated to Catherine Street in the city of Pickens. The main branch of the Pickens County Library system is located in Easley. (Photo courtesy of Pickens County Library.)

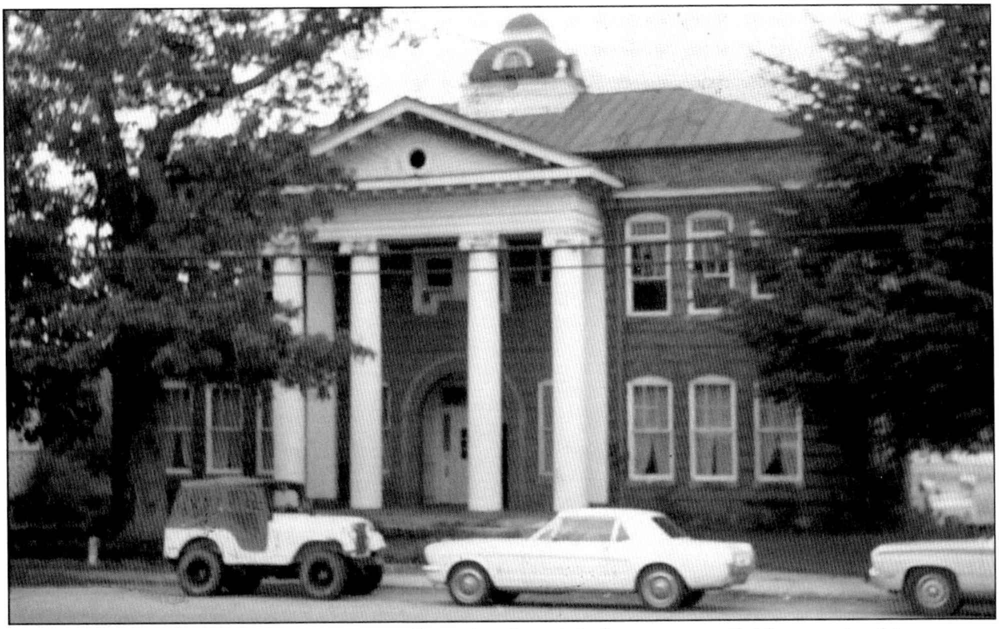

Central Library. In 1960 a new walk-in bookmobile became available to suburbia patrons who were building homes along the highways. The main library was open at night for the first time, and county library branches were established in Central and Clemson. In Central, the first public high school, on Church Street (constructed *c.* 1900s by contractor and brick mason J.H. Hall), was adapted for the library's use in 1962. It was called the Allen Community Library. Now vacant of books, the Central school with its detailed Greek moldings, brick impost entrance, and Greek columns with voluted capitals is a remarkable piece of architecture. (Photo courtesy of Pickens County Library.)

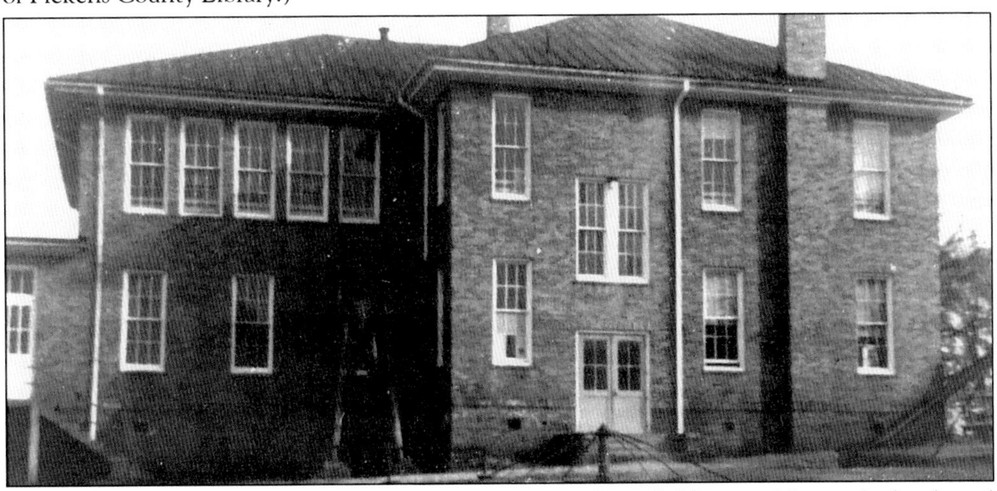

Cateechee-Norris School. In the early years at Cateechee, children could attend school until they reached the eighth grade. Obtaining a higher education meant leaving the community and paying tuition. Most Cateechee parents could not afford boarding schools, so public schools were a welcomed addition by the 1920s. Cateechee had several schools including this one, which is usually referred to as Cateechee-Norris Elementary. While not as grand in construction as the Central School, the building proved to be equally functional in serving the children from Cateechee and Norris. (Photo courtesy of Pickens County Library.)

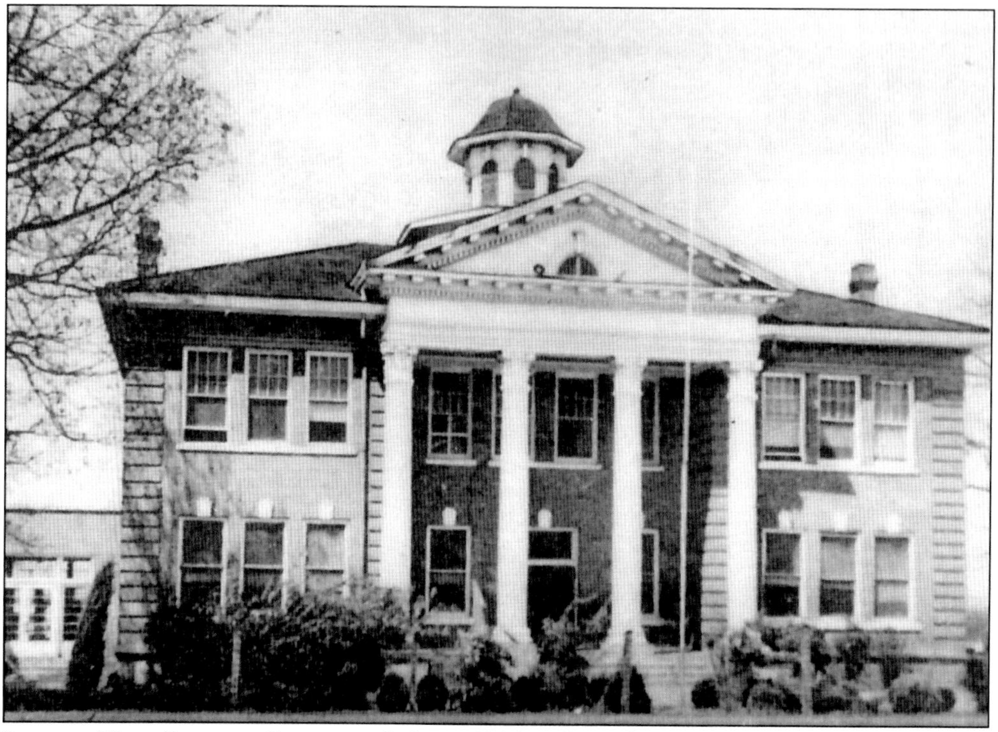

Liberty High School. Constructed about 1906 and razed in 1967, Liberty High School is pictured in this 1950s postcard. Initially, the school existed to teach white children only, but by 1969 Pickens County Schools had integrated. (Photo courtesy of the Audrey Wyatt and Anne Sheriff.)

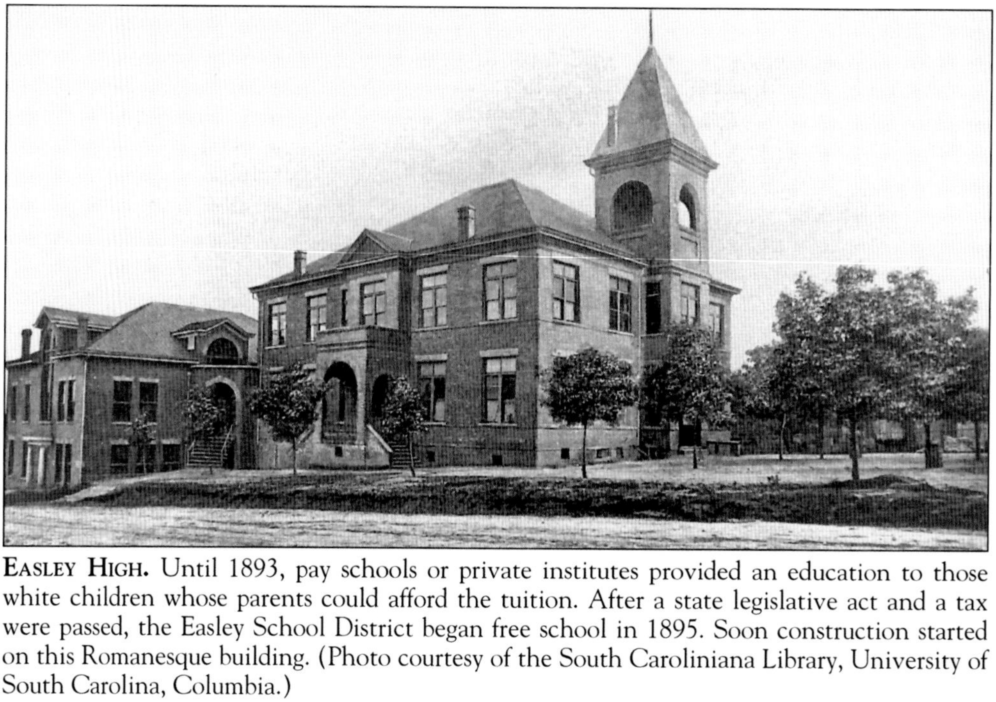

Easley High. Until 1893, pay schools or private institutes provided an education to those white children whose parents could afford the tuition. After a state legislative act and a tax were passed, the Easley School District began free school in 1895. Soon construction started on this Romanesque building. (Photo courtesy of the South Caroliniana Library, University of South Carolina, Columbia.)

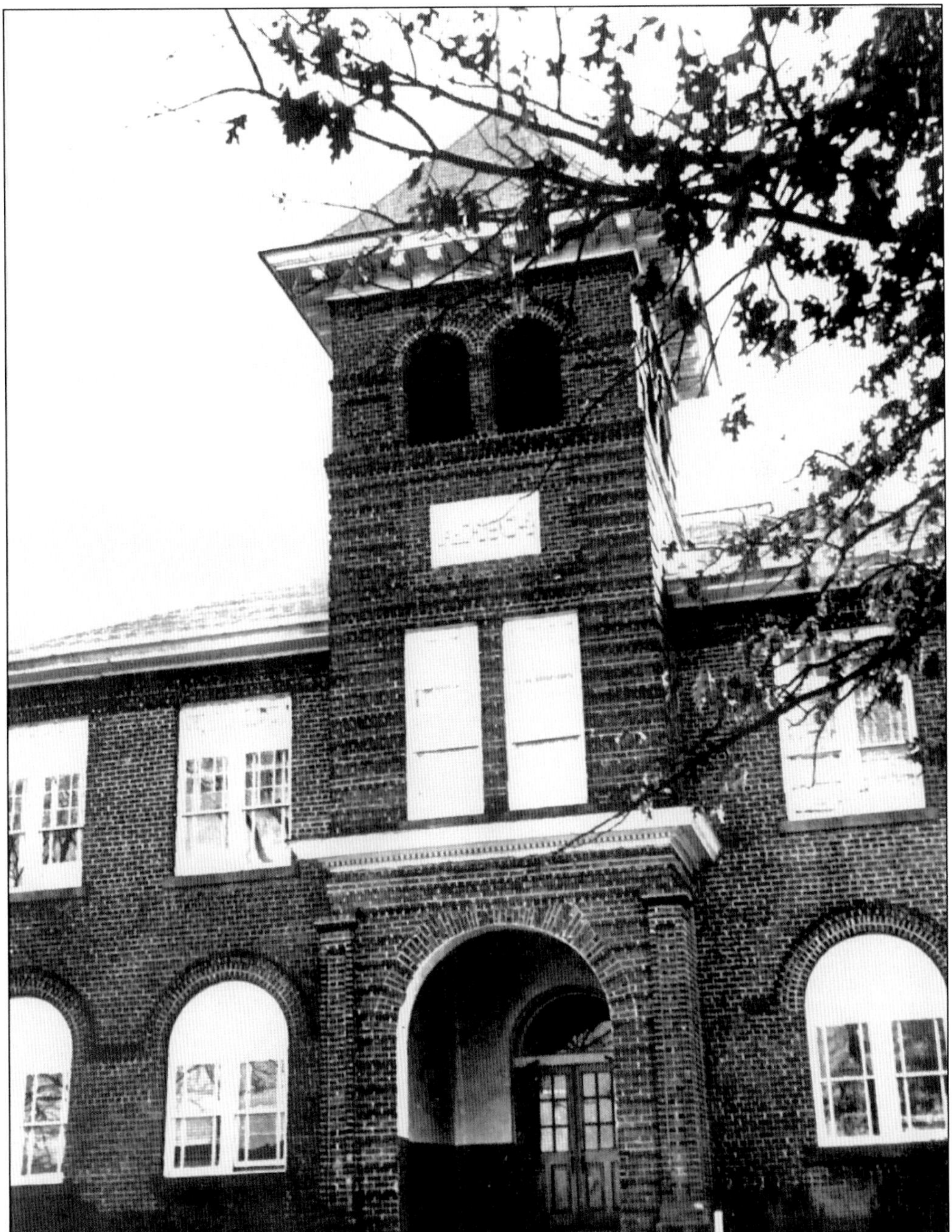

PICKENS HIGH. Clemson's Tillman Hall, with its arched entrances and doorways and its grand clock tower, impacted architects of the Pickens County School Districts. This is the old Pickens High School. According to library documents, the graduating class of 1905 consisted of Jay Robinson, Jesse Looper, Lee Roper, Leroy Grandy, Ella Looper, Mary Newton, Eliza McDaniel, Kate Hester, Viola Gilstrap, Floride Carey, and Eilene Taylor. (Photo courtesy of the Pickens County Library.)

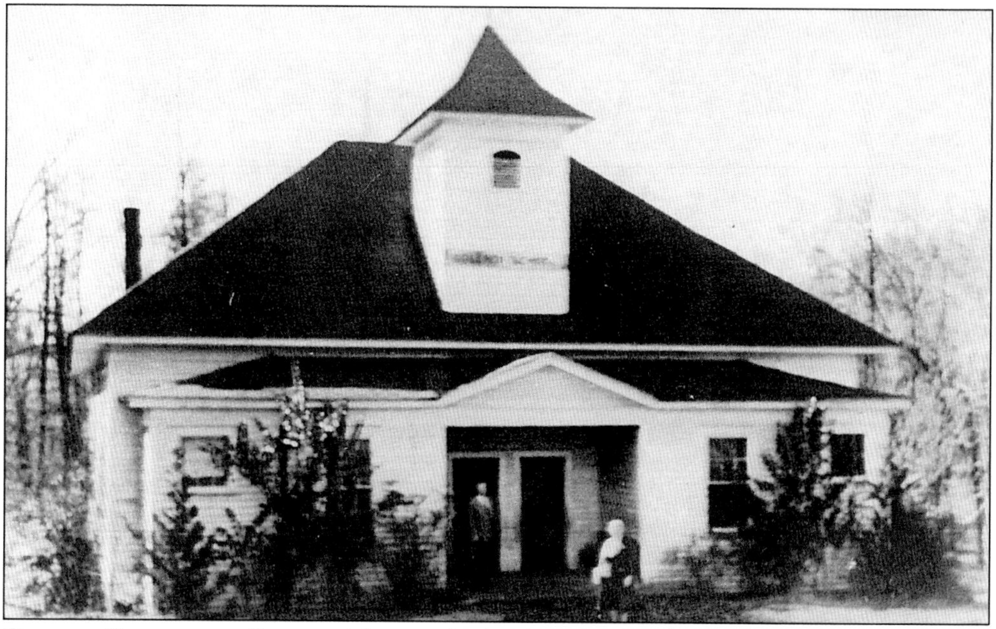

OOLENOY ELEMENTARY SCHOOL. Most rural schools and colored schools were constructed out of wood. As the county grew and facilities became unsafe or outdated, schools like Oolenoy Elementary, pictured here in the 1950s, were ordered to consolidate with larger schools in more densely populated areas. (Photo courtesy of the Pickens County Library.)

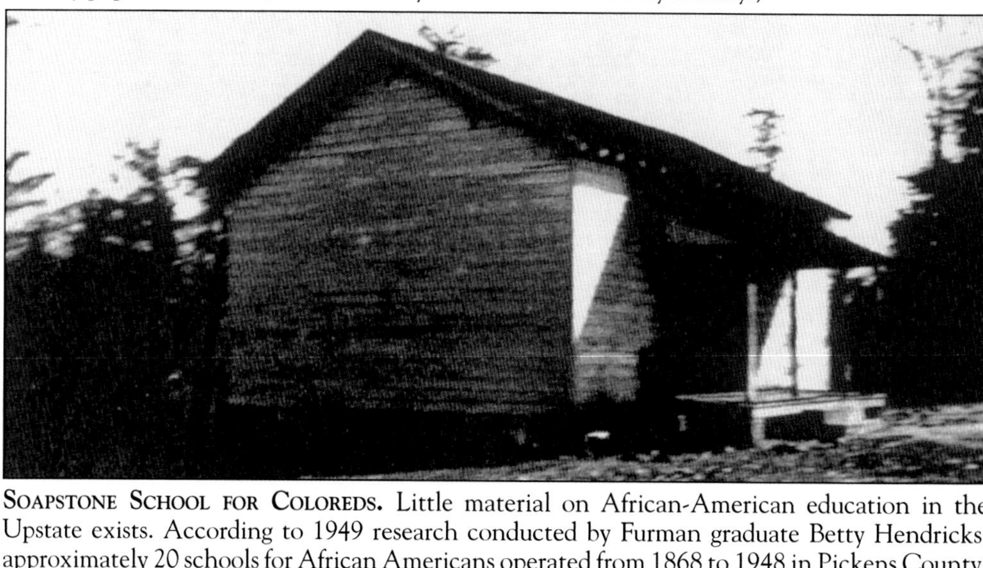

SOAPSTONE SCHOOL FOR COLOREDS. Little material on African-American education in the Upstate exists. According to 1949 research conducted by Furman graduate Betty Hendricks, approximately 20 schools for African Americans operated from 1868 to 1948 in Pickens County. These schools included Cold Springs, Twelve Mile, Cross Roads, Pickens County Training (destroyed by fire in 1966), Dacusville, Cross Plains, Bright Station, Liberty Colored, Simpson School (in Easley), Norris Colored, Calhoun Colored, White Oak, and Dayton. Tradition has it that Soapstone Rock, an actual rock where students gathered, was the first African-American school in Pickens. Later, this structure, Soapstone School, was erected. Many of the African-American schools no longer exist. Some of the buildings constructed from wooden planks either burned to the ground or were recycled into other buildings. (Photo courtesy of Southern Wesleyan University. Hendricks Report filed with PDHRT.)

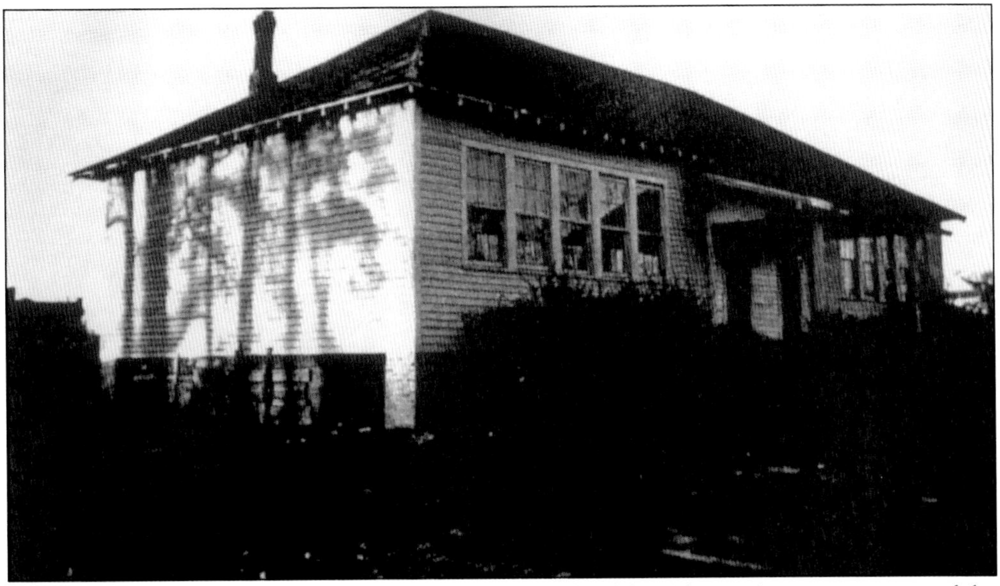

CENTRAL COLORED SCHOOL. **THE** Central Colored School for African Americans is one of the few structures that survived the turbulence of the 1960s. Located on S.C. 93 not far from the Littlejohn Community Center, the Central Colored School, taught by P.S. Little, stands for an unprecedented era of educational reform in the Upcountry. By 1969, Pickens County schools had integrated. (Photo courtesy of the Central Heritage Society.)

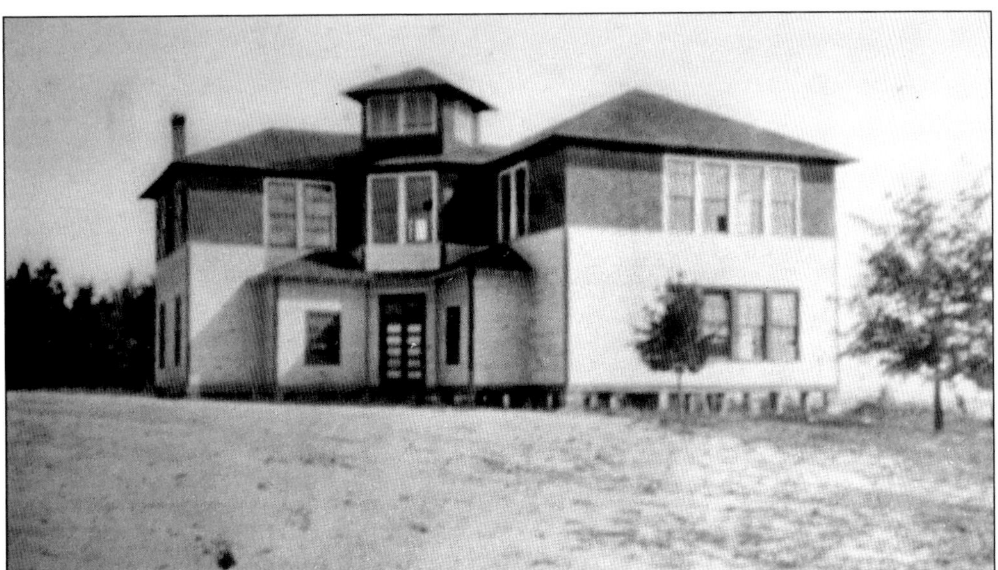

DACUSVILLE ELEMENTARY. Dacusville Elementary, close to Marietta and Greenville, is pictured here. (Courtesy of Pickens County Library.)

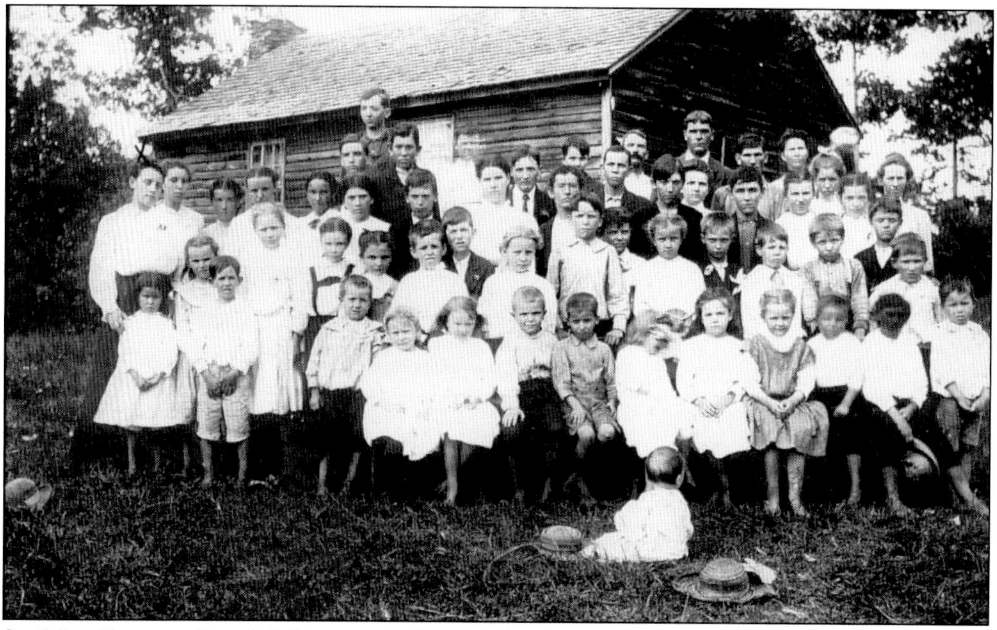

SIX MILE SCHOOL. Rev. L.J. Harrington became Southern Wesleyan University's first president. His daughter, Beth Harrington (Mrs. Henry West), opened the first school in Six Mile around 1910. A small "x" has been inked over Beth's head. The farm children wear no shoes, and the tree foliage indicates that the modest school building and its student body were photographed in the spring or fall. (Photo courtesy of Southern Wesleyan University and the Central Heritage Society.)

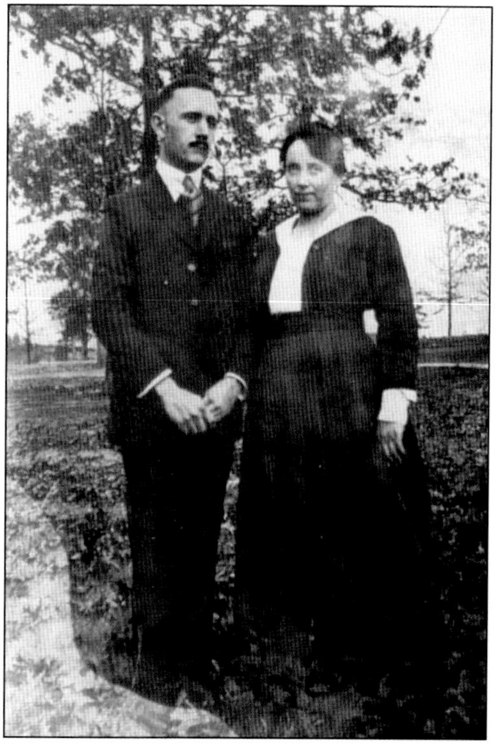

EDUCATION. Students from Southern Wesleyan and Clemson were encouraged by their professors to visit the people within the poor county's interior. Sometimes Clemson cadets met with gristmill operators in order to share the latest news about hybrid grains or nutrients that could enrich flour. Henry West and his wife, Beth Harrington West (right), the daughter of Rev. L.J. Harrington, also worked to better educate the hill people. (Photo courtesy of Southern Wesleyan University and the Central Heritage Society.)

Three

People and Places

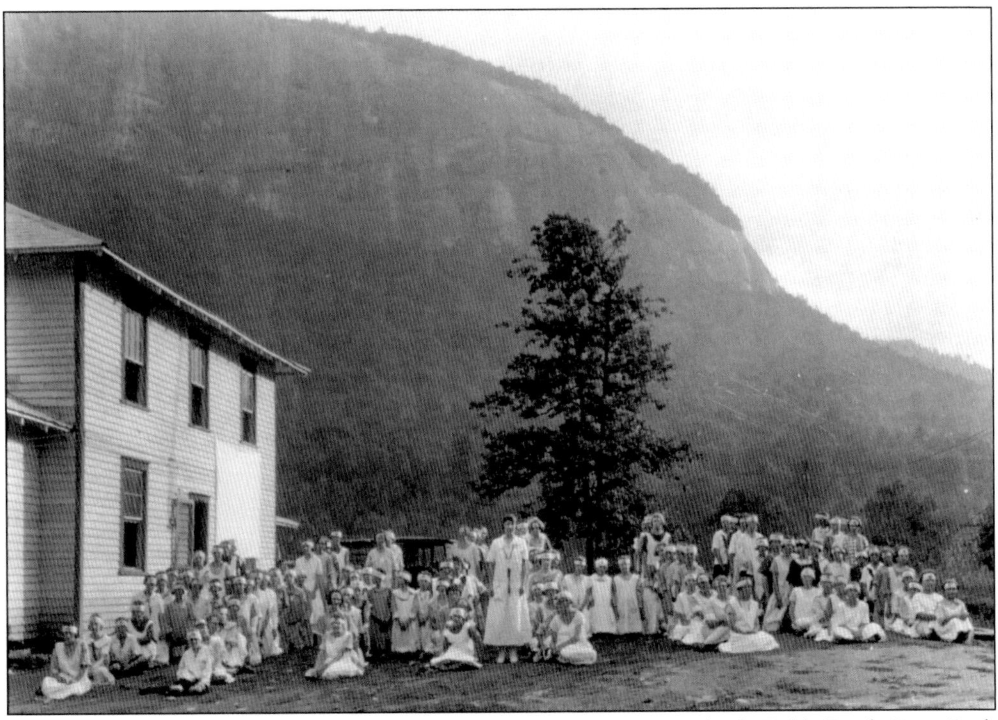

Table Rock Park (c. 1940s). The Civilian Conservation Corps built Table Rock State Park in 1933. It consists of 2,680 acres centered around three peaks with crags as high as 1,000 feet. Table Rock is 3,157 feet high, the Stool is 2,530 feet high, and Pinnacle Mountain stands 3,413 feet above sea level. Beyond Table Rock's top is a sheer drop 1,000 feet down to a water reservoir that serves Greenville. The headwaters of the Saluda River and farmlands were once located in this valley. Near the park is the state's tallest peak, Sassafras Mountain, about 3,548 feet tall, but it is Table Rock that remains Pickens County's most recognizable landmark. (Photo courtesy of the Strom Thurmond Institute, Clemson University.)

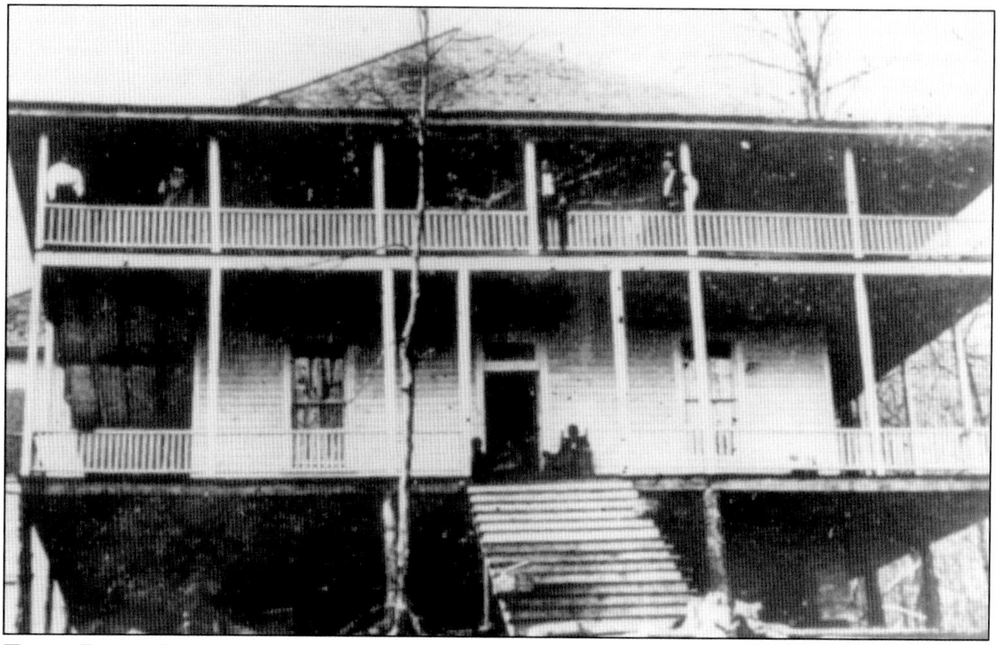

Table Rock Hotel. Hostelries like Table Rock Hotel were scattered throughout Pickens. According to journalist Benjamin F. Perry, Furman students frequently enjoyed excursions to Table Rock because the mountain inspired romance. One trip to Table Rock resulted in four engagements and, in due time, four weddings among Perry's peers. Perry later became provisional governor of South Carolina. Gov. John L. Wilson visited Table Rock in 1824 where he celebrated July Fourth. This Table Rock Hotel (there were two of them) provided lodging for tourists in the 1890s. Later, the hotel burned. (Photo courtesy of PDHRT.)

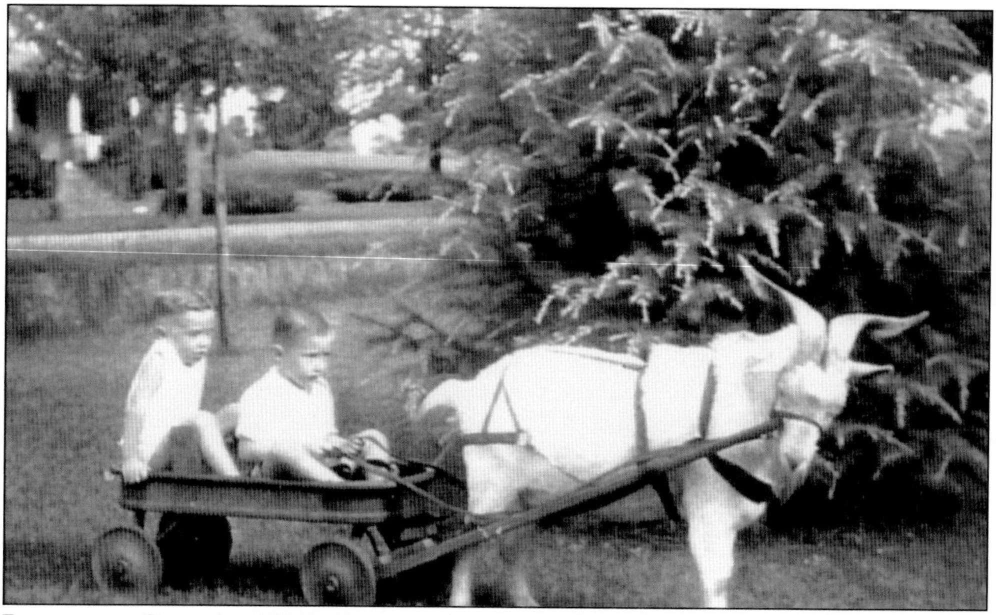

Boys and a Goat (c. 1930). Trains and cars moved people to the mountains, but a good goat and a sturdy wagon could haul two little explorers from Gassaway Street to anywhere in Central. (Photo courtesy of the Central Heritage Society.)

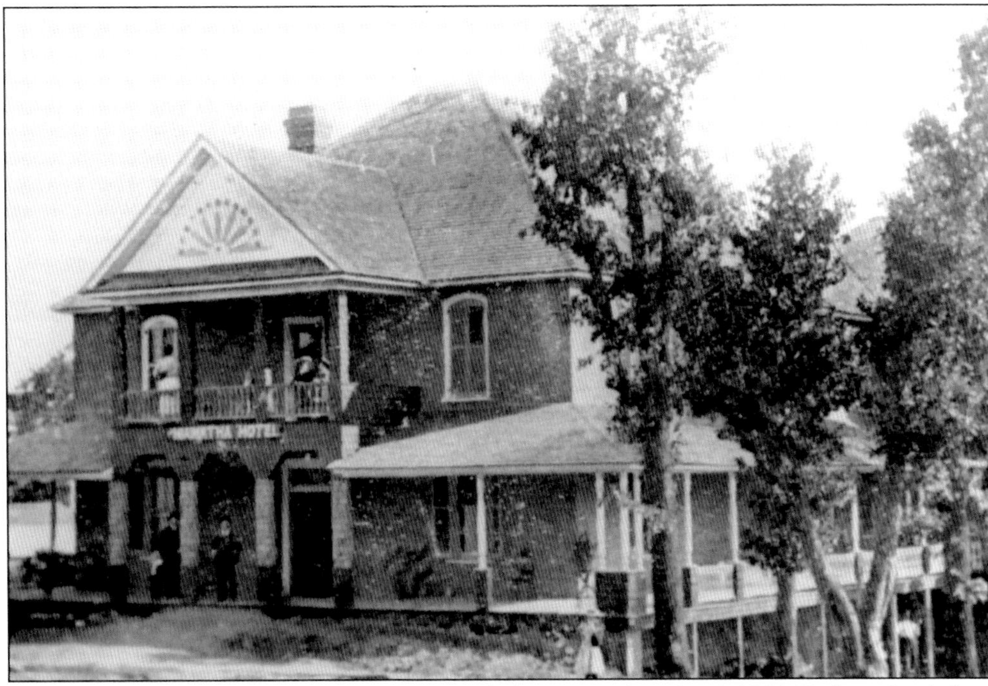

HIAWATHA HOTEL. T.D. Harris Sr. operated the Hiawatha Hotel (Old Hickory Inn) from 1900 to 1904. Square dancing provided entertainment for local and traveling attorneys that visited the courthouse town of Pickens. In 1980, the hotel housed the Pickens County Planning Commission. (Photo courtesy of PDHRT.)

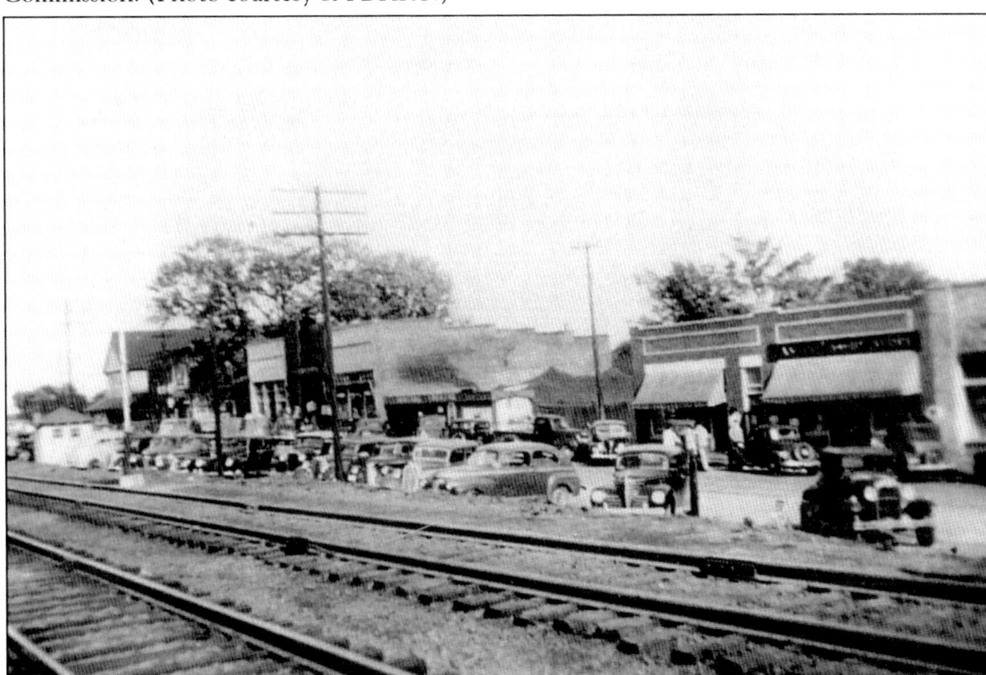

WORLD WAR II CENTRAL. Post-World War II Central expanded between Clemson University and Southern Wesleyan University. (Photo courtesy of the Central Heritage Society.)

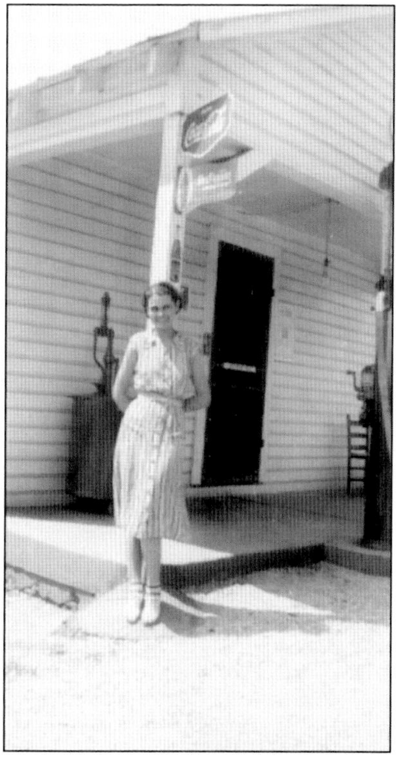

Garrett's. Stores like Garrett's dotted Pickens County in 1938 and provided fuel and food for motorists. These stores were the predecessors of modern convenience stores. (Photo courtesy of the Pickens County Library.)

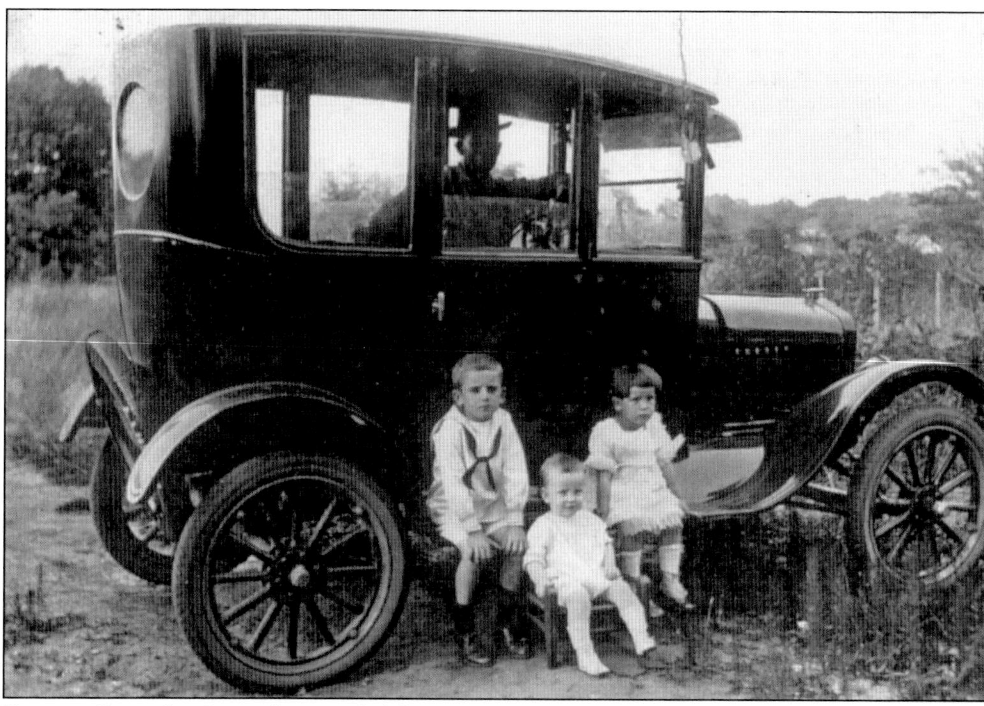

Family Car. In Central, a prideful motorist poses his children on the running board of the family car, a luxury in its day for most citizens. (Photo courtesy of the Central Heritage Society.)

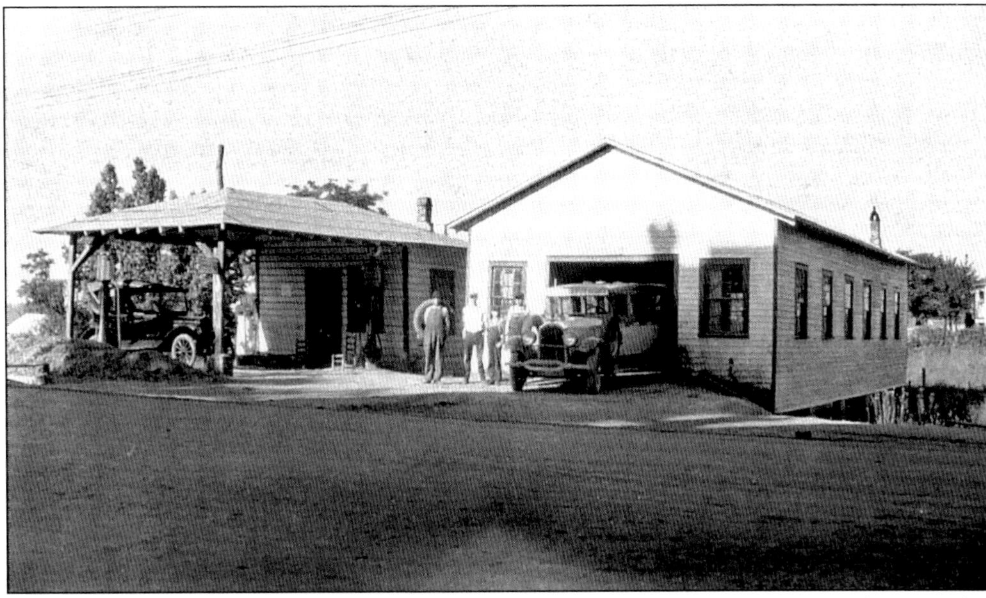

Ray Lynch Garage. Blacksmiths forged horseshoes and wagon wheels out of hot metal, a desirable skill given that when the automobile was invented, mass produced car parts were unavailable. As a result, when a horseless carriage cracked a wheel spoke or broke a nut and bolt, the blacksmith would have to repair the car. As time progressed, blacksmiths became mechanics. Some mechanics opened garages. Pictured is a brand new, modern service station (left) completed by a contemporary garage (right) owned by Ray Lynch & Brothers. (Photo courtesy of the Central Heritage Society.)

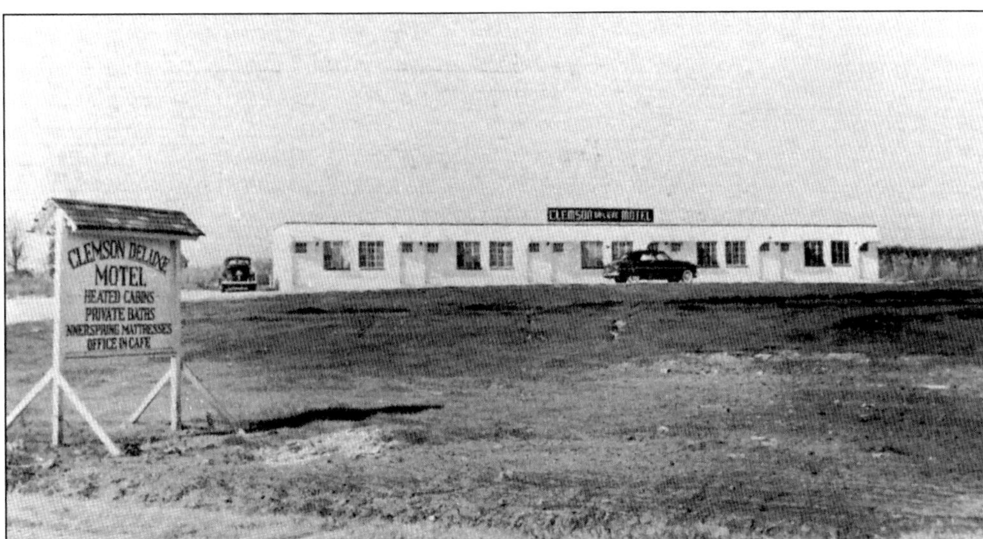

Clemson Deluxe. Clemson's athletics program drew big audiences by the 1950s. Graduates traveled into the area and farmers supported Tiger football with a fury. Motels began to pop up along the new highways. This one, the Clemson Deluxe, was located 2 miles east of Clemson on Highway 123. (Photo courtesy of the South Caroliniana Library, USC, Columbia.)

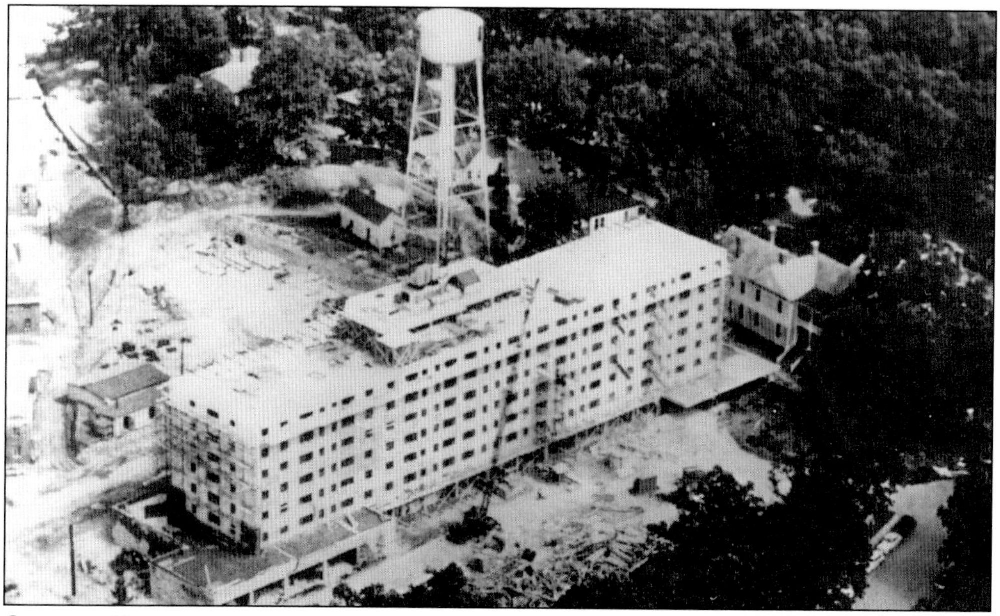

Clemson House High-Rise. In the mid-20th century, Clemson alumni frequently returned to the college to see the Tigers play. Some of them stayed in the luxurious Clemson House designed by William G. Lyles and Bissett, Carlisle and Wolf Architects and constructed on what is commonly referred to as the watertank hilltop. (Photo courtesy of the Strom Thurmond Institute.)

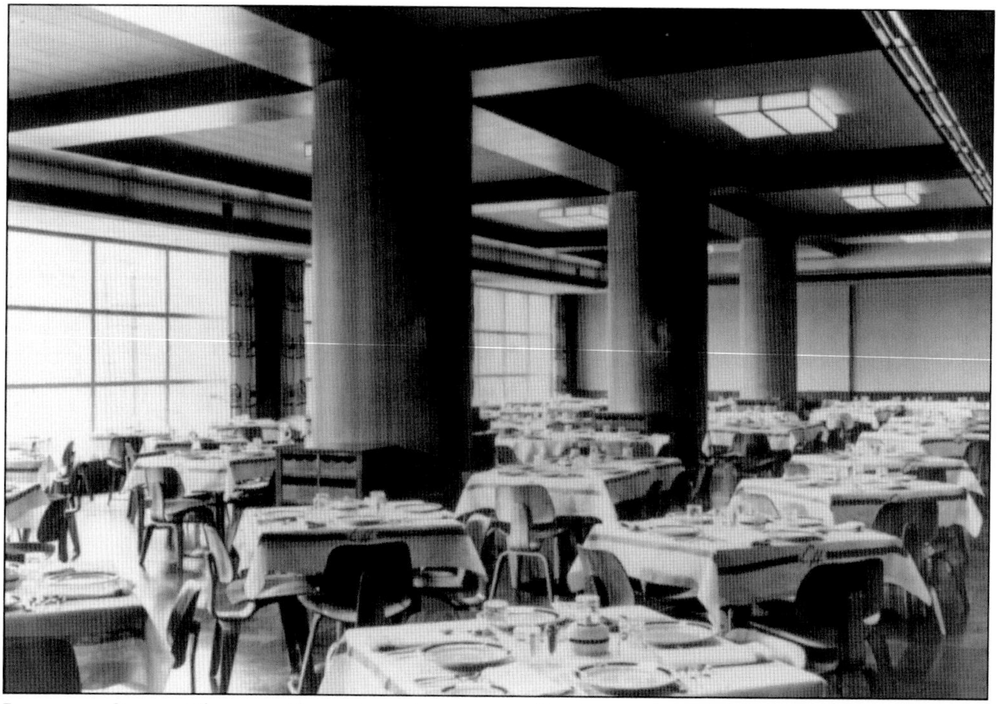

Interior Shot. Clemson House interiors originally featured sleek "hip" furniture that was considered outdated by the late 1980s. The hotel's trademark CH tablecloths added a traditional element to the dining room. (Photo courtesy of the Strom Thurmond Institute.)

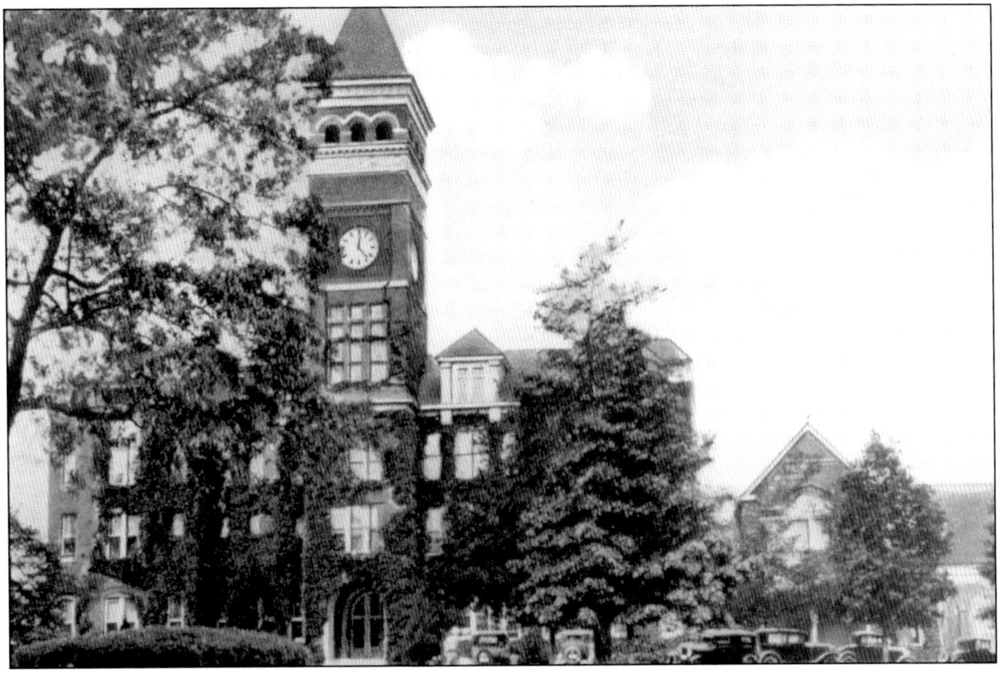

Athletic Programs. Referred to as "Cow College" by some people, Clemson athletic programs earned the all-male agricultural school a bit of respect among more established leagues. At the same time, Clemson became a school noted for excellence in education with the college sponsoring agricultural exhibits, new inventions demonstrations, and livestock competitions for the general public throughout the state. Clemson's Garrison Livestock Arena continues this tradition. It showcases regional and national horse-and-cattle activities with most of the events promoted as free to the general public. (Photo courtesy of the PDHRT.)

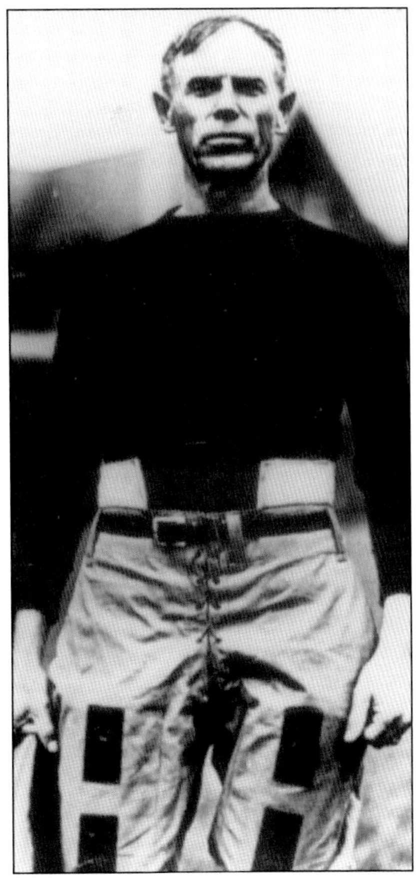

Heisman. Clemson's first four coaches, W.M. Riggs, W.M. Williams, J.A. Penton, and John Heisman (pictured), came from Auburn, so the early football program was strongly influenced by Alabama's style. Clemson's first team organized in 1896 under the direction of Riggs, an engineering professor, but the Tigers became feared under the leadership of John Heisman. Heisman's 1900 team was one of only two undefeated, untied teams in Clemson's history. The other was Frank Howard's creation. Heisman, inducted into the Hall of Fame in 1981, received $1,800 a year at Clemson until Georgia Tech hired the coach away from the Tiger team. In 1904, John Heisman received $2,250 plus 30% of net gate receipts from Georgia Tech. (Photo courtesy of the Strom Thurmond Institute.)

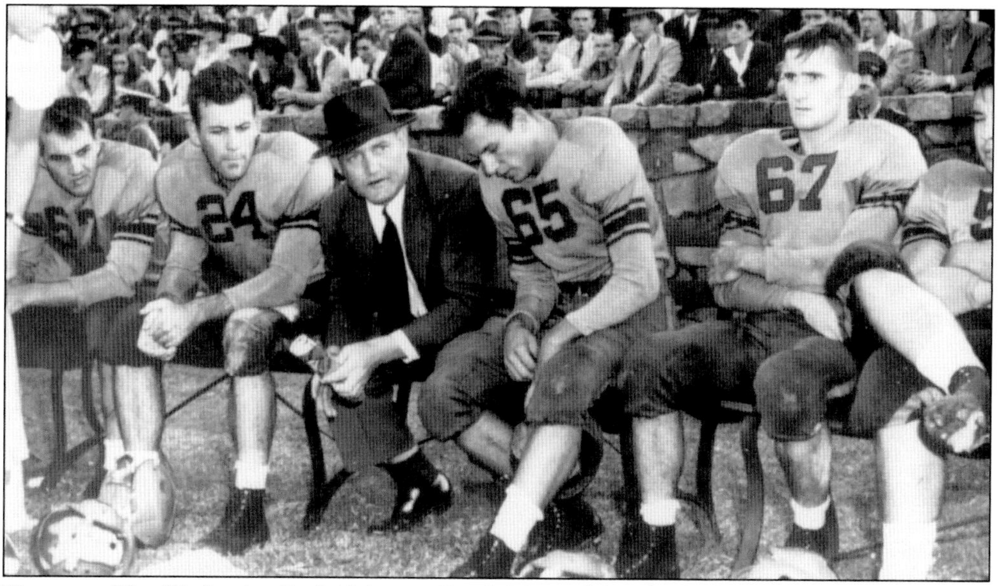

HOWARD. The "little giant" of Alabama, Frank Howard (in the hat), came to Clemson as an assistant to Coach Jess Neely during the 1928–1929 season, but the "Frank Howard" era of Clemson football is considered to be from 1940 to 1969. Before retirement, Howard's success included 295 games, 165 wins, and six bowl teams. Pictured is Frank with his Clemson Tigers in Charlotte, N.C., during a game in 1942. (Photo courtesy of the Strom Thurmond Institute.)

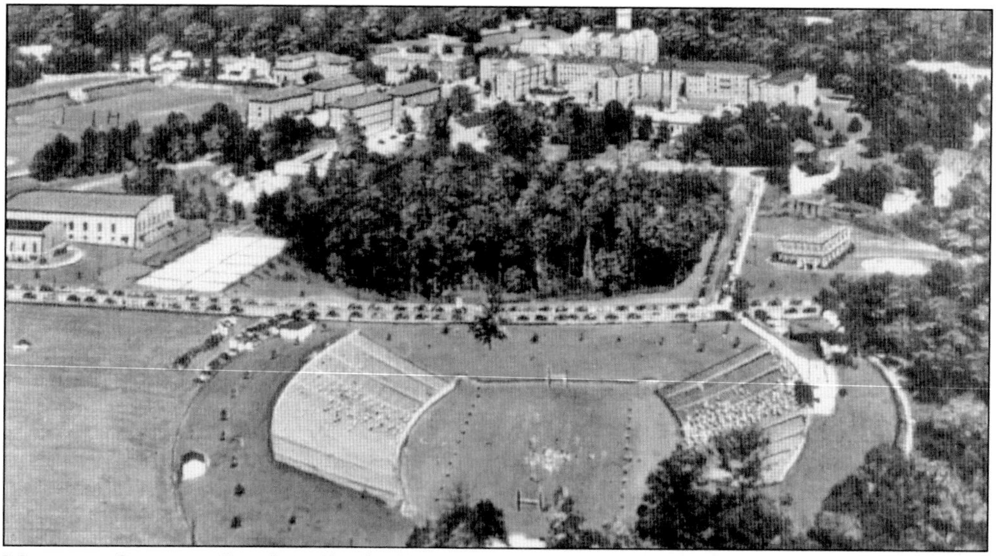

MEMORIAL STADIUM. Death Valley had humble beginnings, but with its contemporary additions Death Valley is a grand piece of structural engineering with the capacity to hold over 81,000 fans. Death Valley is also known as the Frank Howard Memorial Stadium and Football Field. The NFL Carolina Panthers, based in Charlotte, N.C., played their first season here in 1995 while Erikson Stadium was under construction. Notice Riggs Field in the left corner of the image. It was the first mapped and level playing field for the Tigers. Prior to Riggs Field, Clemson cadets hurled the football on the lawns stretched out before Tillman Hall. Riggs Field is still in use, but the campus lawn is for student pedestrians only. (Photo courtesy of Lou Ann Aheron and the PDHRT.)

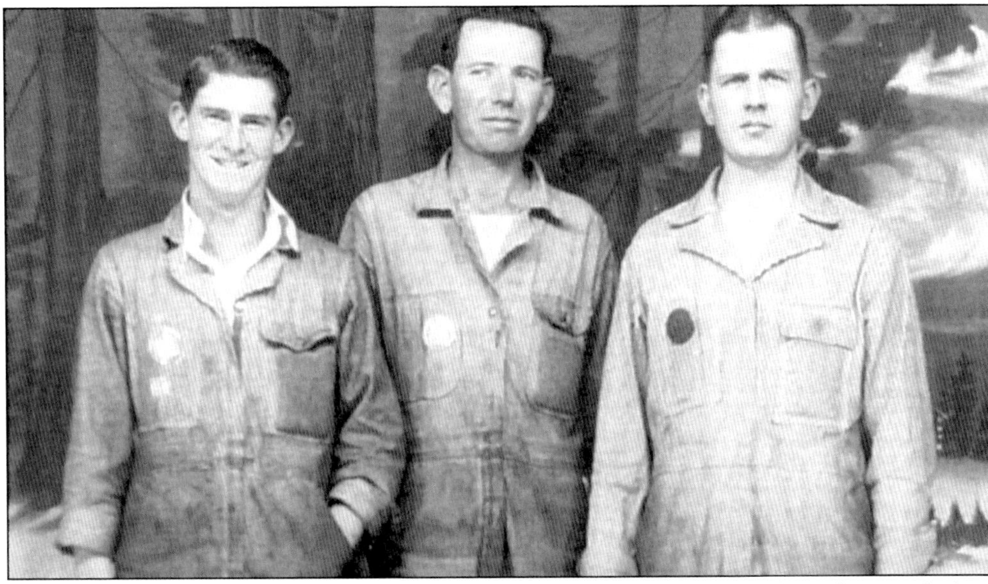

THREE MEN. During World War II, Clemson College recruited locals and trained them as technicians. A certificate would be issued, not a degree, then the individual would be dispatched according to the country's military needs. Shown here, from left to right, are Pickens County residents G.D. Butler, James D. Sheriff, and J.G. Stephenson, who were recruited and trained in welding and shipbuilding. According to war correspondence and the Southeastern Shipbuilding Corp. of Savannah, G.A., Sheriff had a few assignments including work on the SS *Ben Robertson*. Sheriff's pay stub No. 223627 indicates he received a net pay of $95.73 for 69 hours of work on December 20, 1942. (Photo courtesy of the Central Heritage Society.)

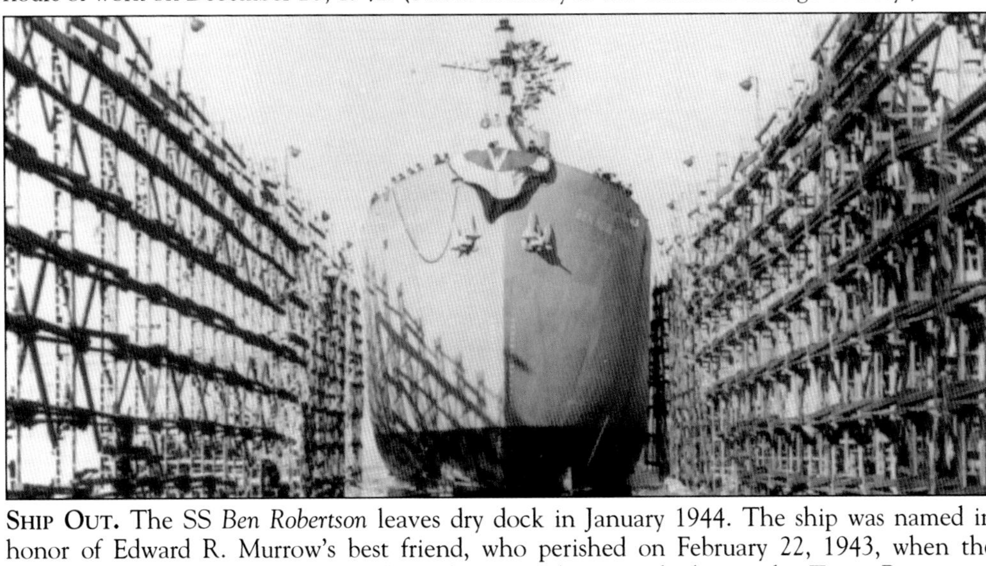

SHIP OUT. The SS *Ben Robertson* leaves dry dock in January 1944. The ship was named in honor of Edward R. Murrow's best friend, who perished on February 22, 1943, when the *Yankee Clipper*, a Pan American "flying boat" airplane, crashed into the Tagus River near Lisbon while attempting an emergency landing during a storm. Ben was scheduled to arrive in England and begin work as chief of the *New York Herald-Tribune*'s London bureau. His untimely death prevented the publication of his third manuscript, titled *The Pilgrim*, that he completed in rough draft at Clemson. (Photo courtesy of the Strom Thurmond Institute, Clemson University.)

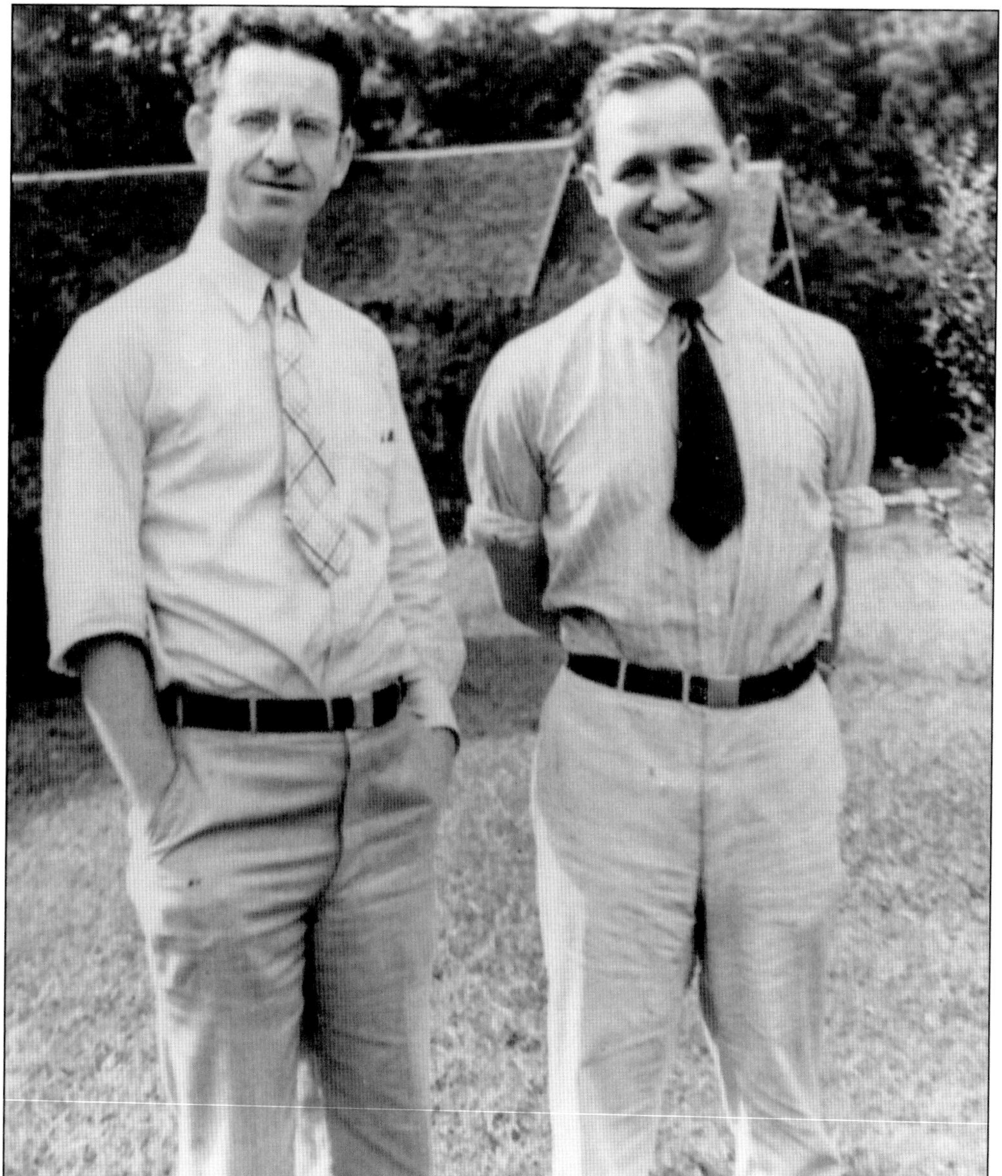

Robertson and Lane. Born in Calhoun or Clemson, Benjamin Franklin Robertson Jr. (1903–1943), received a B.S. degree from Clemson in 1923. Robertson obtained his bachelor of journalism from the University of Missouri in 1926. He worked for various newspapers, then became a correspondent for the Associated Press in the Washington and London offices (1934–1937). Until 1940 he was a freelance writer for national magazines including *The Saturday Evening Post*. Robertson served as a World War II correspondent for London's *PM* newspaper in 1940. While in London, he published reports about German air raids entitled *I Saw England* (1941). He wrote two other books published in the U.S., *Travelers' Rest* (1938) and *Red Hills and Cotton* (1941), a Southern classic still available from the University of South Carolina Press. These books reflect Ben's childhood experiences in the Pickens area during the early 1900s. Ben Robertson (right) stands with his friend John Lane, a Clemson English professor. (Photo courtesy of the Strom Thurmond Institute, Clemson University.)

ALEXANDER BOYS. Pickens is home for many writers including historians Jane B. Morris, Fred C. Holder, and Anne Sheriff. Depicted here is Ed Alexander, a U.S. Navy man during World War II. He poses with his little brother Jerry (right), who would later record history and events as a writer and an artist. Throughout his lifetime, Jerry has worked for newspapers including *The Anderson Independent*. Jerry Alexander, author of several books including *A Little Place Called Cateechee*, continues to publish *The Pickens Sentinel* newspaper as he has done for over 20 years.

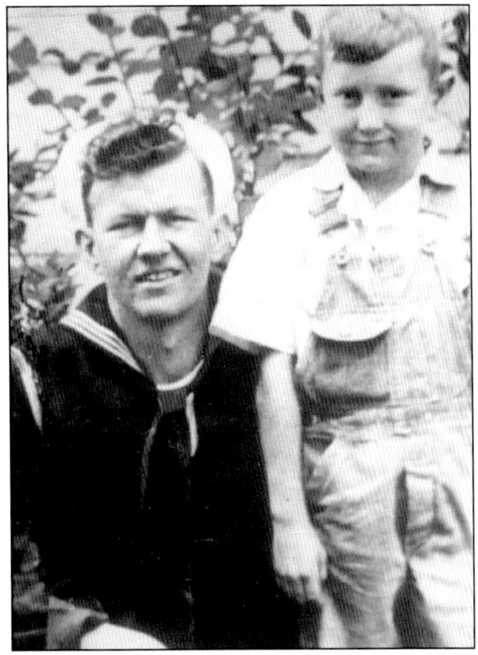

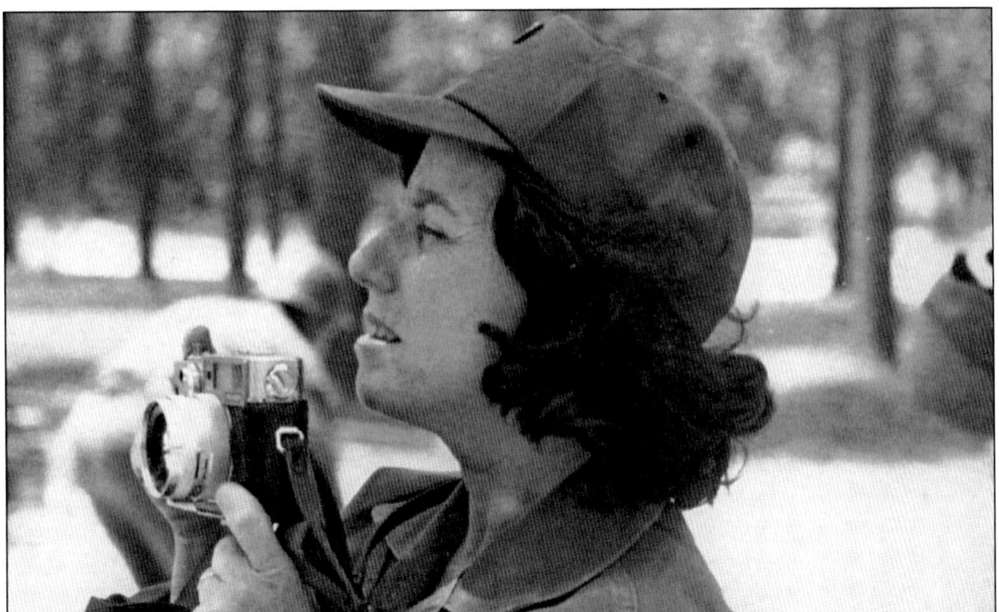

JOURNALIST AND CAMERA. Since the 1960s, Dot Jackson has worked for newspapers. She served as columnist and editor for *The Charlotte Observer*. Under the byline Dot Robertson, she has reported for *The Anderson Independent-Mail*, *Greenville News*, and *The Easley Progress*. Since Dot's ancestors were among the first European settlers in the Keowee River Valley, she co-authored the book *Keowee* (1995), now in its fifth printing, with Michael Hembree. Jackson also co-authored *The Catawba River* (1985) with Frye Gaillard, and in 1991 she won the Foundation Fellowship in Journalism and conducted research in Southern Appalachia economics. Dot continues to write about the region that she loves. She is pictured here photographing troops in training at Fort Jackson during the Vietnam War era.

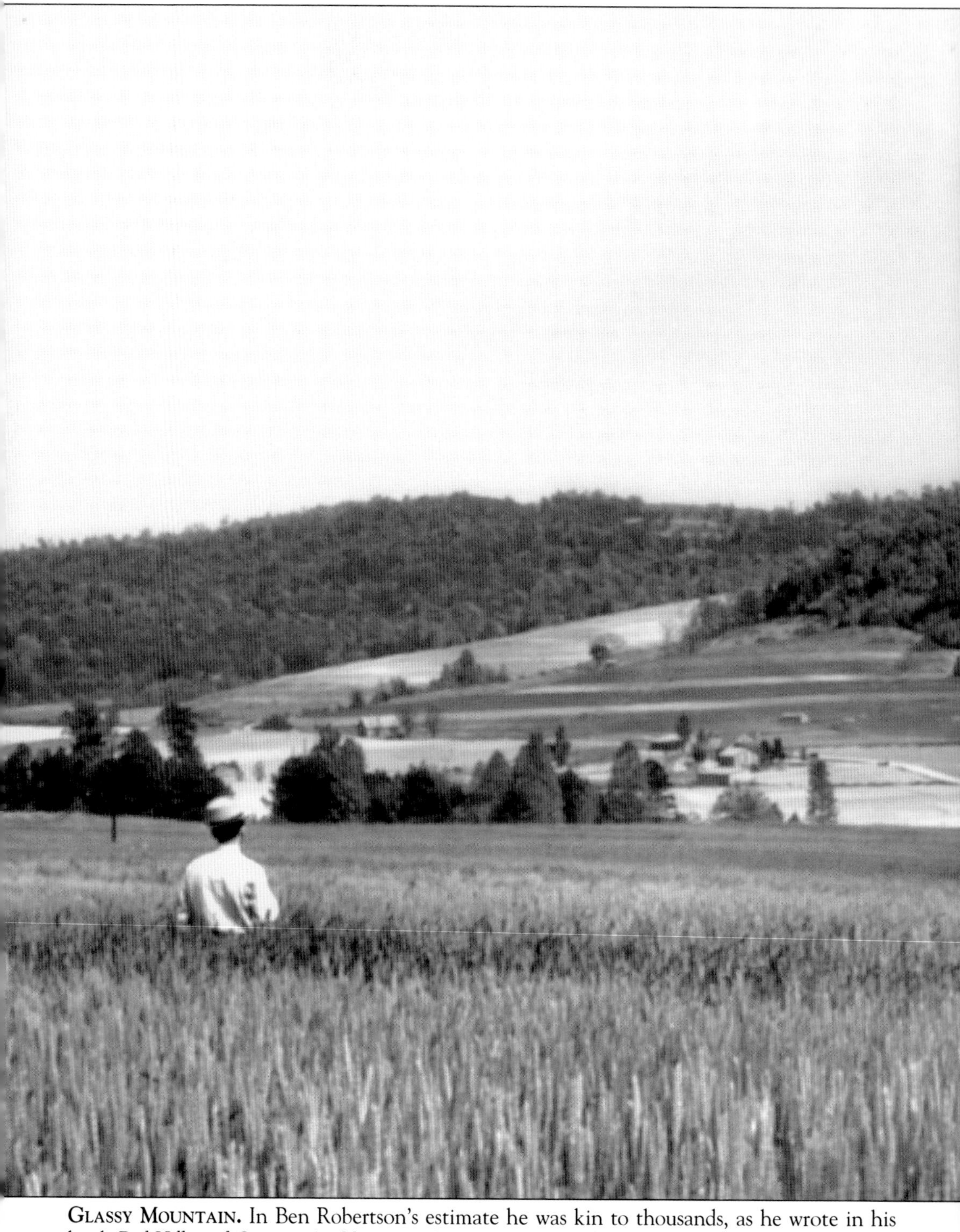

Glassy Mountain. In Ben Robertson's estimate he was kin to thousands, as he wrote in his book *Red Hills and Cotton: An Upcountry Memory*, "Most of my kinfolks, when I was growing up, were located on Pea Ridge between Glassy and Six Mile Mountains on a long rise of fine cotton country between two lonely spurs of pine grown granite—we lived and some of us still

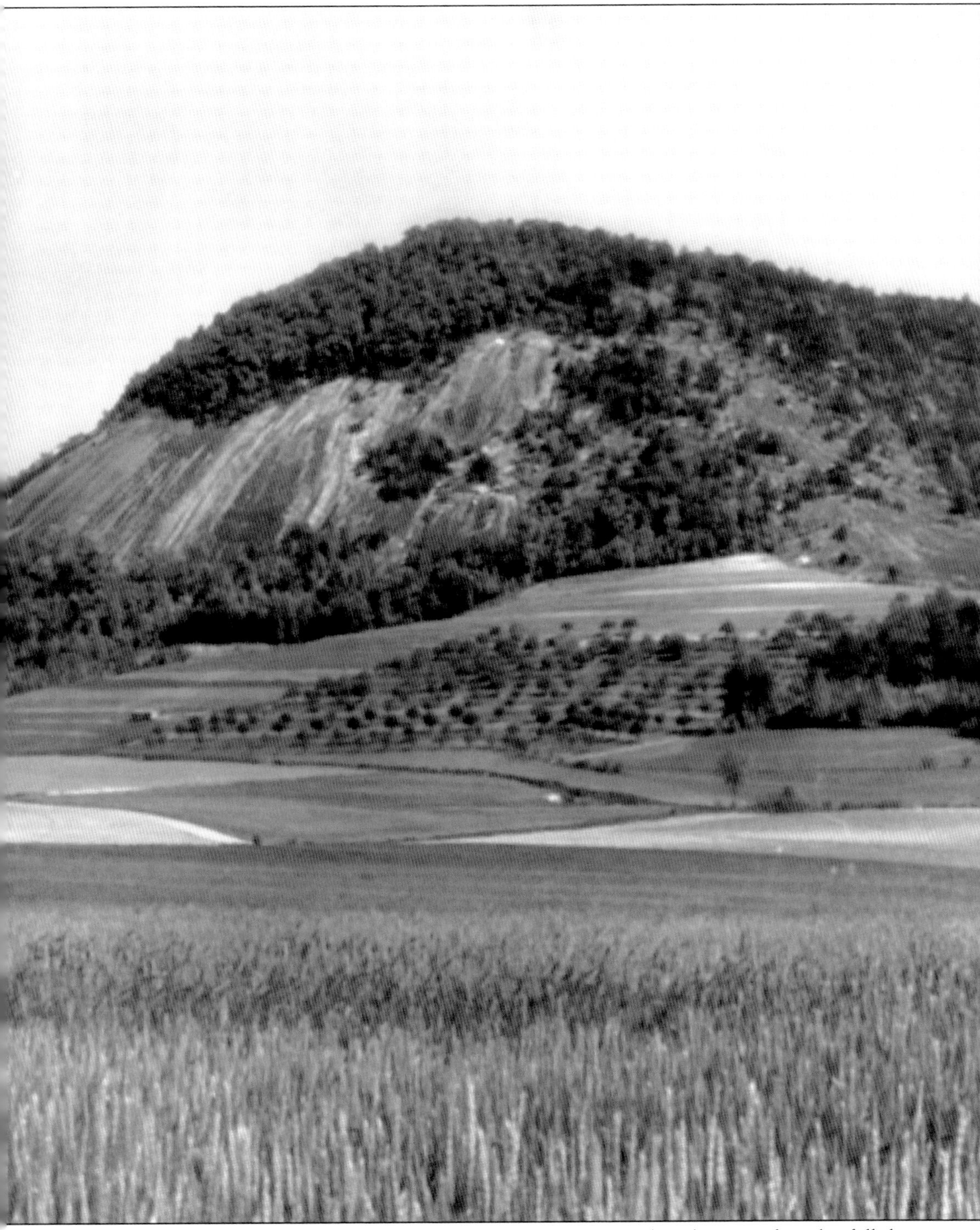

live in the winding open valley of a river called the Twelve Mile. The rest of our kinfolk live to the west of us. They have their houses along both banks of the river Keowee." Pictured here is Glassy Mountain in the 1940s with J.R. Woods standing in the field. (Photo courtesy of the Strom Thurmond Institute.)

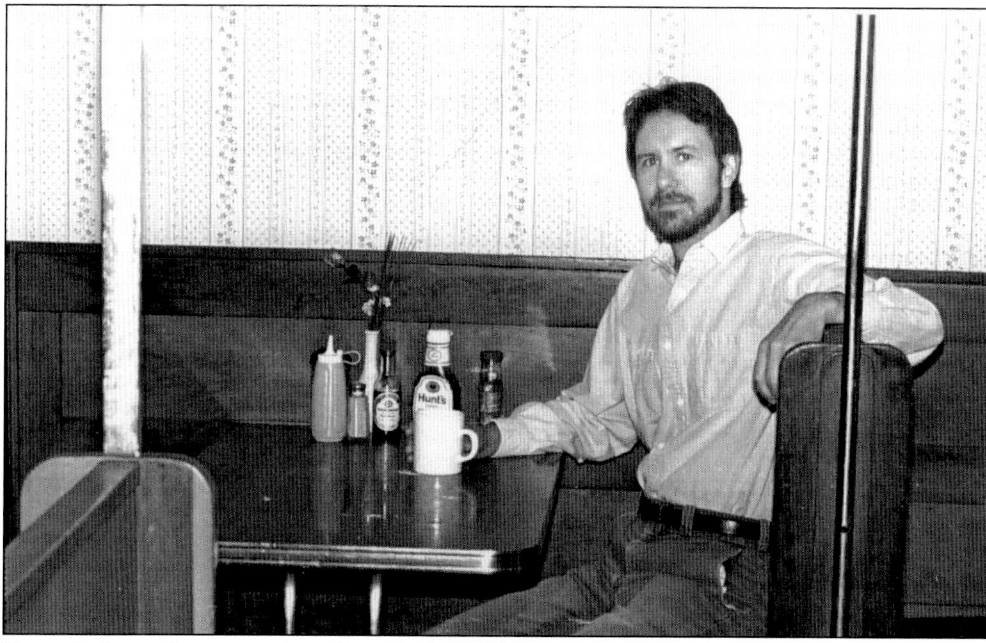

POET. Pickens County resident Ron Rash and his many ancestors have lived in the southern Appalachian Mountains since the mid-1700s. It is this region that is the primary focus of his writing. Recipient of the General Electric Younger Writers Award in fiction (1987), Ron has also received a NEA Poetry Fellowship (1994) and the Sherwood Anderson Prize (1996). His poems and stories have appeared in several journals including the *Yale Review*, *Georgia Review*, *Oxford American*, and *Southern Review*. He is the author of several books including *The Night the New Jesus Fell to Earth* (short stories), *Casualties* (short stories), *Eureka Mill* (poetry), and *Among the Believers* (poetry).

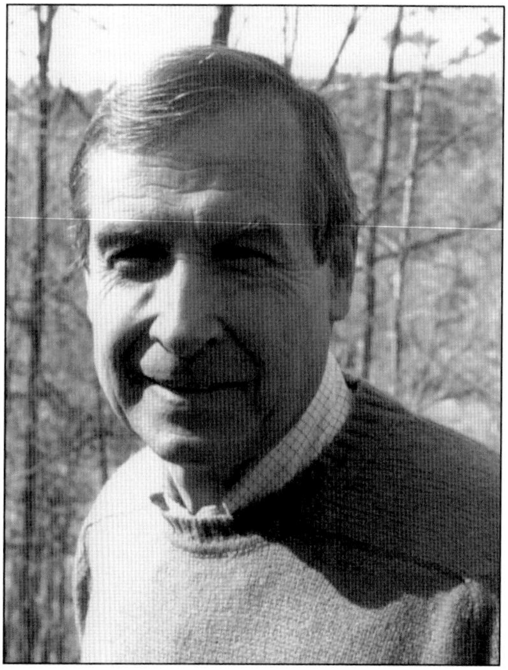

FICTION. A graduate of Emory (1951) and a survivor of the U.S. Navy, Dr. Mark Steadman wrote advertising copy for a couple of years in Atlanta before returning to college on the G.I. Bill. While teaching at the American University in Cairo, Egypt (1968 to 1969), Mark began his third novel, his first to be published, *McAfee County*. Other books, *A Lion's Share* (1977), *Angel Child* (1987), and *Bang-Up Season* (1990), along with a few anthologies, comprise the bulk of Mark's work. As an educator, Mark retired from Clemson as emeritus alumni distinguished professor of English and a writer in residence. He continues to work on numerous projects including the construction of his home in Pickens County. He periodically teaches courses about American humor and fiction writing.

ILLUSTRATOR. Kate Salley Palmer, one of three women members of the American Association of Editorial Cartoonist, makes her home in Clemson. A former *Greenville News* political cartoonist, Kate's work was nationally syndicated in over 200 newspapers until 1987. She is the illustrator of several children's books: *How Many Feet in the Bed* by D.J. Hamm (Simon & Schuster), *Octopus Hug* by L. Pringle (Boyd Mill Press), and *Night of the Five Aunties* by M. Somer (Albert Whitman Co.), just to name a few. Kate also illustrated and authored *A Gracious Plenty* (Simon & Schuster, reprinted by Warbranch Press) and writes novels as well. Chapter one of *Spitfire* won a 1998 South Carolina Fiction Project award. A lecturer and humorist, Kate continues to explore a multitude of outlets for her many talents.

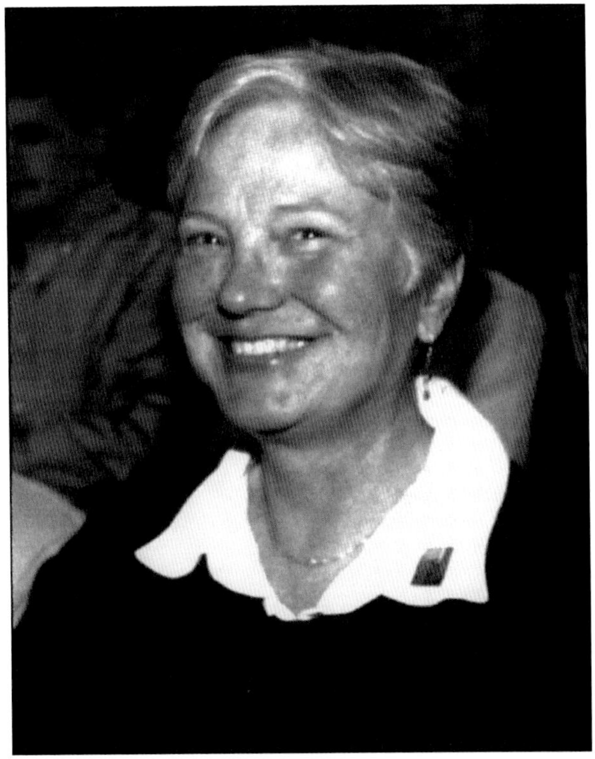

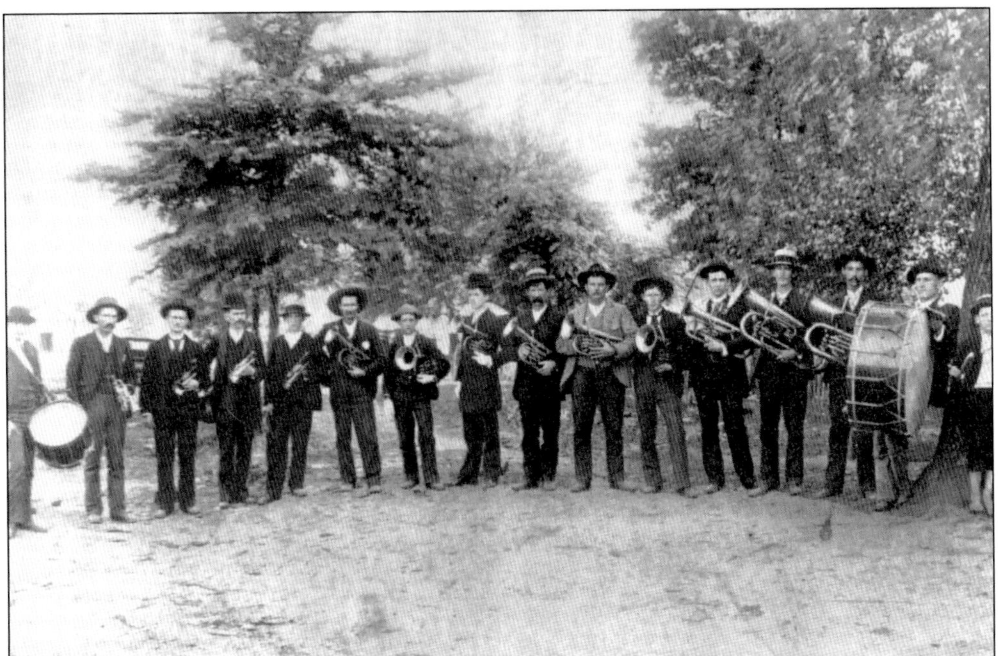

EASLEY BAND. Musicians and music lovers can enjoy WCCP, WSBF, and WELP along with Music Scene Recording Studios and Southeastern Sound Studios headquartered in Pickens County. Pictured is the 1920 Easley Community Band back when "live" and "unplugged" was the only form of entertainment available. (Photo courtesy of Pickens County Library.)

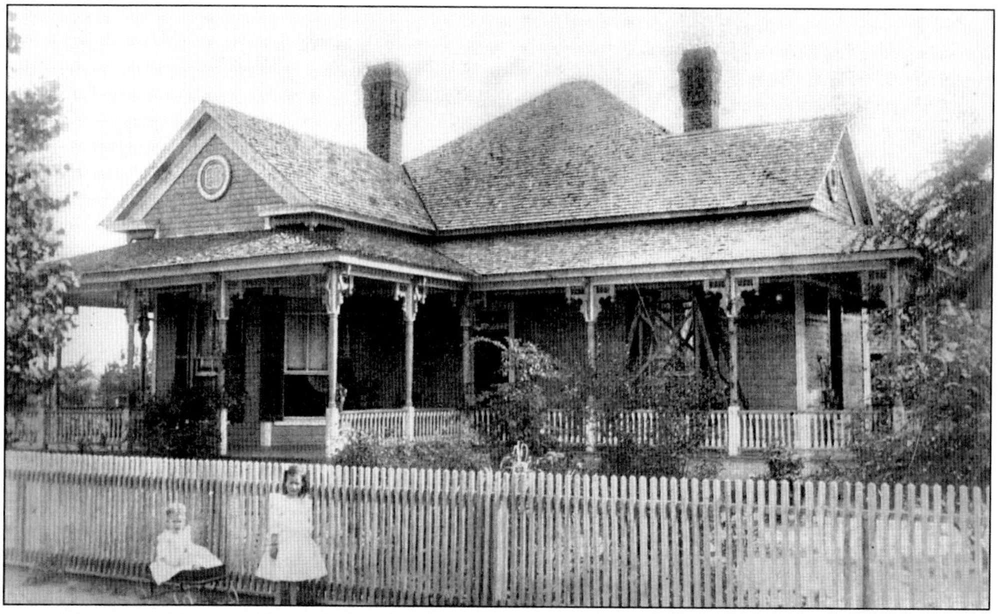

OLD MORGAN HOUSE. One of the local points of interest is the late-19th-century Central Heritage Museum (Morgan House), the former property of Central merchant J.N. Morgan. It remained the home of his daughters, pictured here as children. Jessie and Jennie Morgan continued living in the house and took over operations of his mercantile store. (Photo courtesy of the Central Heritage Society.)

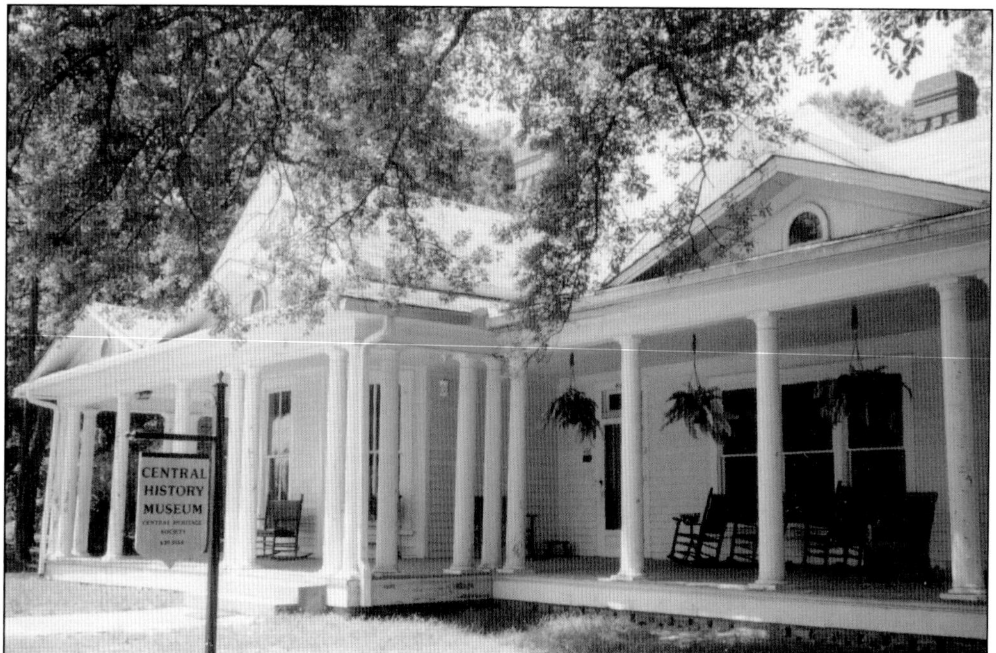

MUSEUM. In April 1995, the Central Heritage Society purchased the Morgan House and its furnishings through the generosity of Milton and Betty Holcombe and their foundation. Artifacts from the railroad town of Central and its surrounding farmlands are displayed throughout the large house, which has been methodically restored. (Photo by P.E. Peters.)

ROCKING CHAIR MATRONS. Minnie Morgan, the mother of Jessie and Jennie, owners of the Morgan Store, entertains a guest on the porch of their home in Central. (Photo courtesy of the Central Heritage Society.)

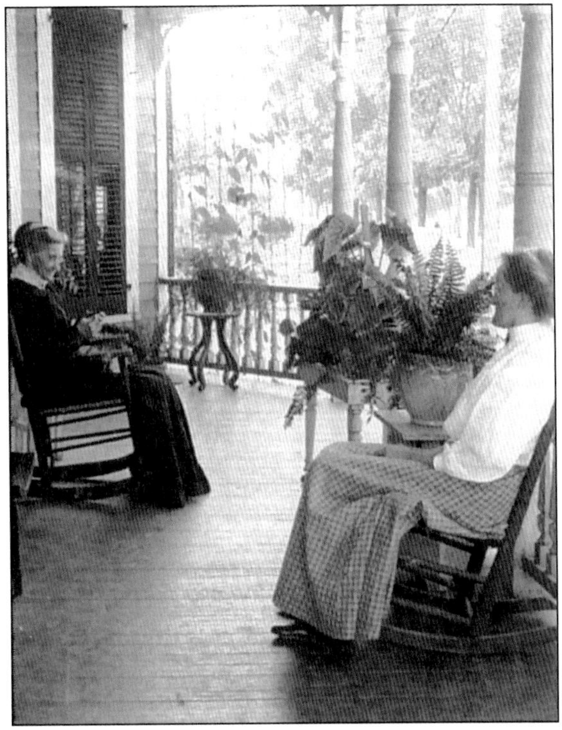

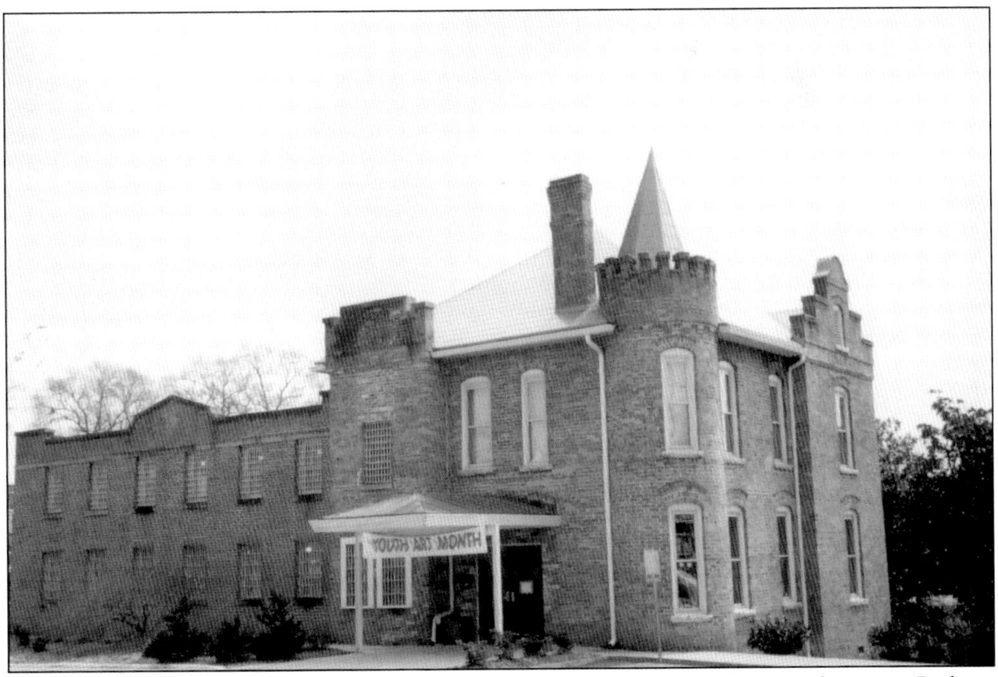

CASTLE. To children, this is a castle, not a jail constructed in 1902. A non-profit entity, Pickens County Museum of Art and History is located at 307 Johnson Street. It maintains the Pickens County Heritage Collections on the first floor and an art museum upstairs. The art museum offers changing exhibits throughout the year. Also, historic Hagood Mill is maintained through the museum's membership. (Photo by P.E. Peters.)

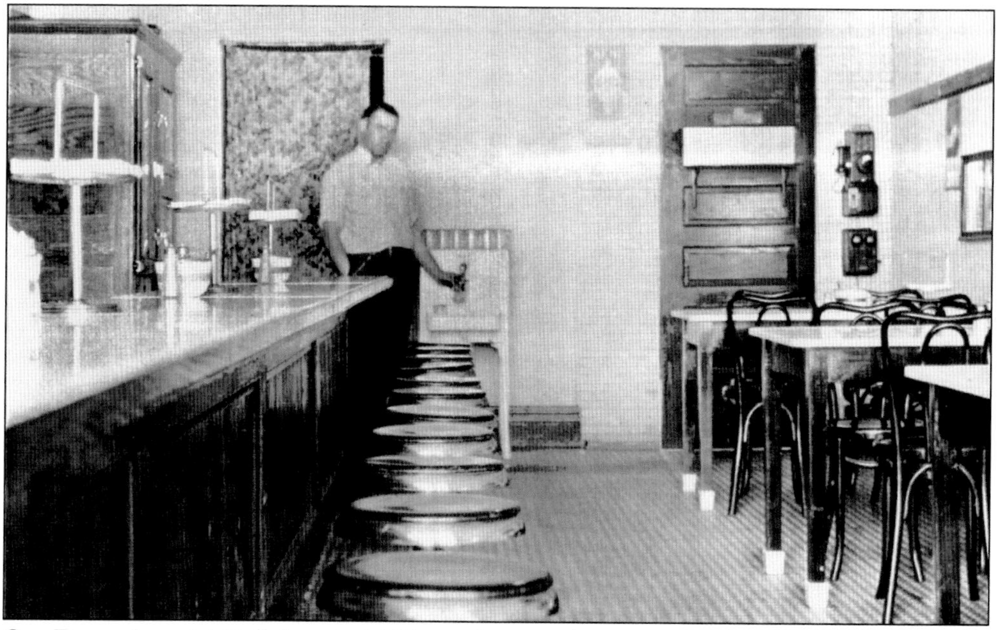

OLD DINER. Leon McCall, born in 1905, stands in a café reconstructed within the building that once contained the Keowee Bank. The curtained area behind Leon is the old vault, which Leon used as a pantry. About 1958, Bobby Garren began to work for Leon. Eventually, Bobby would own the quaint café at 312 E. Main Street in Pickens. (Photo courtesy of Judy Alexander Black and Jerry Black.)

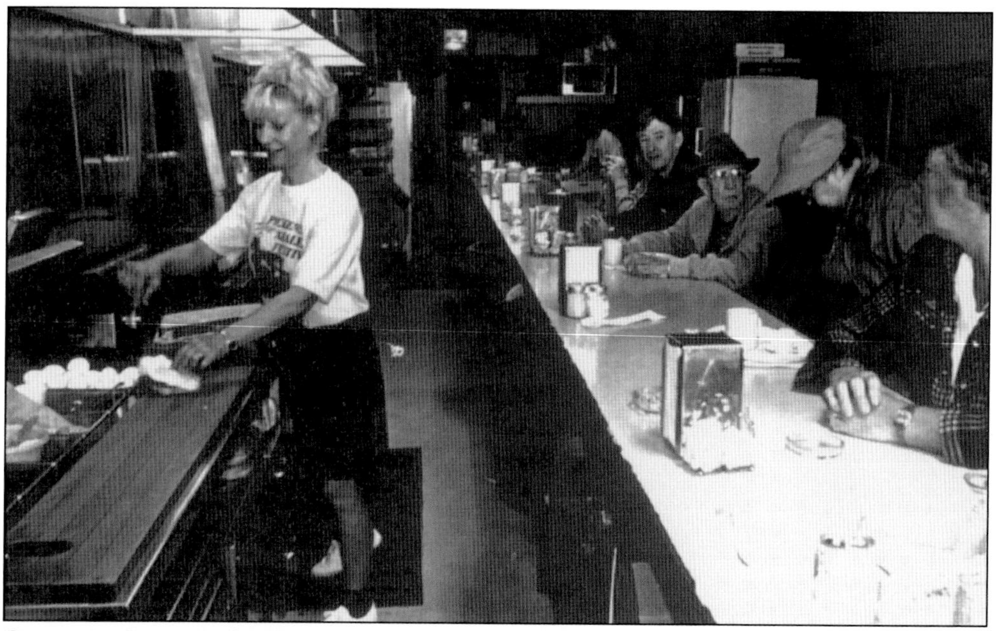

GARREN'S CAFÉ. A family business, Garren's Café survived the emergence of restaurant franchises during the 1950s and 1960s. Ms. O.M. "Gig" Garren Alexander now owns the building. Judy Alexander Black and her husband Jerry cook and serve the customers sitting on bar stools installed in 1927. Judy scrambles eggs in this snapshot. Garren's Café remains a favorite neighborhood grill. (Photo courtesy of Judy Alexander Black and Jerry Black.)

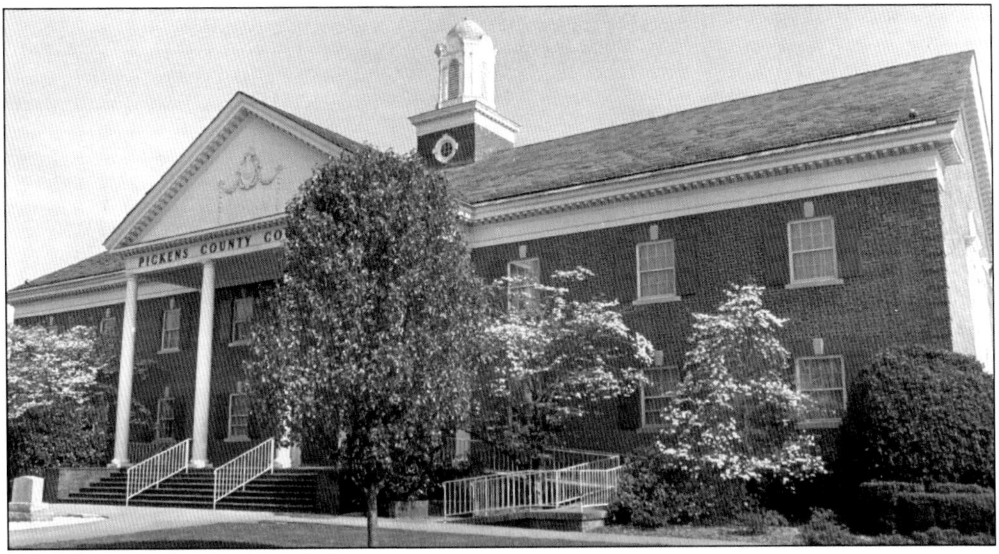

PICKENS COURTHOUSE. Pickens County was originally seated on the Keowee River near the Duke Energy complex along Highway 183 in Oconee. A courthouse centered the frontier town until 1868, when the county split at the river. The first courthouse was abandoned and a second courthouse was built 14-miles east of Keowee. A third courthouse, erected between 1891 and 1892, was replaced by this structure that has undergone renovations and additions in the latter half of the 20th century. (Photo courtesy of Judy Alexander Black and Jerry Black.)

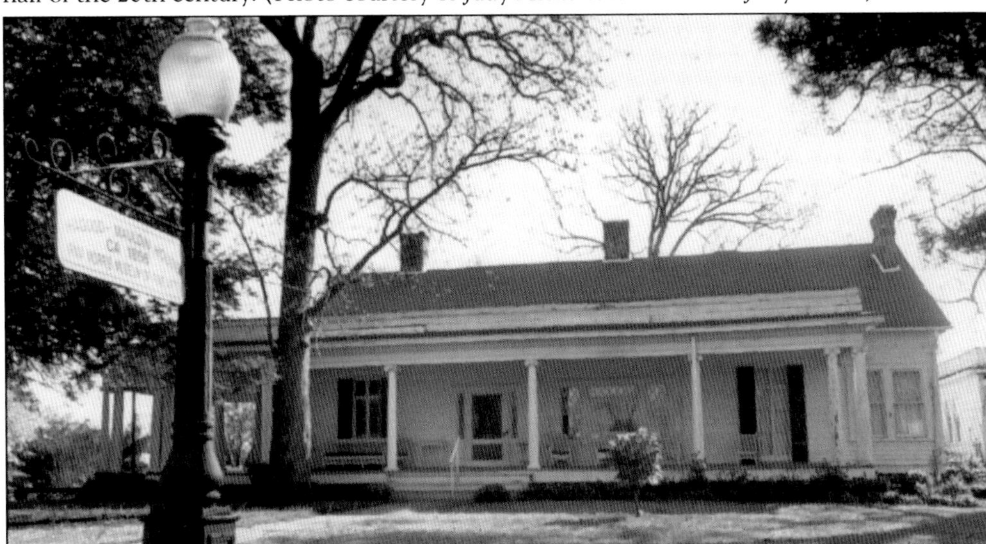

HAGOOD-MAULDIN HOUSE. Hagood-Mauldin House is located at 104 N. Lewis Street in Pickens. Listed on the National Register of Historic Places, the house was built in the frontier town of Pickens on the river Keowee. It was moved to its present location in 1868. The house was the property of James E. Hagood, the first clerk of court of the Pickens District. His daughter, Frances Miles Hagood, married Judge T.J. Mauldin and took possession of the house around 1904. Mauldin was judge of the 13th Judicial Circuit. Mrs. F.M. Hagood Mauldin was one of the chief supporters of the Tamassee-DAR Industrial School established for the benefit of the hill children in Oconee. (Photo courtesy of Judy Alexander Black and Jerry Black.)

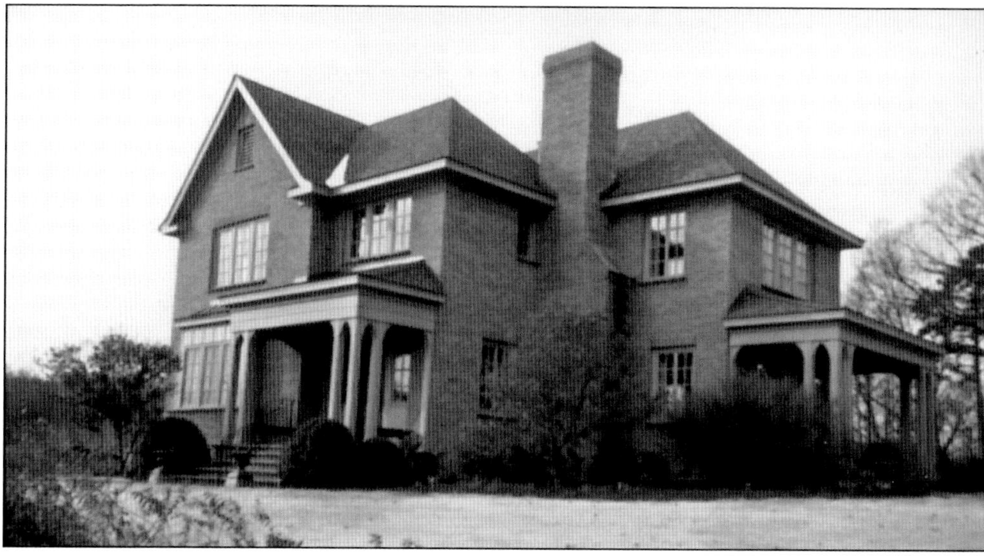

Discovery Center. In the late 1950s, a camellia collection grew on a landfill near the Clemson campus. The 44-acre site was named for its founder. When the Dr. T.L. Senn Horticultural Gardens consolidated with the Forestry Arboretum and adjoining Clemson properties, it became the South Carolina Botanical Garden, encompassing 270 acres of natural landscapes and providing year-round public education programs. The garden contains a variety of walking trails, many labeled in Braille, running through bogs, meadows, and groves. Pictured is the Wren House situated in the wild flower meadow of the South Carolina Botanical Gardens. The Wren House (Fran Hanson Visitor Center), a discovery center for the South Carolina Heritage Corridor project, is just off Perimeter Road. (Photo by P.E. Peters.)

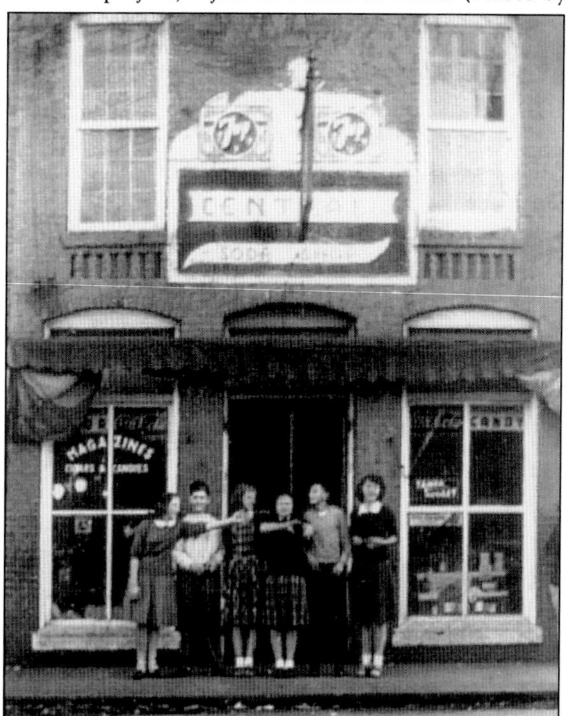

Central Soda Shop. Dolls in bobby socks greet guys at the Central Soda Shop owned by Hugh Dudley in 1946. The store also served as a bus stop on Main Street, and with the railroad tracks and depot close by, business was brisk. (Photo courtesy of Mary Eugenia Dudley Stone and the Central Heritage Society.)

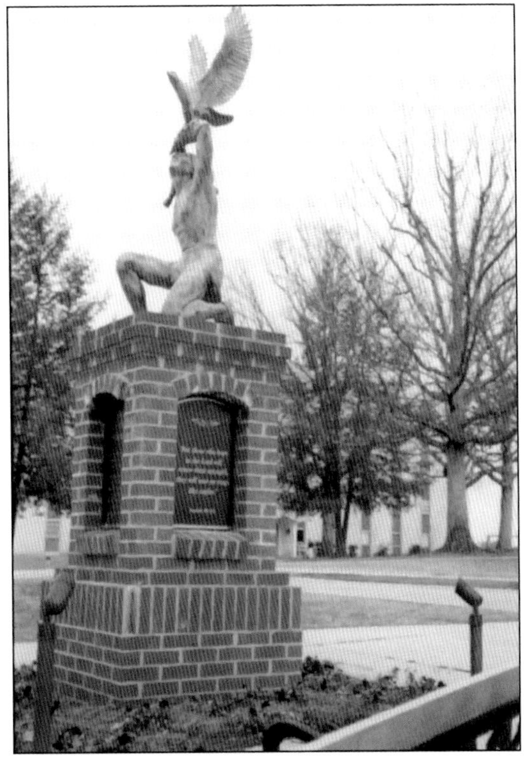

AMERICAN INDIAN STATUE. On the campus of Southern Wesleyan University is a sculpture of an American Indian warrior with a Biblical inscription from Isaiah 40:31. Behind the sculpture and beyond the plaza is Stuart-Bennett Hall, erected in 1967 and named for two female students who perished in a fire at McDonald Hall. (Photo by P.E. Peters.)

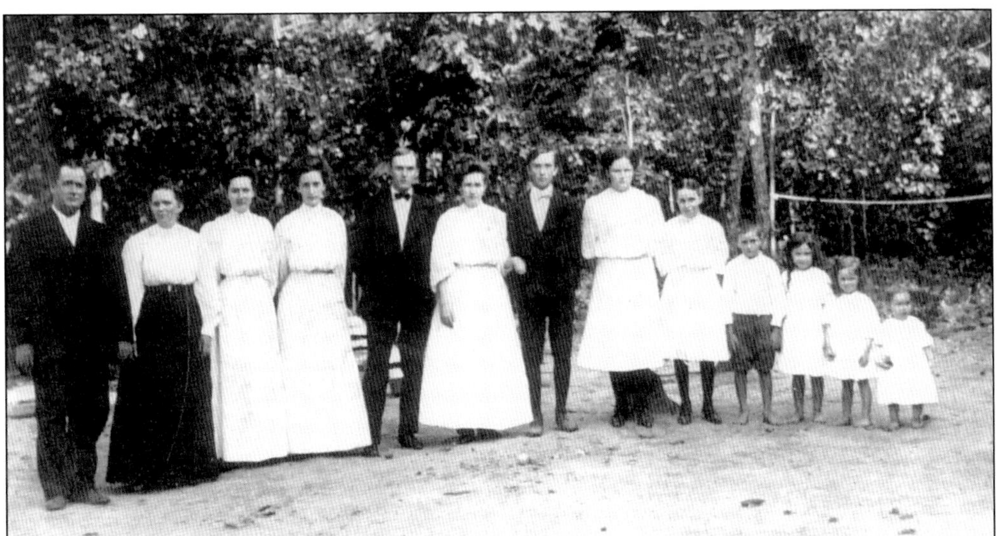

CLAYTON FAMILY. Southern Wesleyan University relies on the generosity of many families and communities in order to continue its mission, which is providing high quality education in a Christian environment. The Clayton family donated their money, their property, and their services to the school and the Central community throughout the 20th century. Shown here, from left to right, are Dr. Lawrence Clayton (founding father of Southern Wesleyan), Martha Adelaid "Addie" Smith Clayton, and their children—Nita, Grace, Silas, Christine, Van, Ethel, Faith, Harold, Eunice, Cleone, and Angie Clayton. (Photo courtesy of the Faith Clayton Room, Southern Wesleyan University, Central.)

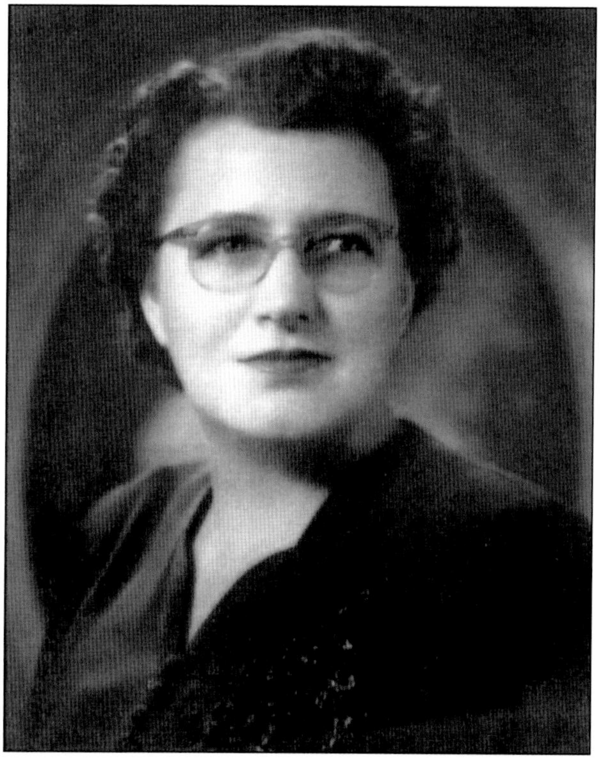

PORTRAIT OF FAITH CLAYTON. Original historical documents, photographs, and books about the Upstate, particularly Pickens County and the formation of its local schools, are among the items available to researchers at the Faith Clayton Family Research Room. Faith Clayton, former industrial commissioner of South Carolina, followed in the footsteps of her father, Dr. Lawrence Clayton. Motivated to help others obtain knowledge, Faith assembled and indexed information for the Rickman Library at the Wesleyan University. (Photo courtesy of Southern Wesleyan University, Central.)

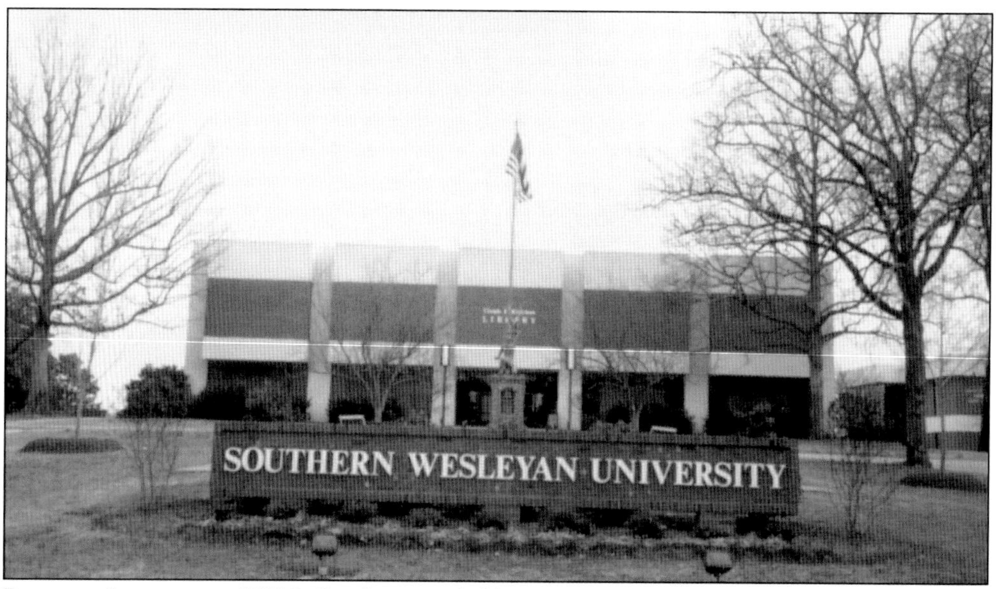

RICKMAN LIBRARY AT SWU. On the site of old Grimes Hall, the Claude R. Rickman Library at Southern Wesleyan University houses the Faith Clayton Family Research Room. Southern Wesleyan University is just off Highway 93 between the cities of Central and Liberty. Until 1995, Southern Wesleyan University was called Central Wesleyan College. The name change provided location clarification for out-of-state parents and students since many thought the school was located in the middle of South Carolina, near Columbia, and not in the Upstate area. (Photo by P.E. Peters.)

Strom Thurmond. Joe Derithat, J.M. Stallworth, and J. Strom Thurmond (third man from the left) sit beside a guest speaker (standing) at Clemson College. Born in Edgefield in 1902, Thurmond graduated Clemson in 1923 to teach school. He became a South Carolina state senator (1933 to 1938 and 1954 to 2001), decorated World War II veteran (1942 to 1946), South Carolina governor (1947 to 1951), presidential candidate (States Rights Ticket, 1948), and president pro tempore of the Senate (1981 to 1987). Throughout his career, Thurmond frequently visited Pickens County and Clemson University. (Photo courtesy of PDHRT.)

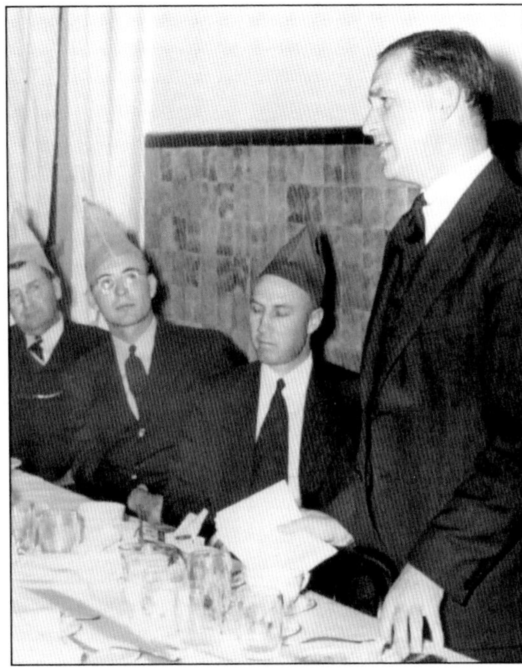

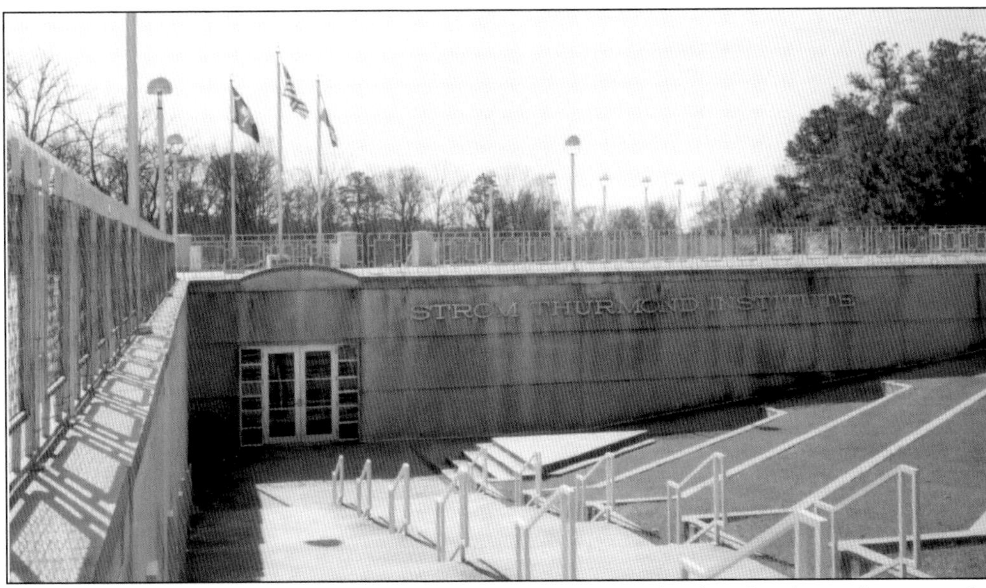

Strom Thurmond Institute. James Strom Thurmond, a schoolteacher by profession and a politician by fate, supported the educational needs of the Upstate, an area drained of resources due, in part, to the economical depression that enveloped the rural community in the 1920s. Thurmond supported Clemson and Southern Wesleyan, but it is the Strom Thurmond Institute, dedicated in 1989, that is his primary beneficiary. Built partially underground, the institute and its archives, located off Perimeter Road, are a part of the Cooper Library Systems on the Clemson campus. The institute houses many artifacts and documents pertaining to the Upstate's development. Strom Thurmond Institute also maintains detailed information about the development of a land-grant college determined to positively impact rural communities through its cooperative agricultural extension services. (Photo by P.E. Peters.)

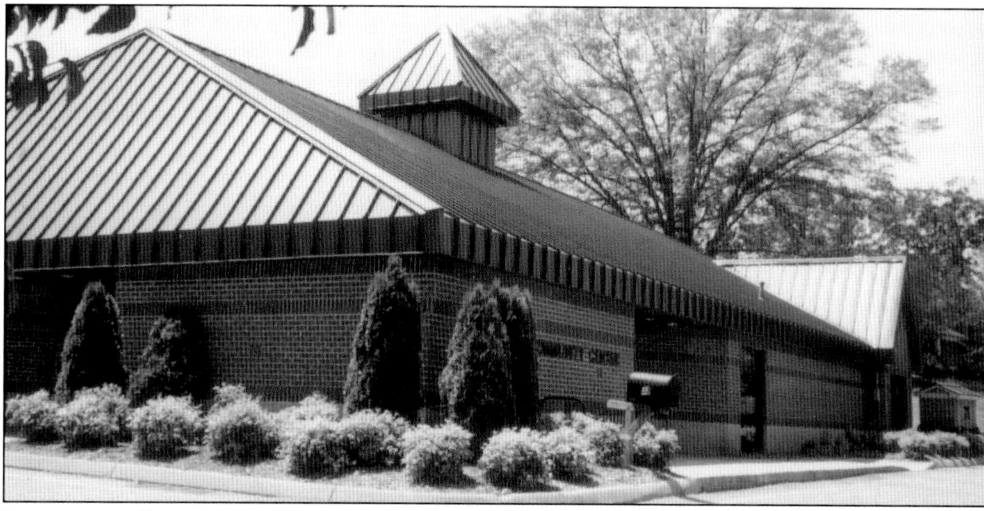

LITTLEJOHN COMMUNITY CENTER. The African-American Heritage Walking Tour begins in Pendleton with other points of interest designated throughout the Upstate area. In Pickens County, the site of the Littlejohn Grill, on Highway 93 between Clemson and Central, is a part of the tour. A club built by Horace Littlejohn was a stop on the black music circuit. Greats like Ray Charles, James Brown, Harry Belafonte, and "Piano Red" played for the patrons of the Littlejohn Grill, now razed. The contemporary Littlejohn Community Center sits on the site of the grill. (Photo by P.E. Peters.)

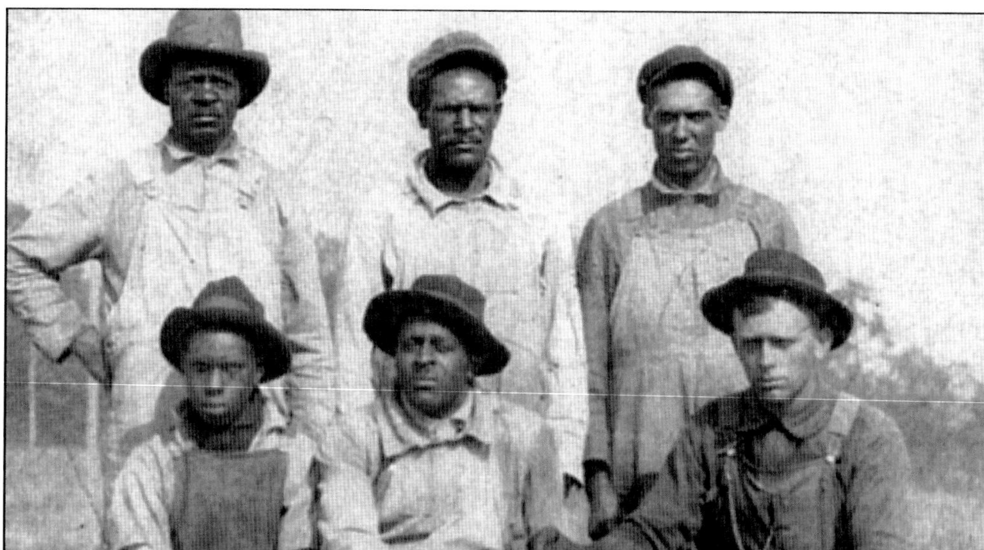

PORTRAIT OF RAILROAD CREW. Scottish-Irishmen built the Pickens short-line railroads between the 1830s and the 1850s, but freed African Americans constructed the Southern Railway in Pickens. Little is known about their individual contributions, but cultural study groups and researchers, including those at the Houston Center for the Study of the Black Experience at Clemson, are beginning to clarify history with original documentation. The Pendleton District Historical Recreational and Tourism Commission, located at 125 E. Queen in Pendleton, and the Pendleton Foundation for Black History and Culture also keep accurate records and original documentation concerning African-American experiences in the Upstate area. (Photo courtesy of the Central Heritage Society.)

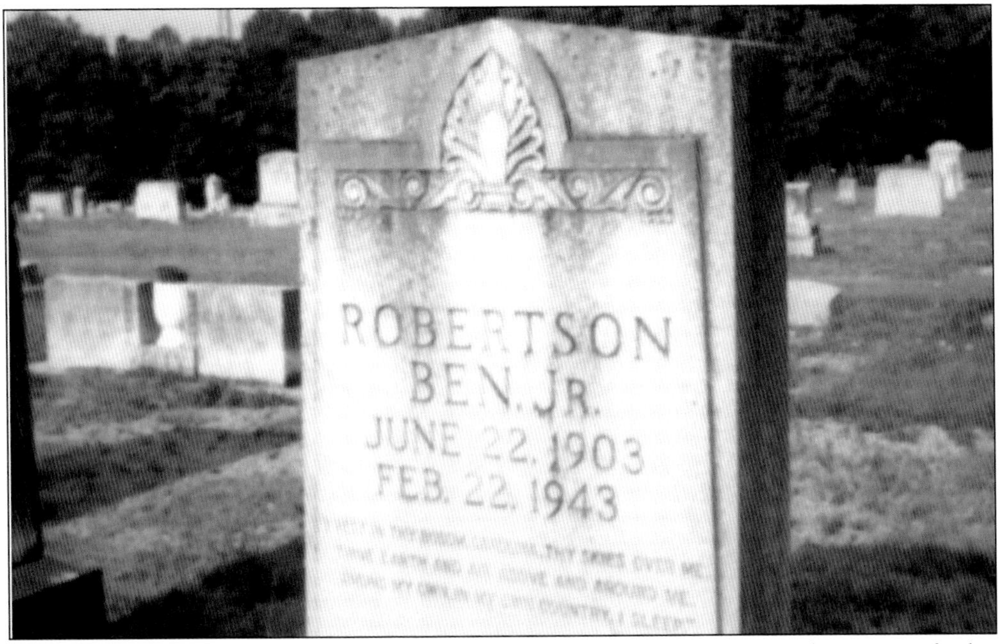

Robertson's Grave. Greenville native Harry Ashmore, who won the Pulitzer Prize for his pro-integration editorials, suggested a different subtitle for *Red Hills and Cotton*, "Epitaph of the Upcountry—In Loving Memory Of a World That Existed Only in the Minds of a Few of Us." Ben was inducted into the South Carolina Academy of Authors in 1992. The epitaph on his tombstone is from his first book, *Travelers' Rest*. (Photo by P.E. Peters.)

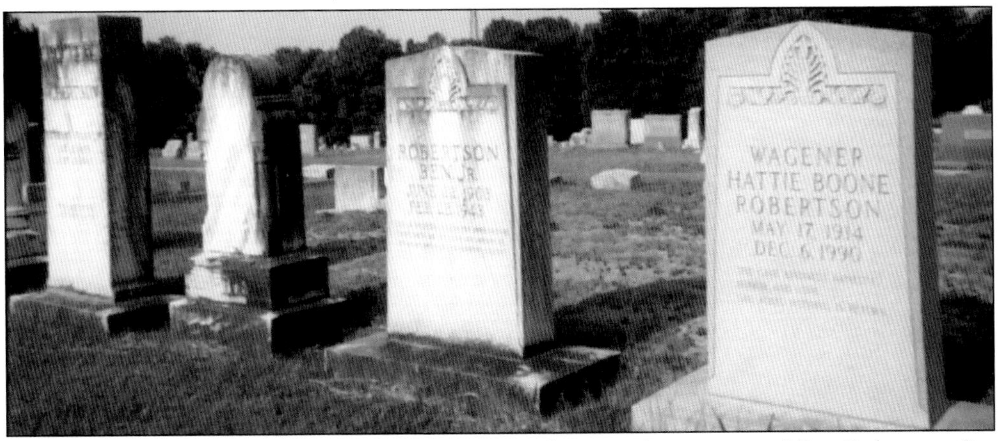

Robertson's Family Grave. Mary Bowen, a Winthrop graduate, married Ben Robertson Sr., a Clemson cadet from the class of 1896. They had a son together and Mary died in 1910. Ben Sr. worked as a chemist on the Clemson Agricultural Extension Service staff (1912 to 1942). He received national recognition for his scientific research that led to the development of new fertilizers. He remarried to Hattie Boggs of Liberty in 1913, but it would be Mary's parents, the W.T. Bowens, that played a vital role in Ben Jr.'s upbringing. Besides visiting his grandparents, Ben Jr. enjoyed trips to the Clemson College Library. The modest library offered books that sparked Ben's imagination. As an adult Ben would visit Hawaii, Java, and Australia. By the 1940s he had traveled to India, Africa, and the Soviet Union. His natural talents can be read in his travelogues. Pictured here is the Robertson family plot in Liberty on Old Norris Road. (Photo by P.E. Peters.)

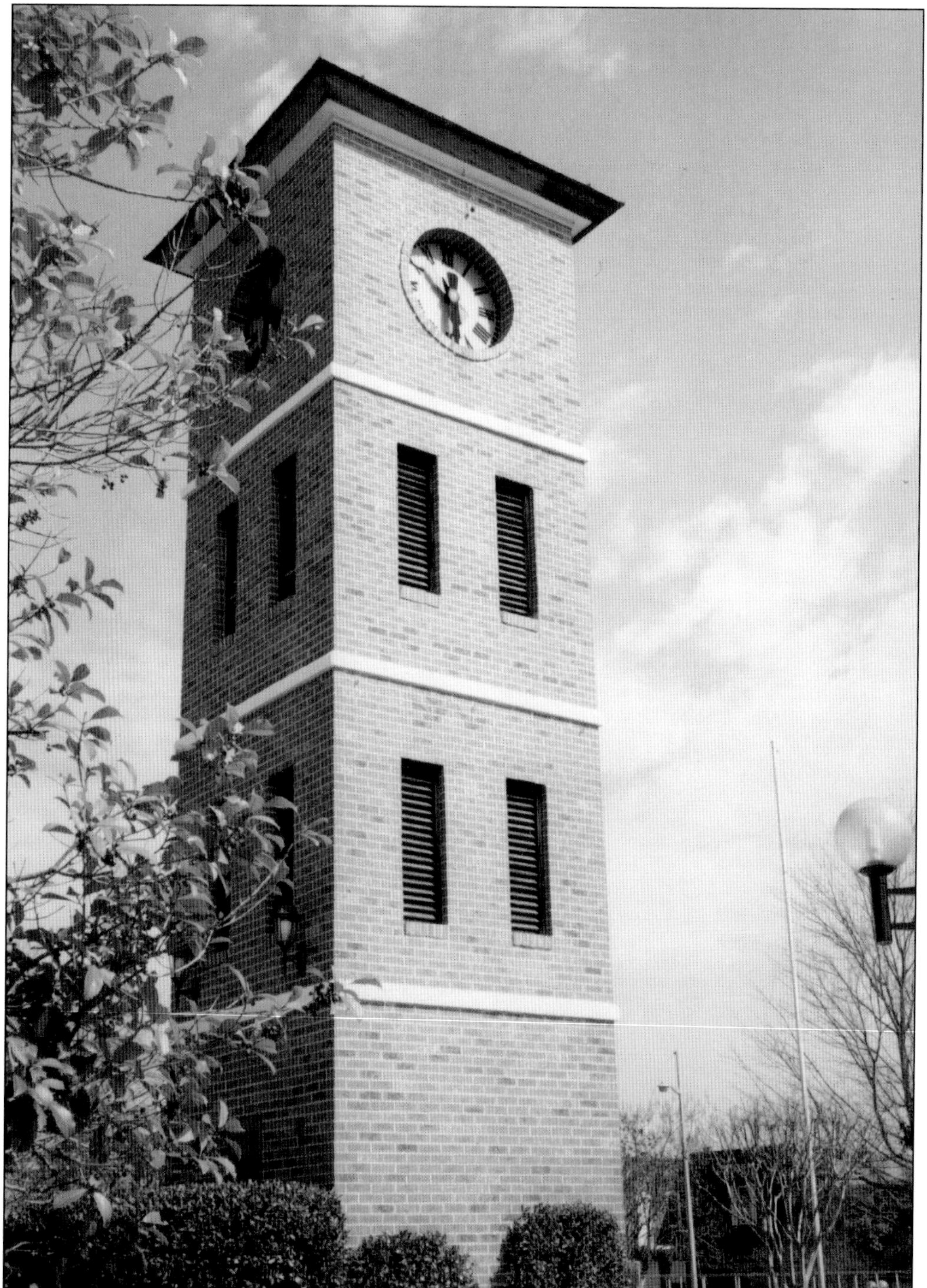

CLOCK TOWER IN OLD MARKET SQUARE. The clock tower at historic Old Market Square in Easley is a reminder that times change. Easley's downtown underwent renovations in the latter half of the 20th century in an effort to divert consumer traffic from the highway strip malls to pedestrian-friendly Main Street. (Photo by P.E. Peters.)

Five

Changes and Challenges

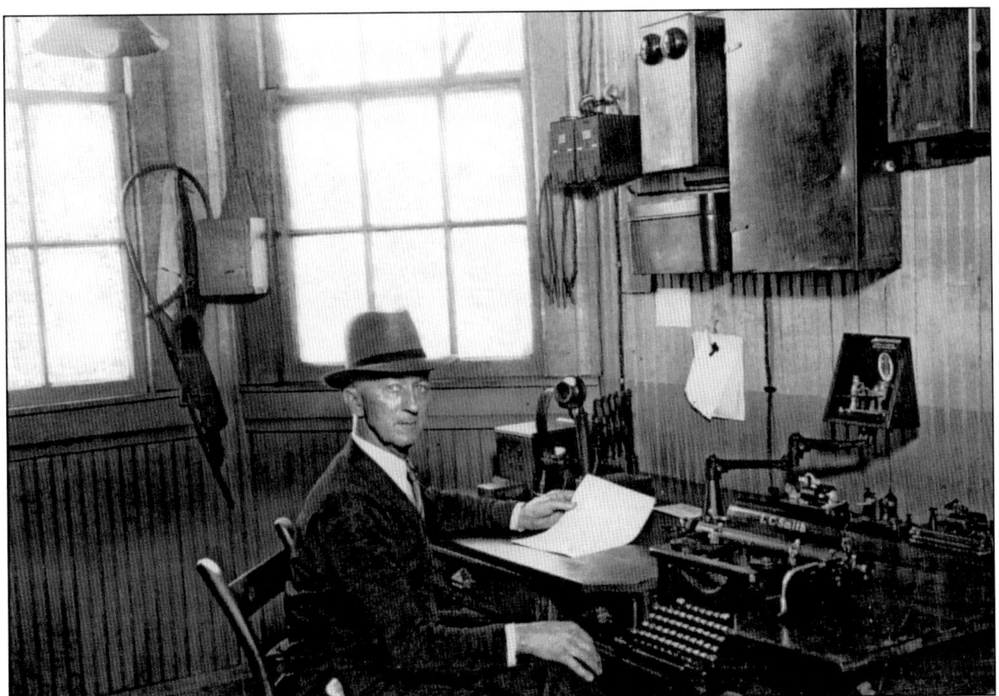

Telegraph Operator. Mr. John Nathan Sims worked in an efficient, modern telegraph office in Central at the beginning of the 20th century. The manual typewriter made by L.C. Smith made paper work easy. The telephone was portable with its go-anywhere extension springs, and the single bulb chandler gave light on a cloudy day. (Photo courtesy of Cathy and Buddy Sims and the Central Heritage Society.)

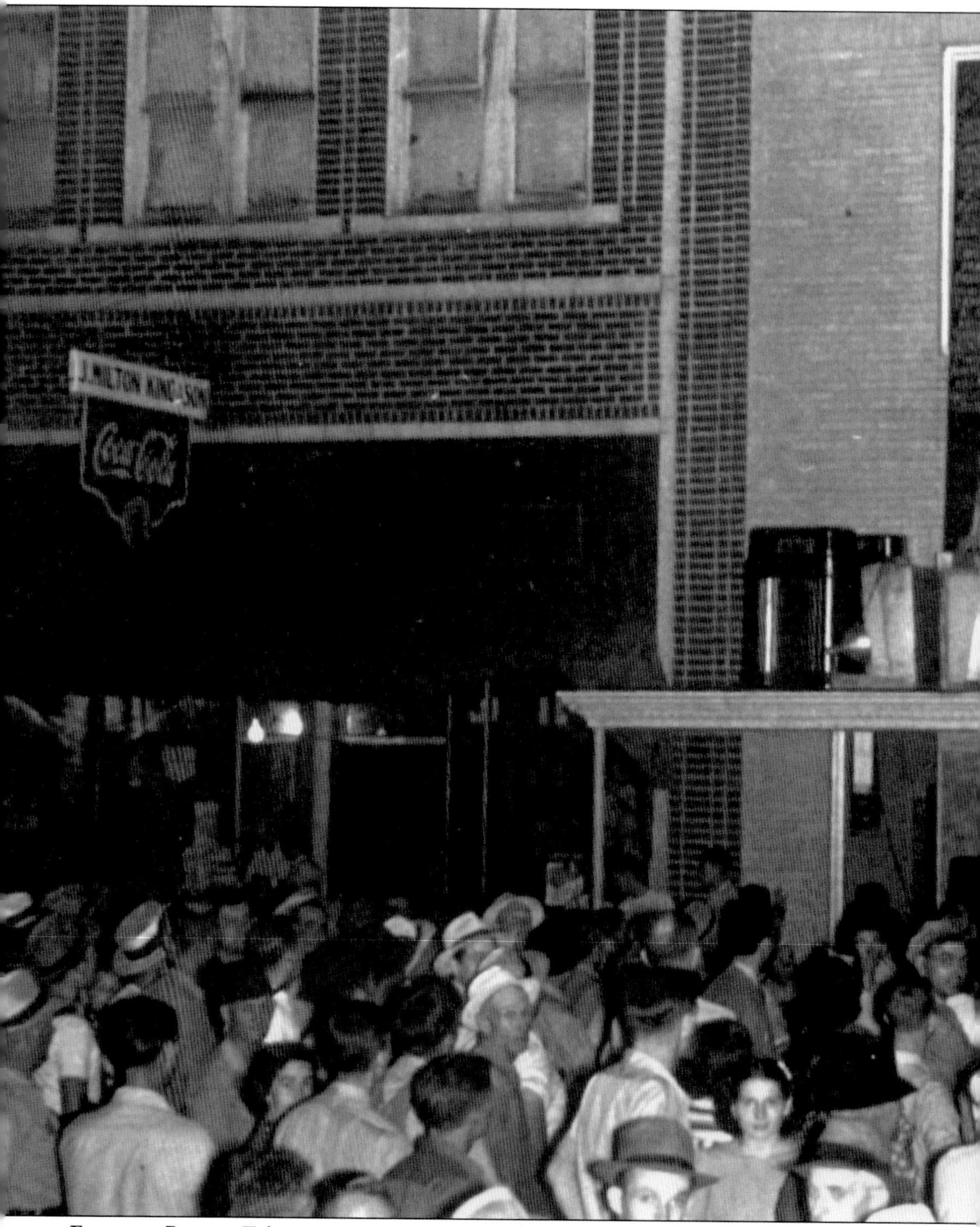

ELECTION BOARD. Television was expensive in the mid-20th century. Most folks got their news from the radio or from the newspaper. In this photo, election results are scribbled on a chalkboard for all the people to see. In the 1940s, at the time this photo was taken, television reporting was in its infancy and precincts had no computerized ballot/voting box systems.

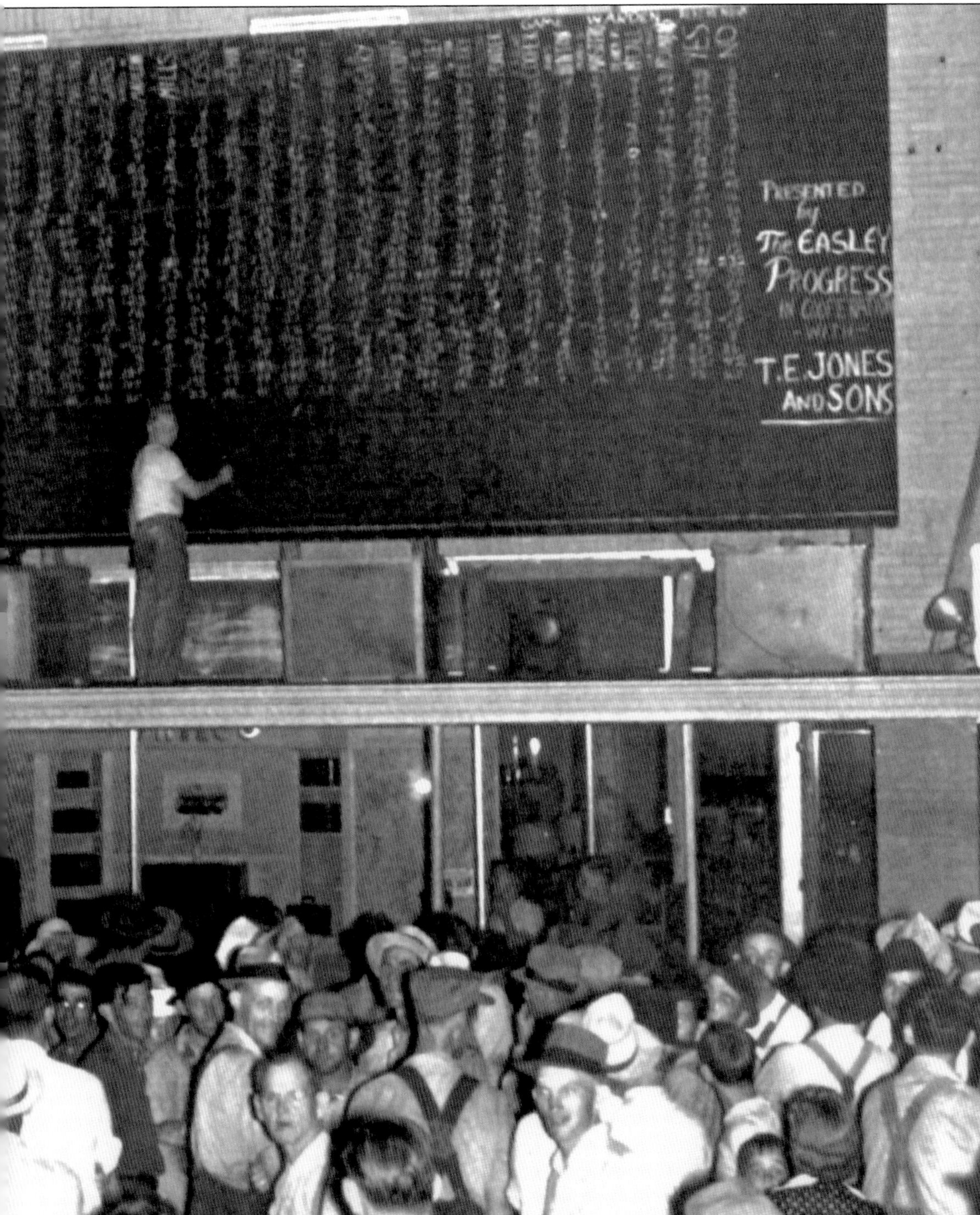

Paper and pencils were used to cast votes and then precincts manually counted each piece of paper and wrote the final results on this chalk election board presented by *The Easley Progress* and T.E. Jones & Sons. (Photo courtesy of the Pickens County Library.)

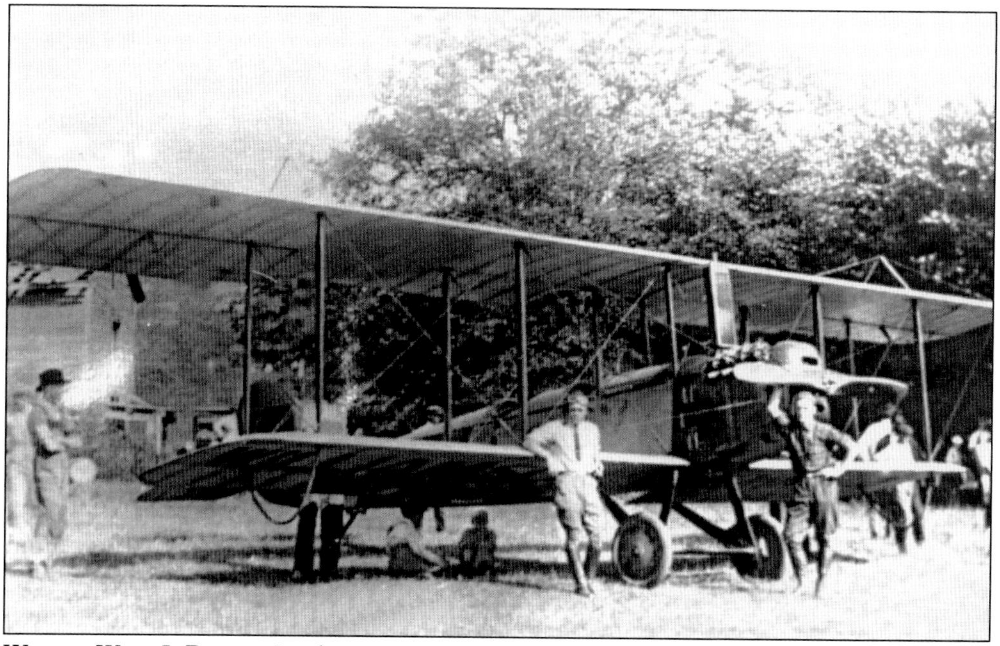

World War I Plane. In the 1920s, pilot Ben Johnson sold rides over Dacusville and Pumpkintown in his World War I airplane. (Photo courtesy of PDHRT.)

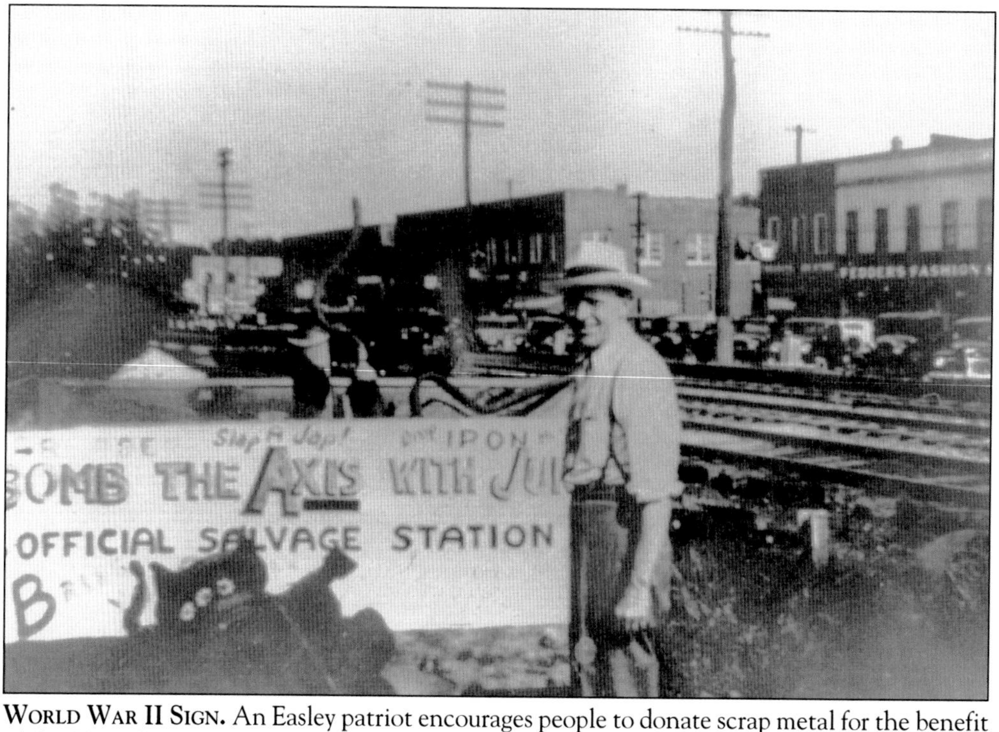

World War II Sign. An Easley patriot encourages people to donate scrap metal for the benefit of the United States during World War II. The metal was used for the construction of bullets, bombs, boats, and airplanes. The airplane became a common method of transportation after World War II. (Photo courtesy of PDHRT.)

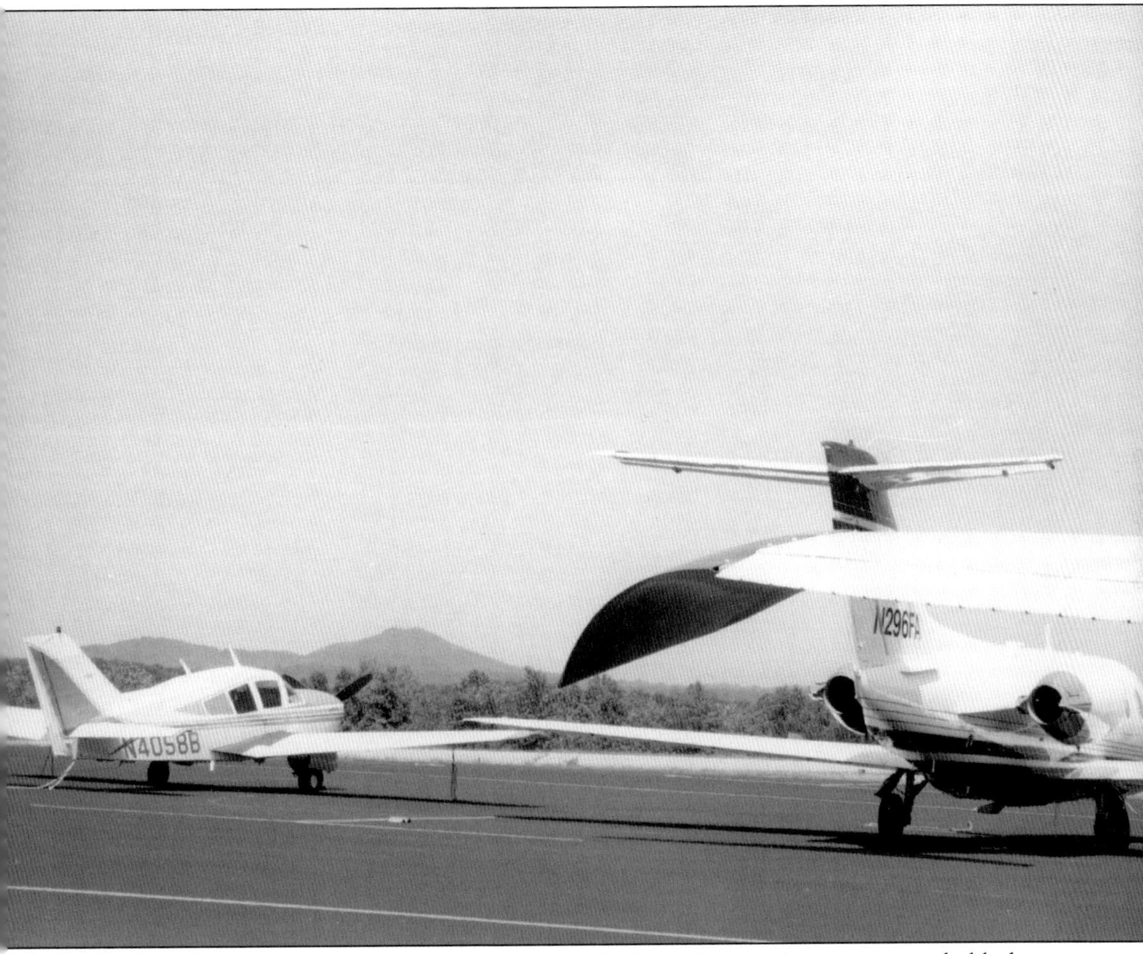

AIRPORT. Located 2 miles north of Liberty, the Pickens County Aero is approachable by car from Airport Road just off U.S. 178 between Pickens and Liberty. With no control tower, the airport relies on the nearby Greer Radar for weather advisements. It has a 5,002-foot-long runway, has approximately 250 takeoffs and landings per day, and offers tie-downs and hanger storage. Service and repair are readily available and there are three flight instructors on duty to assist a wanna-be pilot. Aircraft used for flying lessons include two Cessna 150s for beginners, one 172 Cessna for advanced flyers, and one Piper Archer for rentals. Situated on a high plateau, the Pickens County Aero also offers a breathtaking view of the Blue Ridge Mountains. (Photo by P.E. Peters.)

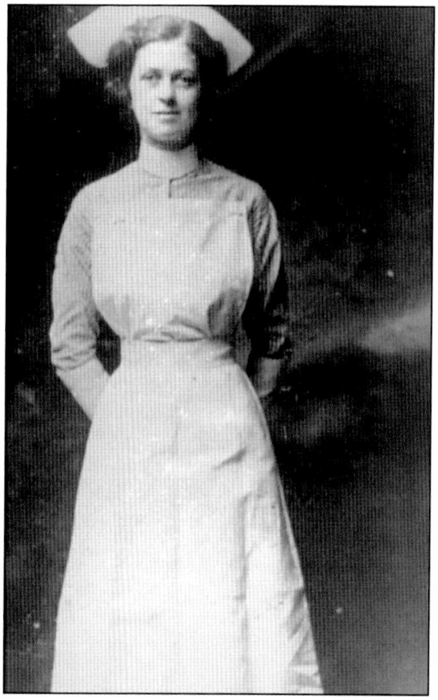

Nurse. Iva Hendricks was a nurse in Pickens County in 1915. At the beginning of the 20th century, nurses were few and technology was primitive. Drugs were expensive, and doctors were always busy because the demand outweighed the amount of qualified surgeons in the area. Finding good healthcare remains a challenge for the people in the Upcountry. (Photo courtesy of PDHRT and Pickens County Library.)

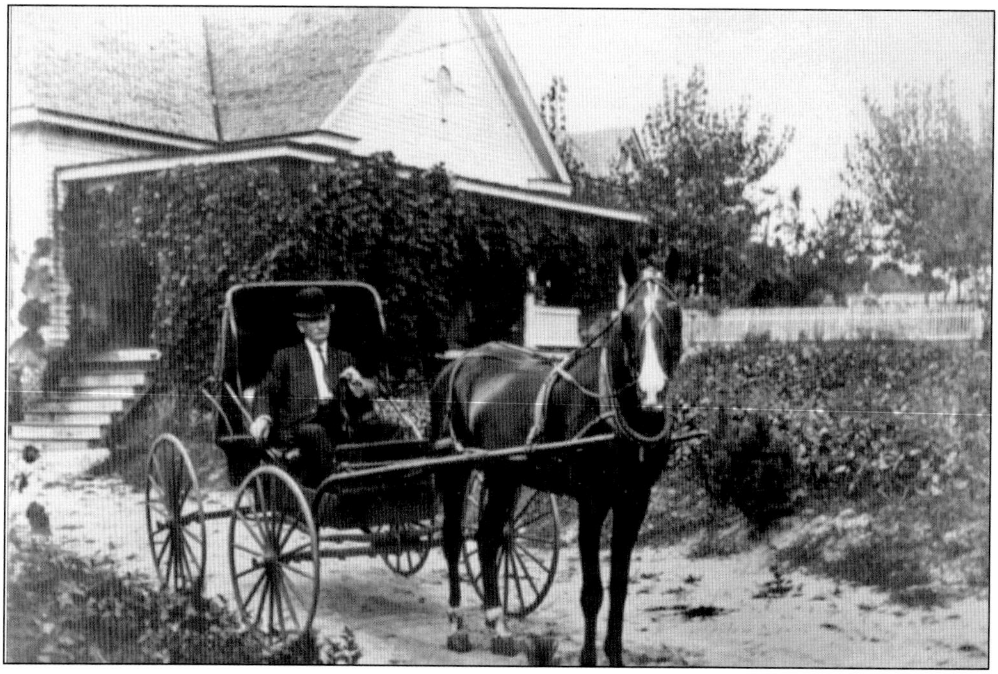

Man, Horse, and Buggy. Dr. Edward F. Wyatt drives his horse "Dandy" out the driveway of his home at 501 W. Main Street in Easley. Doctors made house calls throughout Pickens County. According to *The Journal of the South Carolina Medical Association*, Dr. Lawrence Clayton of Central would practice medicine on horseback. He would net quail from his saddle and take them to his patients. He would prescribe quail broth for the convalescing. (Photo courtesy of the Pickens County Library and the South Carolina Medical Association.)

Dr. Peek. Born in North Carolina, Dr. David E. Peek (1892 to 1942) strikes a pose in 1918. He graduated from Emory School of Medicine and in November 1925, he opened a hospital with 15 beds in Six Mile. In addition to his medical practice, Peek owned and operated a diary farm near Six Mile. He perished from a stroke while attending to a patient. (Photo courtesy of Pickens County Library)

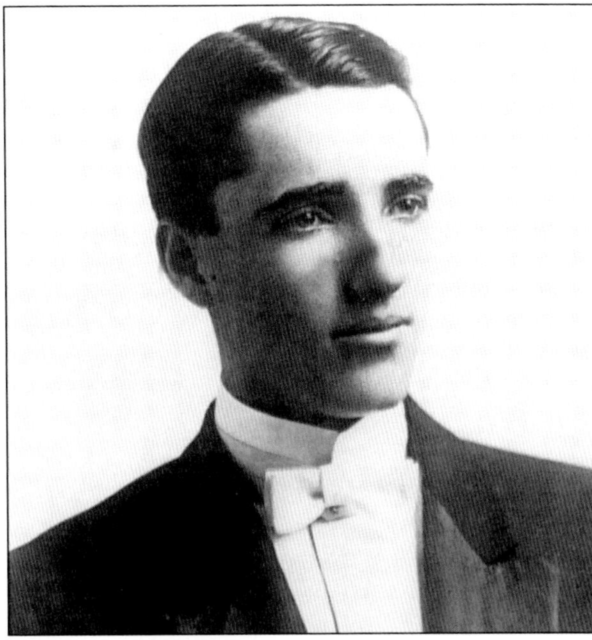

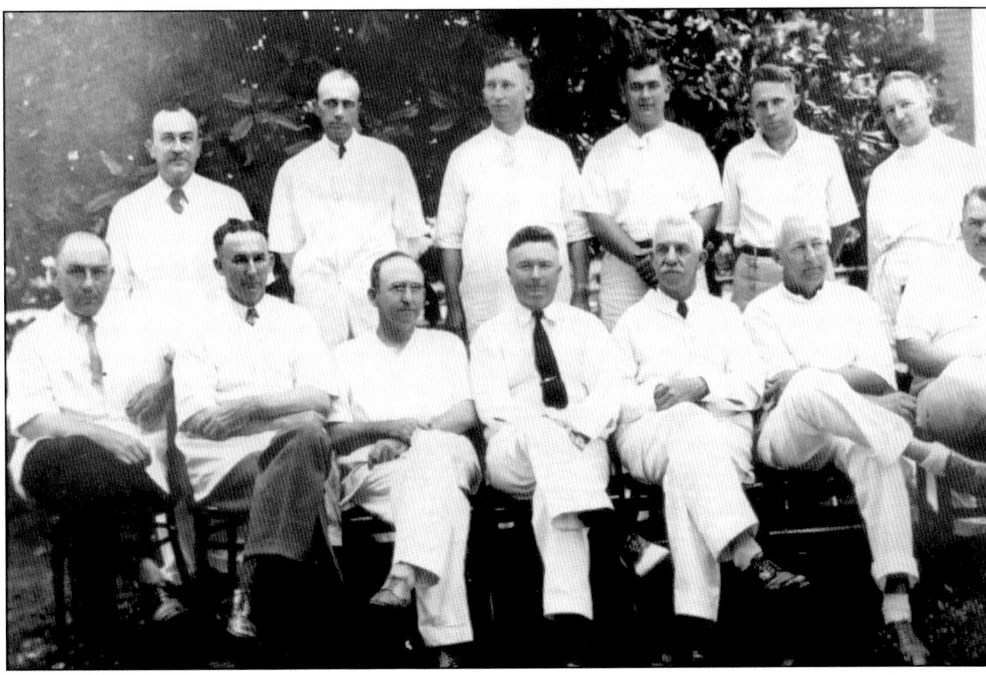

Doctors. In the early 1930s, doctors would travel from across the county to Clemson to give the cadets their physicals. The examinations were free and a courtesy of the community. Shown here, from left to right, are the following: (seated) Dr. Webb of Townville/Seneca; Buck Pressley of Due West; Dr. Lewis Sandy of Greenville; Dr. Lee Milford at Clemson; Dr. E.A. Hines of Seneca; and Dr. Samuel C. Dean of Anderson; (standing) Dr. Mack Sanders; unidentified; Dr. Homer Melvin Daniel; Dr. John Martin; Dr. Thomas R. Gaines; and Dr. Erwin Olin Hentz. (Photo courtesy of Delle Daniel Kelly, Anderson, South Carolina, and the PDHRT.)

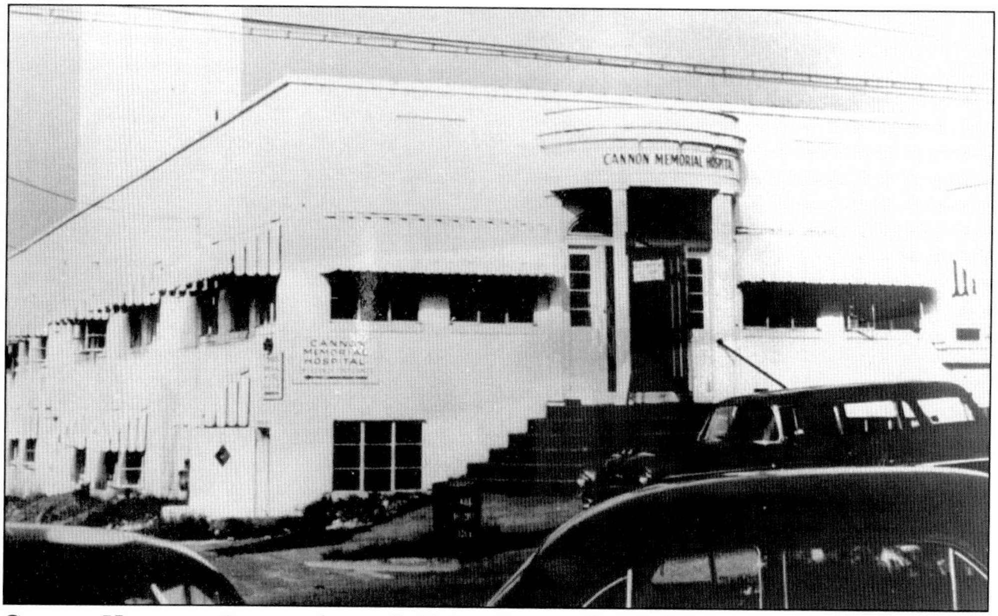

CANNON HOSPITAL. Country doctor E. Gaine Cannon founded Cannon Hospital and named it for his father, Dr. James Cannon. The non-profit community hospital began in 1947 on Pendleton Street in this structure. By 1982, the facility and staff relocated to 123 Medical Park Drive. In 1991, outpatient services were added. Located between Pickens and Liberty, Cannon Hospital continues to serve regional residents with on-site labs, short-term rehab facilities, and a competent staff of specialists ranging from orthopedics to gastroenterology. (Photo courtesy of the Pickens County Library.)

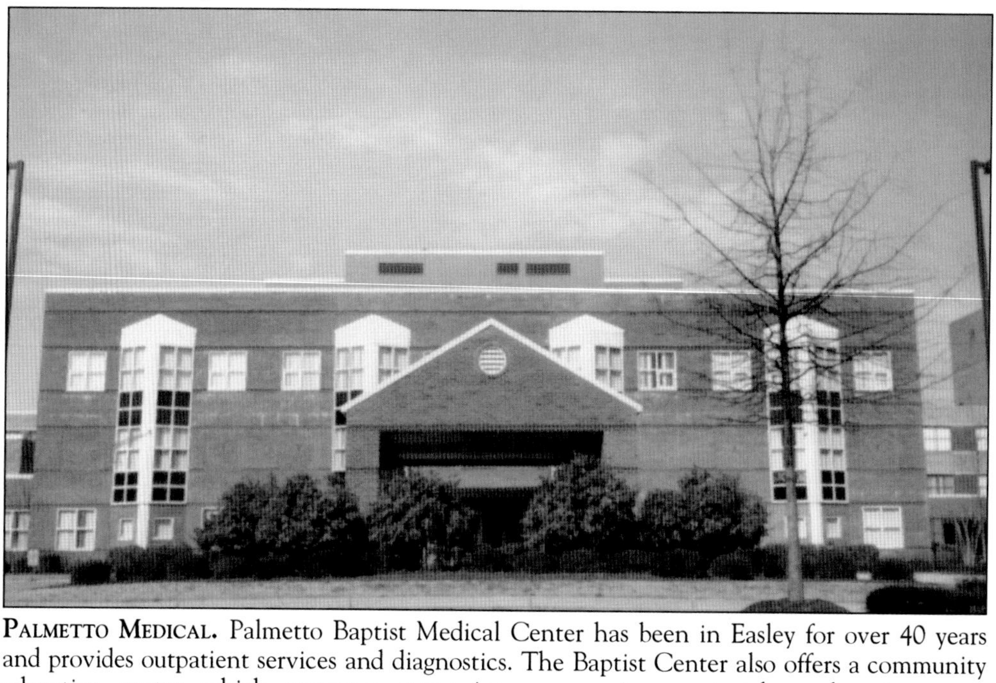

PALMETTO MEDICAL. Palmetto Baptist Medical Center has been in Easley for over 40 years and provides outpatient services and diagnostics. The Baptist Center also offers a community education center, which promotes preventive care services, materials, and maintenance programs. (Photo by P.E. Peters.)

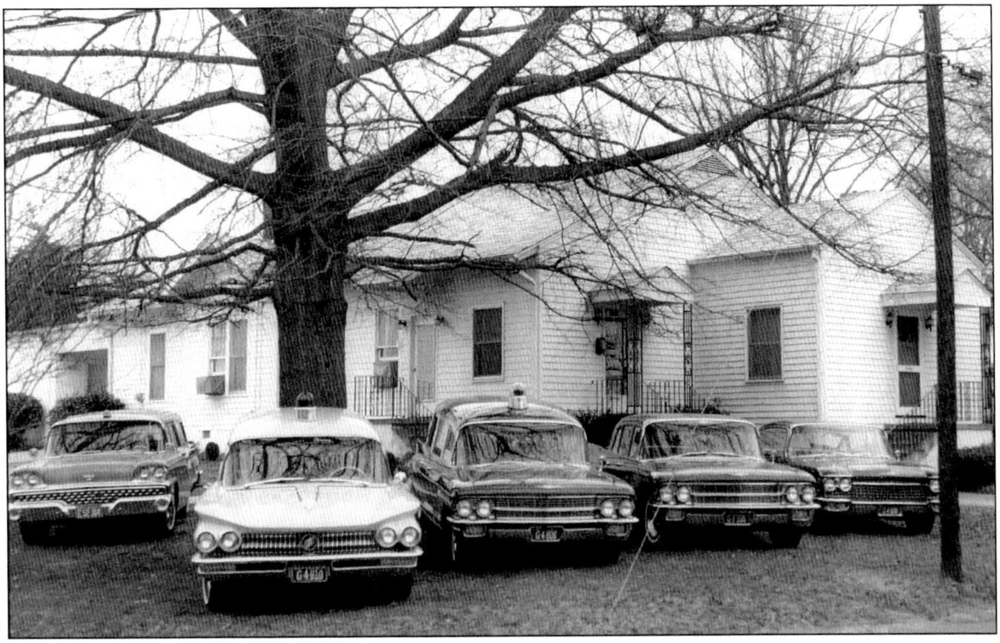

Central Ambulances. By the 1940s doctors made fewer house calls. Local communities like Central purchased fleets of vehicles designed to serve as squad cars or ambulances. Fast transit vehicles allowed doctors to trade travel time by horse and buggy for more hours to treat the injured and the sick. (Photo courtesy of the Central Heritage Society.)

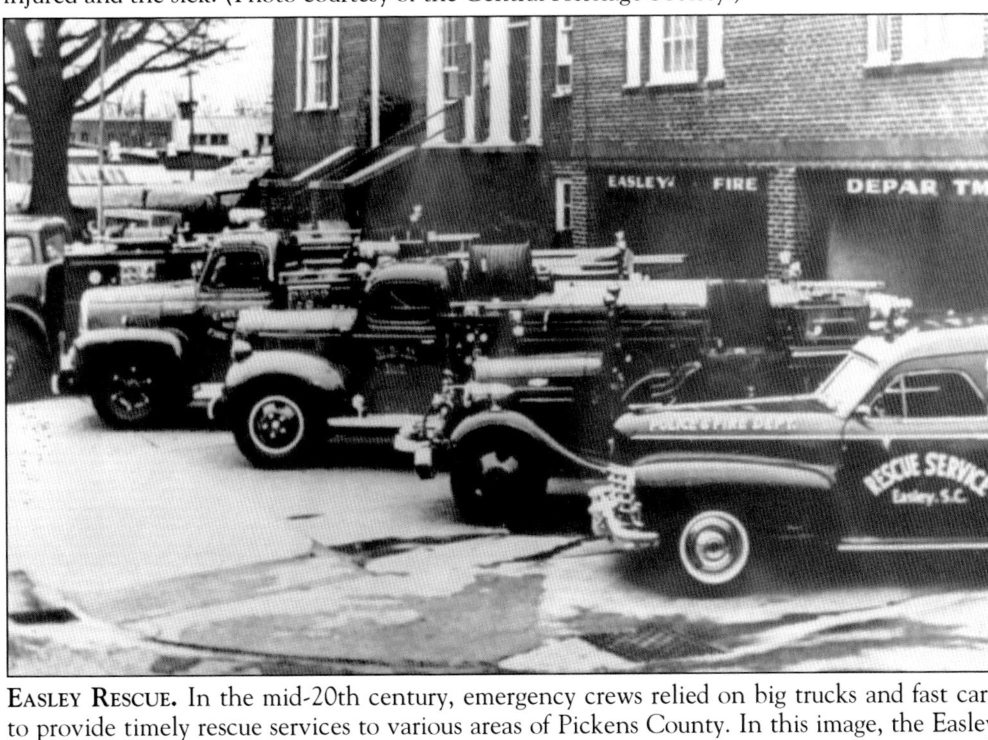

Easley Rescue. In the mid-20th century, emergency crews relied on big trucks and fast cars to provide timely rescue services to various areas of Pickens County. In this image, the Easley Police and Fire Department prepare the transportation equipment for inspection. (Photo courtesy of PDHRT.)

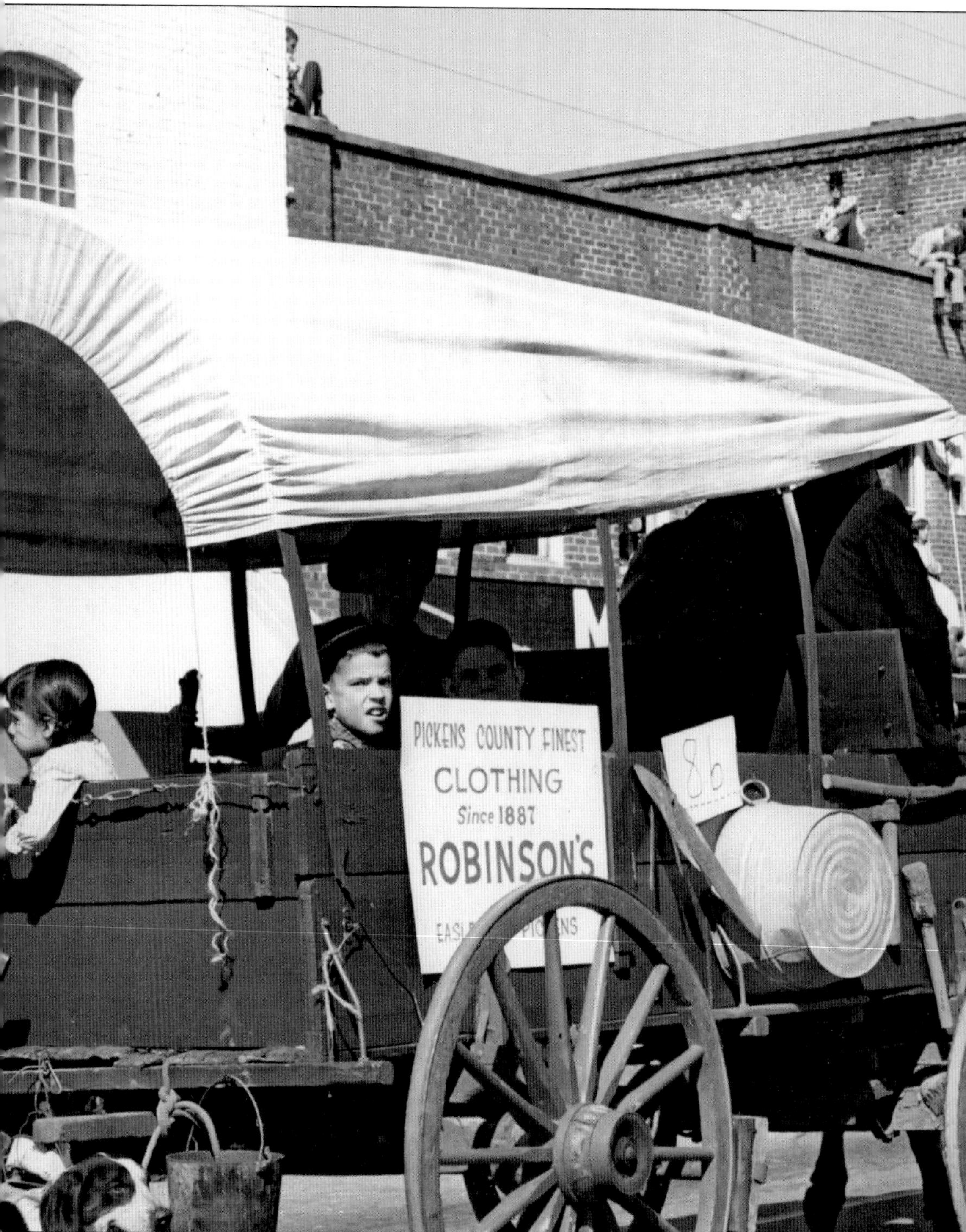

CENTENNIAL PARADE. The Vietnam War raged as Pickens folks celebrated the county's changes and future challenges with the 1968 Centennial Parade. The stores at the left include the Goldsmith 5&10, Rexall Drugstore and Department Store, Collins Store, and

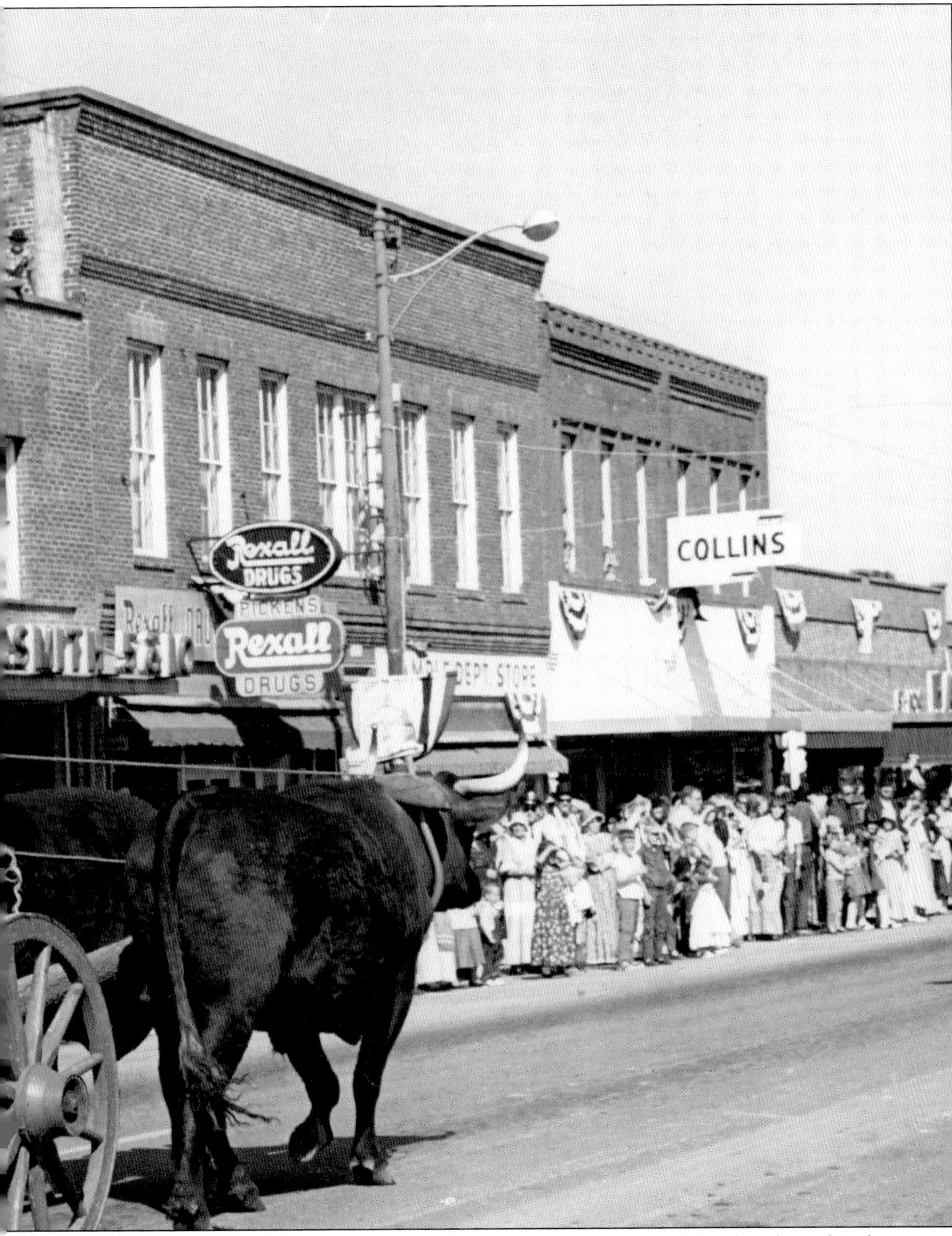

Harpers 5&10. The town folk are dressed in costume in honor of the founders of Pickens County. (Photo by William E. Payne.)

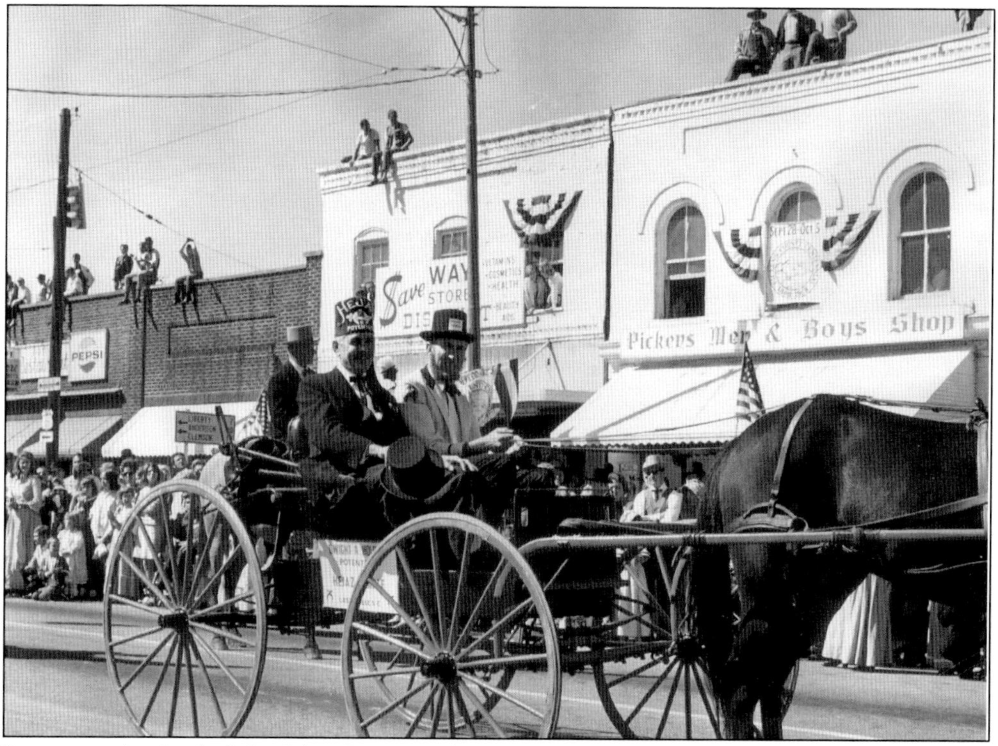

JUNCTION. At the far left of this Centennial Parade image is the junction of U.S. 178 and S.C. 183. Highway 178 leads to Liberty and Clemson. Scenic state road 183 leads to Six Mile, then goes on to Oconee County and the original site of the old courthouse town of Pickens on the Keowee River. (Photo by William E. Payne.)

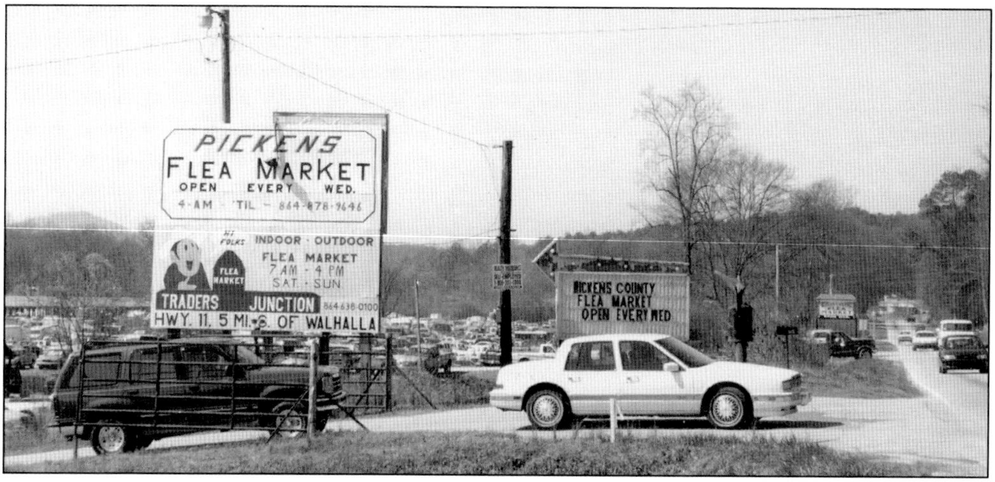

FLEA MARKET. Mill stores and mercantiles provided goods in the late 1800s and the early 1900s. In the middle of the 20th century, village five-and-dimes and soda shops met the babyboomers' needs. From the mid-1960s to the late 1980s, the era of the credit card, shopping malls, and strip malls spread along the major highways. Presently, aging babyboomers and college tech students prefer pedestrian-friendly town stores and the indoor-outdoor Pickens Flea Market beside the Twelve Mile River. The Pickens Flea Market is open only on Wednesdays and is located outside of the city of Pickens on S.C. 183. (Photo by P.E. Peters.)

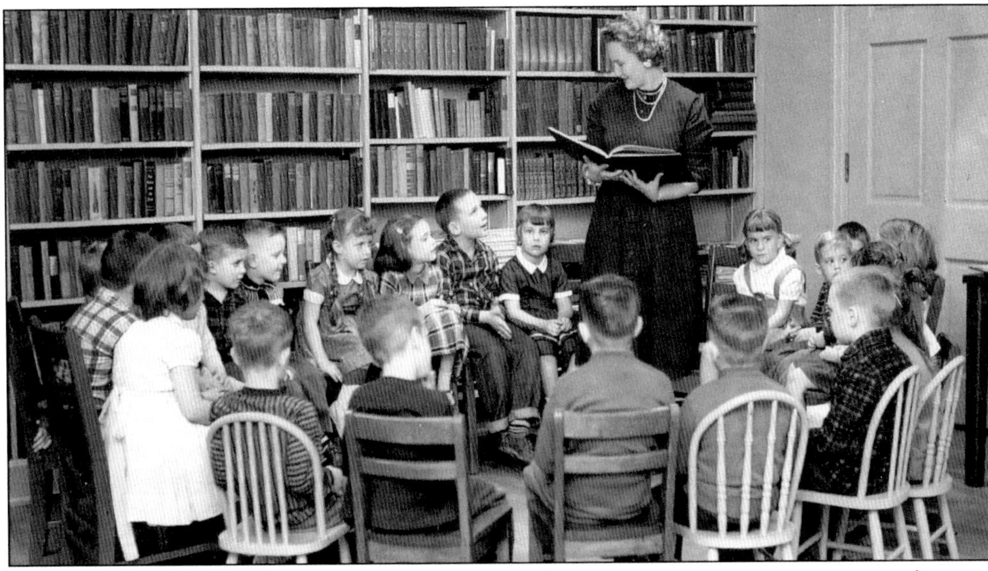

Reading Circle of Kids. Faceless government embraces education as an institutional system and not as a distinguished value cherished by an individual. Like T.G. Clemson, many citizens of Pickens realized that knowledge was paramount to personal and communal success, but few people anticipated the reformation in public education that began in the late 19th century. Land-grant colleges developed, paid schools became free public schools, free schools finally integrated, and the public library was founded for the benefit of all socio-economic communities throughout the county. Pictured here is Marsha Garrison conducting story hour. (Photo courtesy of the Pickens County Library.)

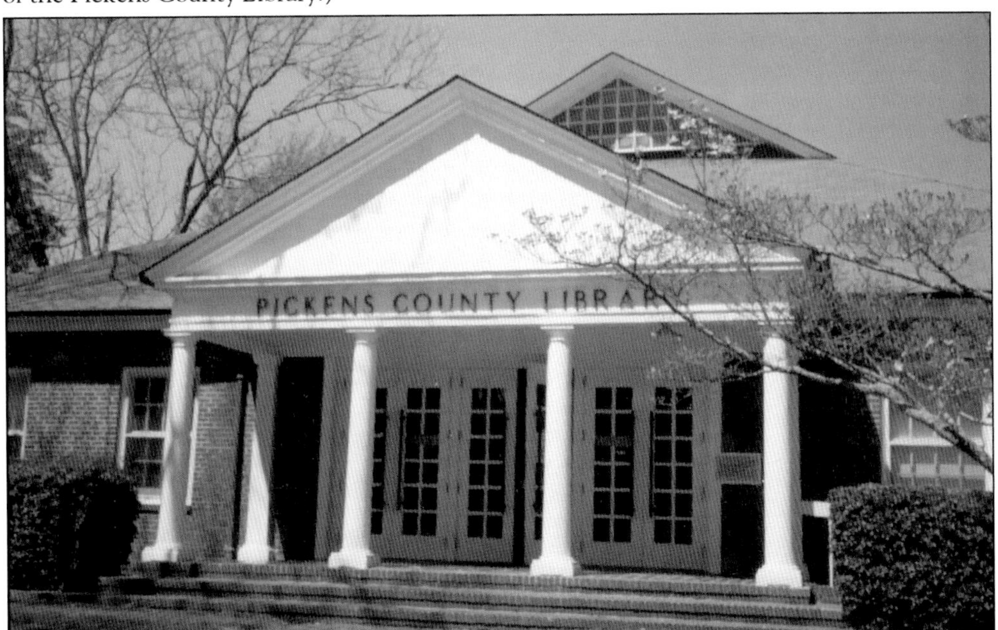

Pickens Co. Library. The Pickens County Library System has manuscripts and photographs that pertain to development of Pickens in its South Caroliniana Room. The majority of these items are housed at the main branch in Easley. (Photo by P.E. Peters.)

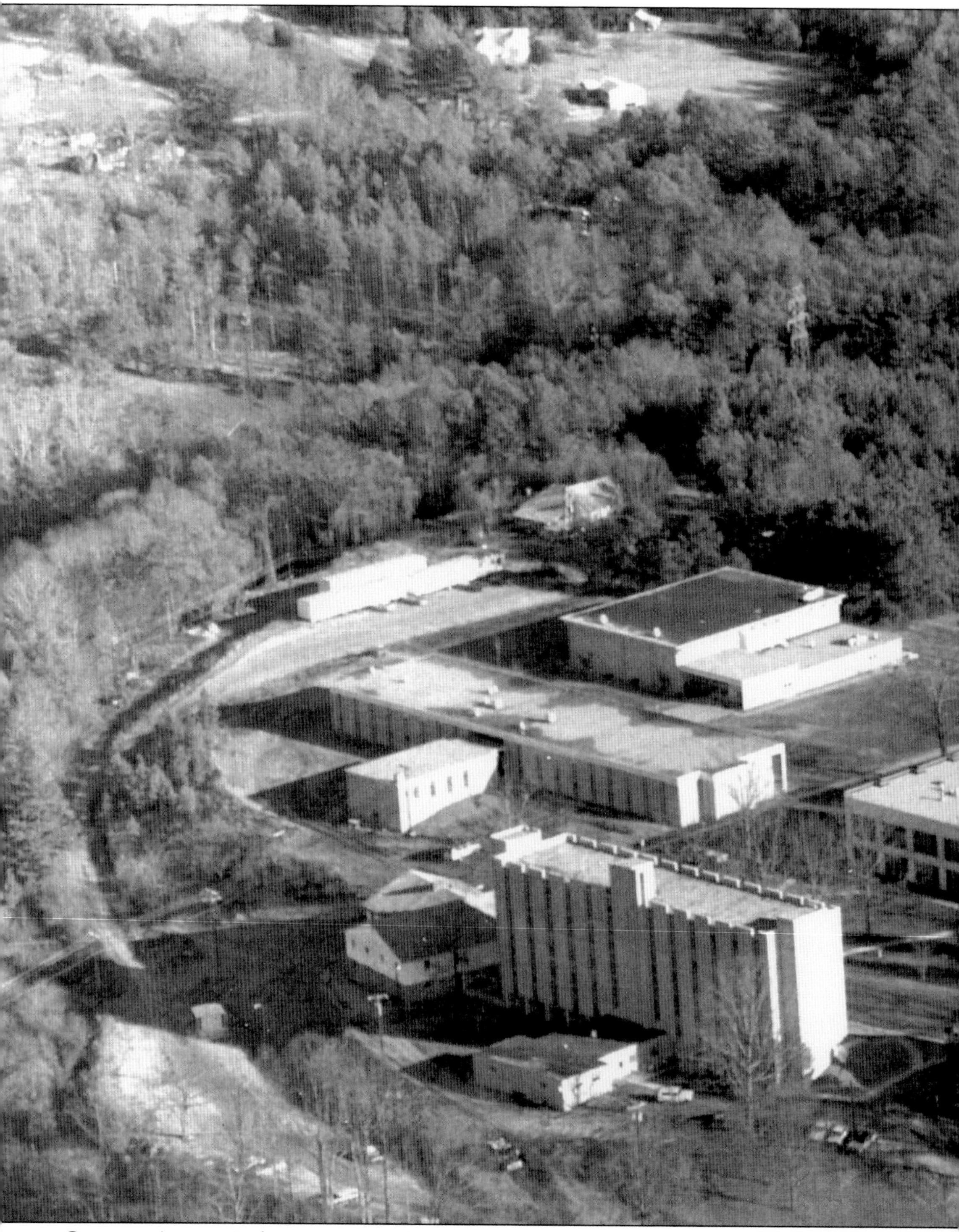

Central Aerial. Pickens County is blessed with two universities. Shown here is College Hill as it appeared during the Vietnam War era. Southern Wesleyan University was Central Wesleyan College from 1962 to 1994. Sponsored by the Wesleyan Church, Southern Wesleyan

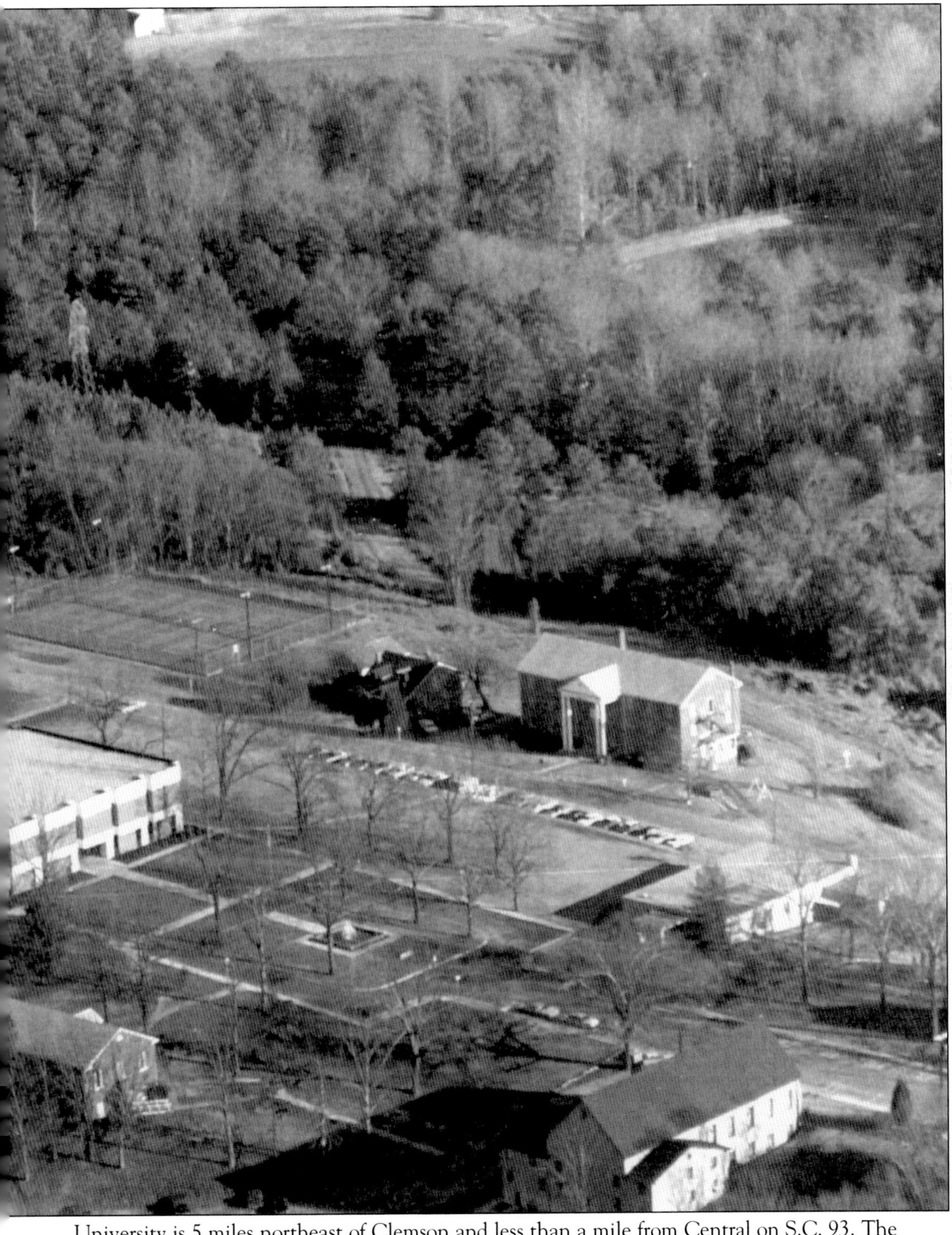

University is 5 miles northeast of Clemson and less than a mile from Central on S.C. 93. The four-year liberal arts institution is dedicated to the concept that God is the source of all truth and wisdom. (Photo courtesy of Southern Wesleyan University.)

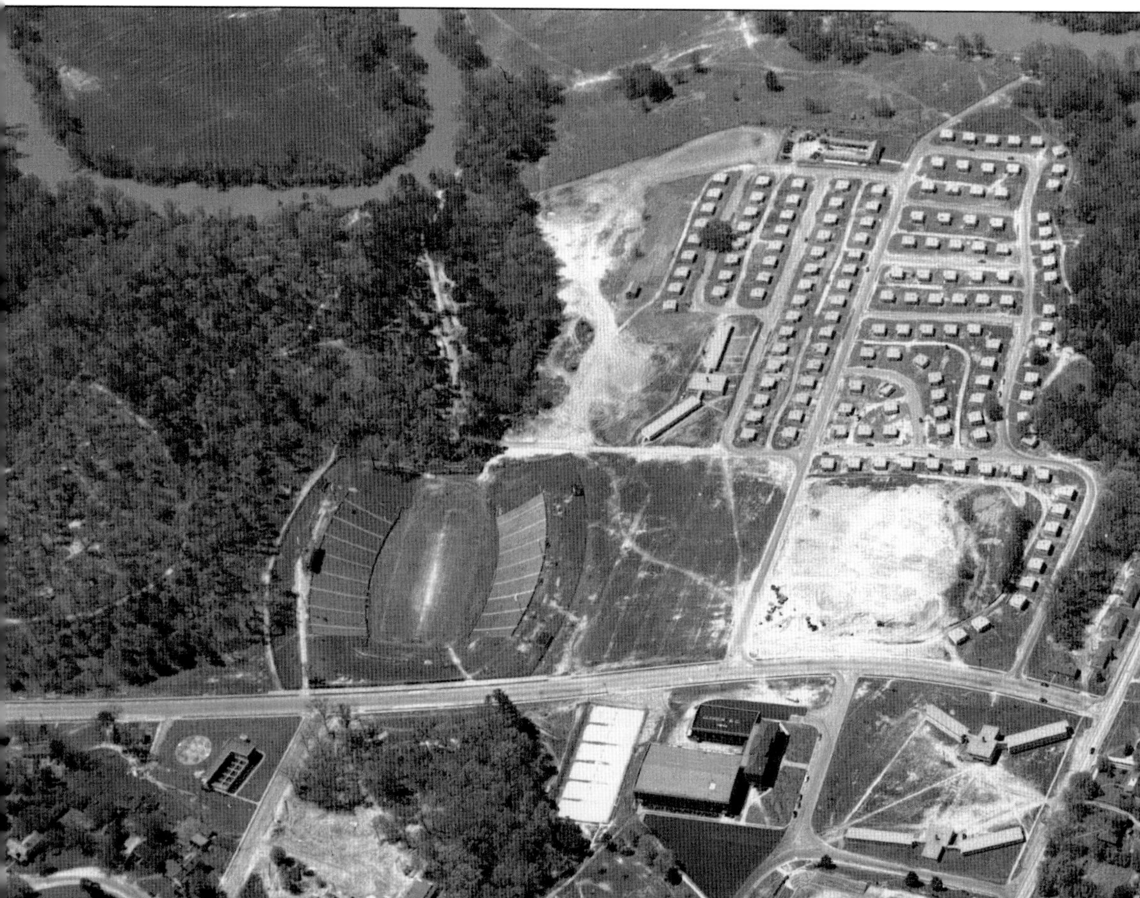

CLEMSON AERIAL. In the beginning, Clemson was located in the Pickens County District. It became a part of Oconee in 1868, then the college rejoined Pickens County in 1968. Clemson College remained an all-male military school until 1955, when it was reclassified as a "civilian" college. Clemson became a coeducational institution and 9 years later it was renamed Clemson

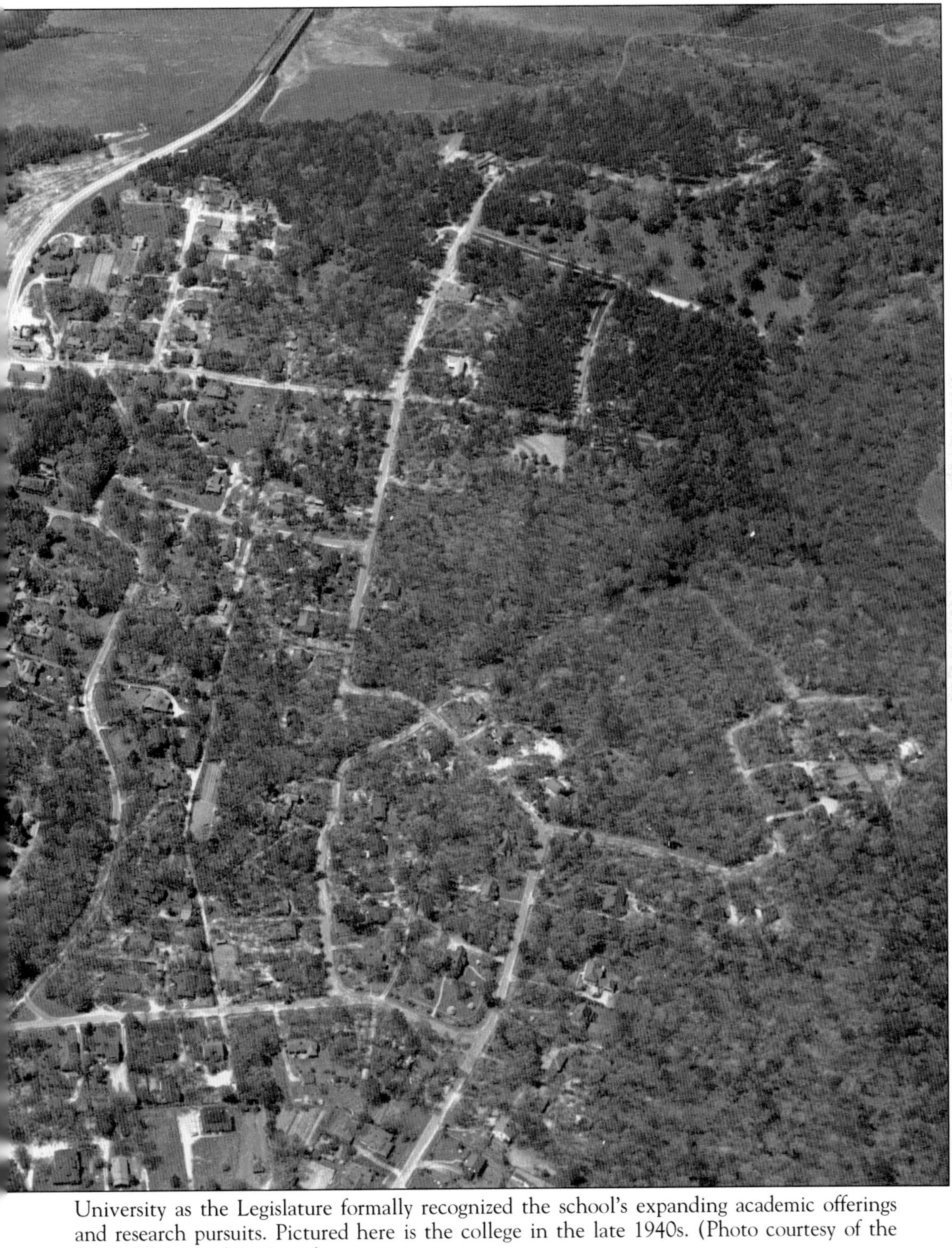

University as the Legislature formally recognized the school's expanding academic offerings and research pursuits. Pictured here is the college in the late 1940s. (Photo courtesy of the Strom Thurmond Institute.)

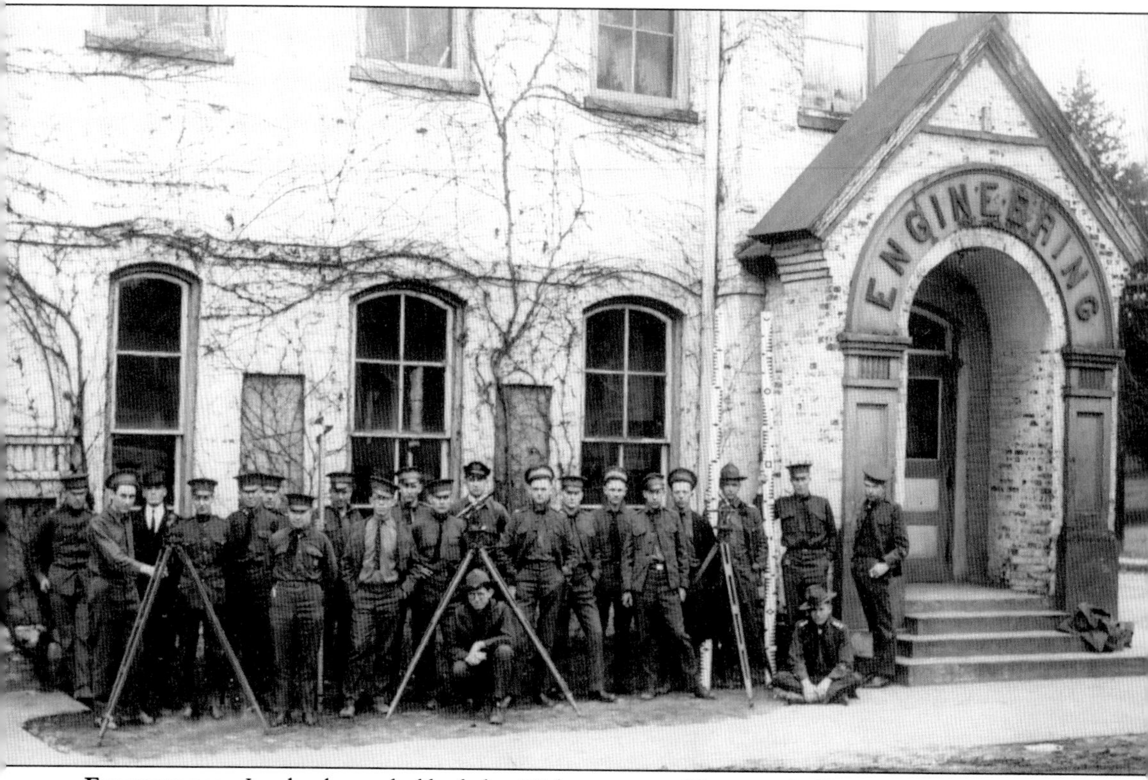

ENGINEERING. In the latter half of the 20th century, Clemson College constructed many buildings and developed additional schools. In the late 1990s the Flour Daniel Engineering Innovation Center was added to a campus located on 1,400 acres of rolling hills. Clemson University features five different colleges including agriculture, forestry, and life sciences; architecture, arts, and humanities; business and public affairs; engineering and science; and health, education, and human development. As of July 1999, Clemson's enrollment of 16,327 represented 47 states and 67 foreign countries. As part of the vision outlined by T.G. Clemson in his Last Will and Testament, Clemson University is the leading university in the southeast and the 11th in the nation in generated revenue from patents and intellectual properties (according to the *Wall Street Journal/Southeast Journal*). Clemson University and its Co-operative Extension Services have achieved far more than Thomas G. Clemson would have ever imagined. Pictured here is the first engineering school at Clemson (*c.* 1900s). (Photo courtesy of Strom Thurmond Institute.)

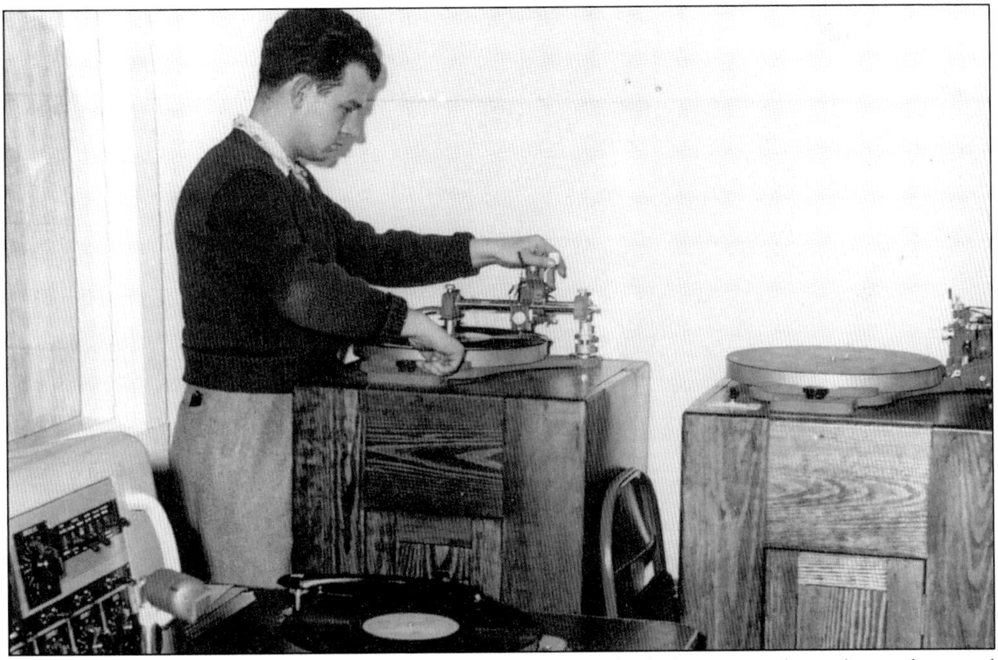

TURNTABLES. Local radio stations and newspapers supplied the news throughout the rural community. Schools and colleges prepared students to utilize their talents in journalism and media relations. In this view (*c.* 1958), a Clemson announcer prepares several records for airplay over WSBF, the Student Broadcast Facility, located on the Clemson campus. A state-of-the-art studio of the time period contained three turntables and a control panel of tubes and electro-mechanical sound equipment. In the late 1960s, tape machines would be used; by the 1990s computer-chip technology made huge turntables and mixing panels obsolete. (Photo courtesy of Strom Thurmond Institute.)

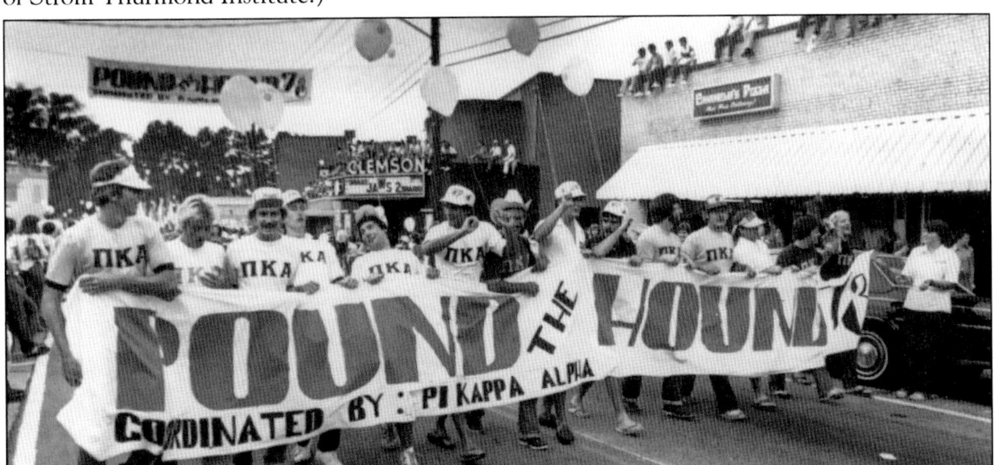

POUND THE HOUNDS. The town of Clemson, once known as Calhoun, is conducive to pedestrian traffic. In this 1978 view, Clemson revelers march down asphalt streets that were narrowed in the mid-1980s. Renovations included brick junctions and antique lamp posts. Notice the Clemson Theater and Channello's Pizza, one of the first pizzerias in the Upcountry. The theater and the pizza place are long gone but the buildings still stand. (Photo courtesy of Strom Thurmond Institute.)

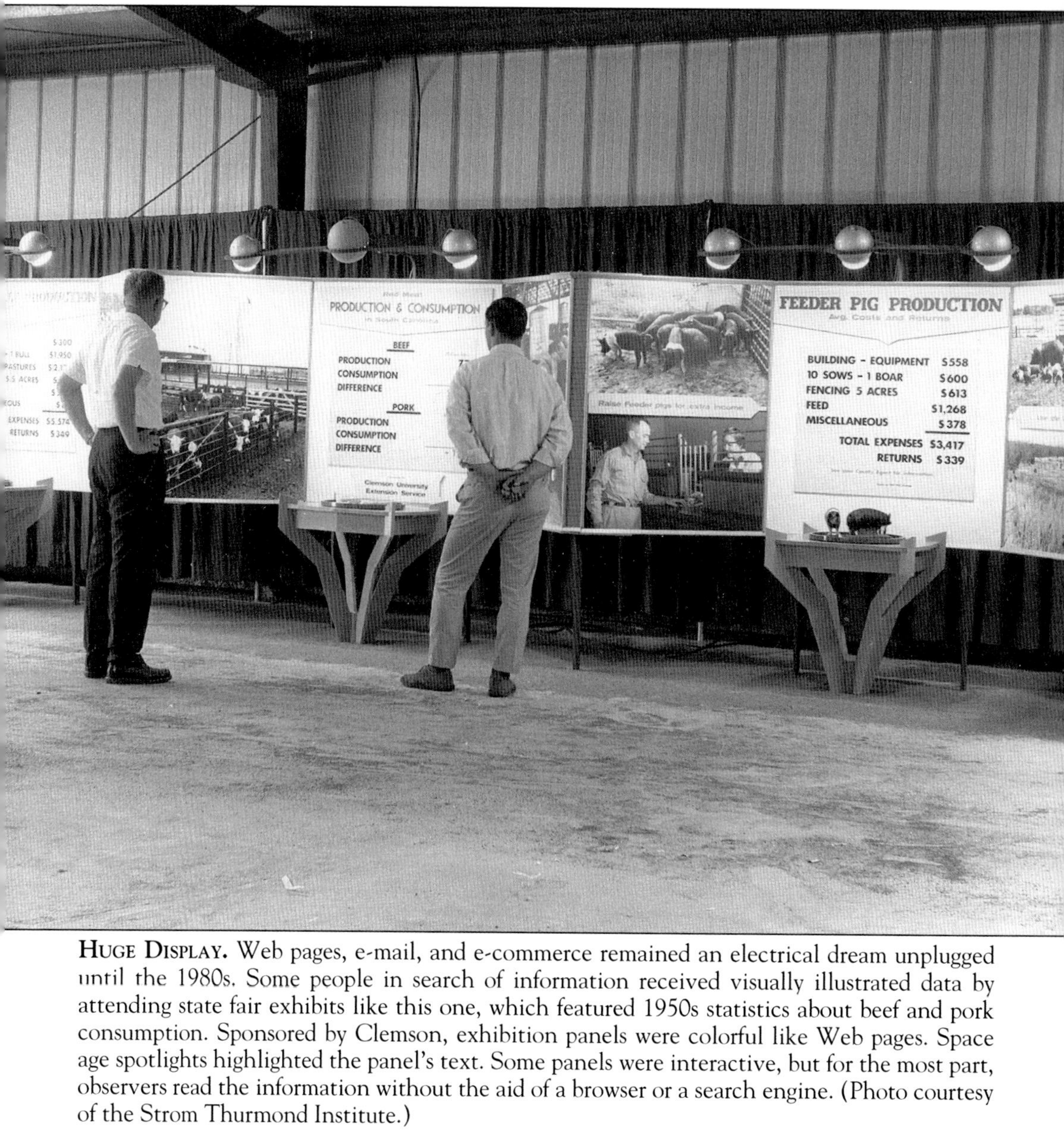

Huge Display. Web pages, e-mail, and e-commerce remained an electrical dream unplugged until the 1980s. Some people in search of information received visually illustrated data by attending state fair exhibits like this one, which featured 1950s statistics about beef and pork consumption. Sponsored by Clemson, exhibition panels were colorful like Web pages. Space age spotlights highlighted the panel's text. Some panels were interactive, but for the most part, observers read the information without the aid of a browser or a search engine. (Photo courtesy of the Strom Thurmond Institute.)

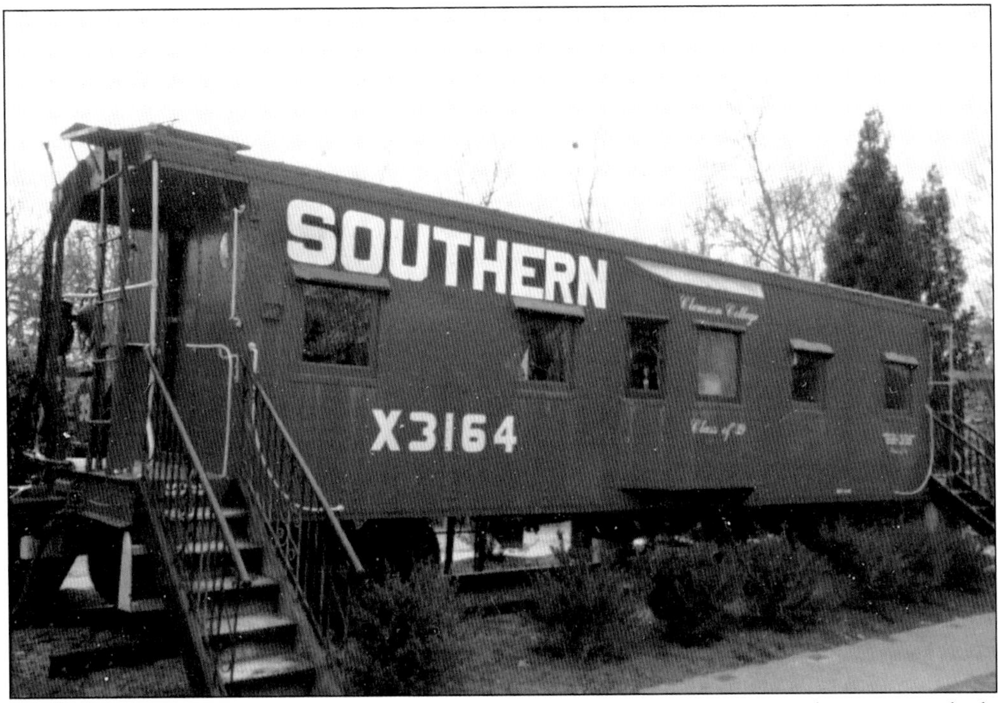

Red Caboose. Trains are still admired and appreciated in Pickens County. There are two little red cabooses in Pickens County that remain open to the public. One sits beside Main Street in Central. The other is a part of the South Carolina Botanical Garden. (Photo by P.E. Peters.)

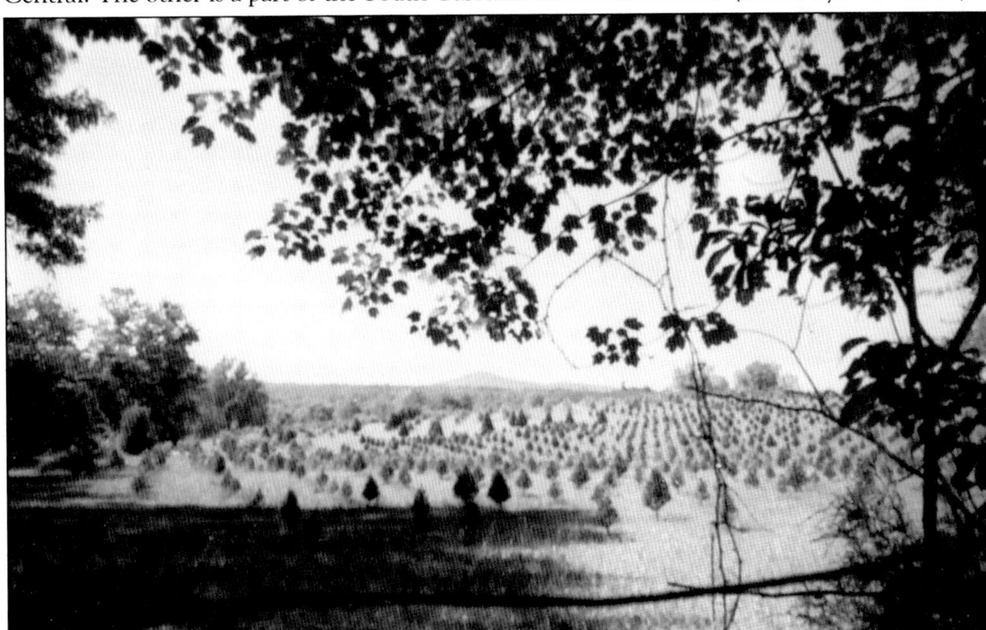

Christmas Trees. Christmas tree farms have replaced the cotton fields of the past. This Christmas tree farm in Norris is one of several in Pickens County. Much of the county's income is now generated by tourists visiting the beautiful mountain parks and lakes. (Photo by P.E. Peters.)

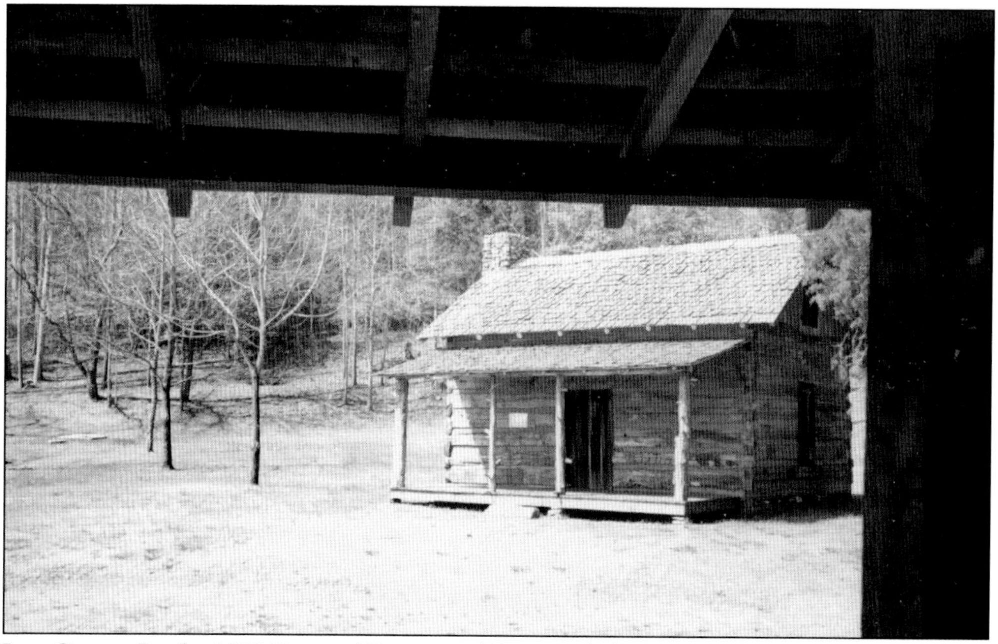

Log Cabin. On the 1972 National Register of Historical Places, Hagood Mill operates as it did in the 1800s. The gristmill is the only mill in the state that uses its original wheel components. Looking out from the gristmill one can view the cabin and grounds where the annual Heritage Day Festival is celebrated on the third Saturday in September. Music, crafts, and reenactments offer a fun education for all participants interested in the region's history. (Photo by P.E. Peters.)

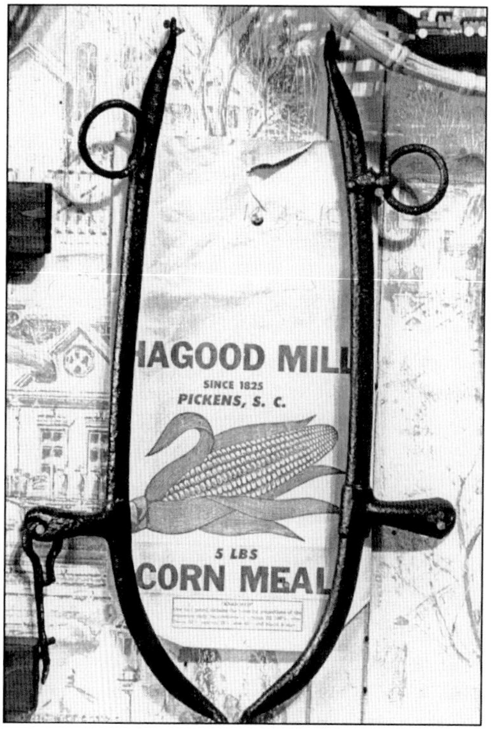

Harness and corn. Heritage Day is celebrated at Hagood Mill, but Dacusville Farm Days at Robinson Field is regionally known for including a large and varied display of vintage farm implements and machinery. The three-day festival is held each Labor Day weekend. Events include a tractor parade, antique car show, plowing contests, and tractor pulls. Dacusville is located on S.C. 186 near the Saluda River in northern Pickens County. Pictured here is an antique livestock harness used as a frame around an old corn meal sack. (Photo courtesy of the Judy Alexander Black and Jerry Black.)

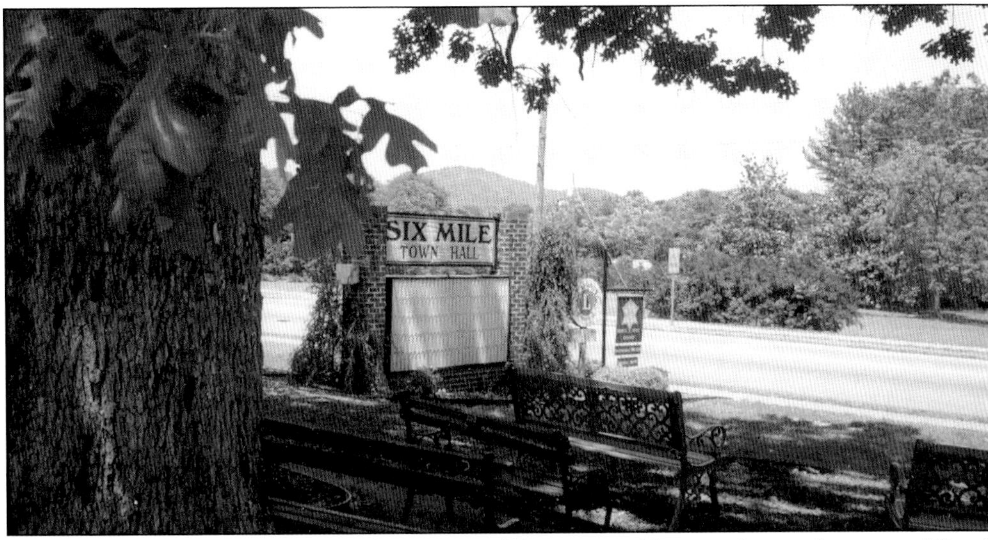

TOWN HALL WITH A VIEW. Six Mile Town Hall has a view like no other in the state of South Carolina. Six Mile is located on scenic S.C. 137 northwest of Norris. Unlike most towns, Six Mile has no major festivals associated with the village. The Azalea Festival, a one-day event in mid-April, is affiliated with the town of Pickens. The Liberty Fest is held in early May in downtown Liberty and is sponsored in part by the South Carolina Arts Commission. Easley's Old Market Square hosts the city's annual Fourth of July celebration. Dacusville supports the Farm Days celebrations. The Heritage Festival, organized by the Pickens County Museum, takes place in mid-September. The Pumpkin Festival is celebrated the second weekend in October in Oolenoy. Although they have no major festivals, Six Mile villagers quietly celebrate each day living among the hills and valleys of this remote community. (Photo by P.E. Peters.)

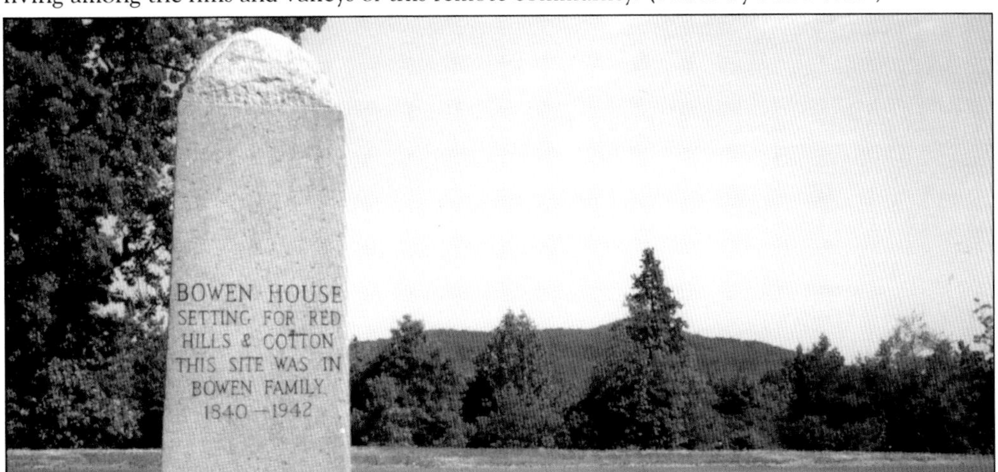

BOWEN HOUSE MARKER. Although moved from its original location where it was dedicated, the Bowen House Markers on Ireland Road in Pickens are backdropped by the landscaped that Ben Robertson described in his book *Red Hills And Cotton*: ". . . when I think of the country we lived in, I always remember the exotic . . . the jasmine and hyacinths and roses, the buckets of warm foamy milk and the smells of the hay barns . . . of tomatoes cooking, of fresh cornbread . . . of kerosene lamps . . . The dusty unpaved roads . . . We lived in a wild, wonderful country . . . Our country is so easy on us and so hard. But it is ours, it is home, and from the depths of us we love it." (Photo by P.E. Peters.)

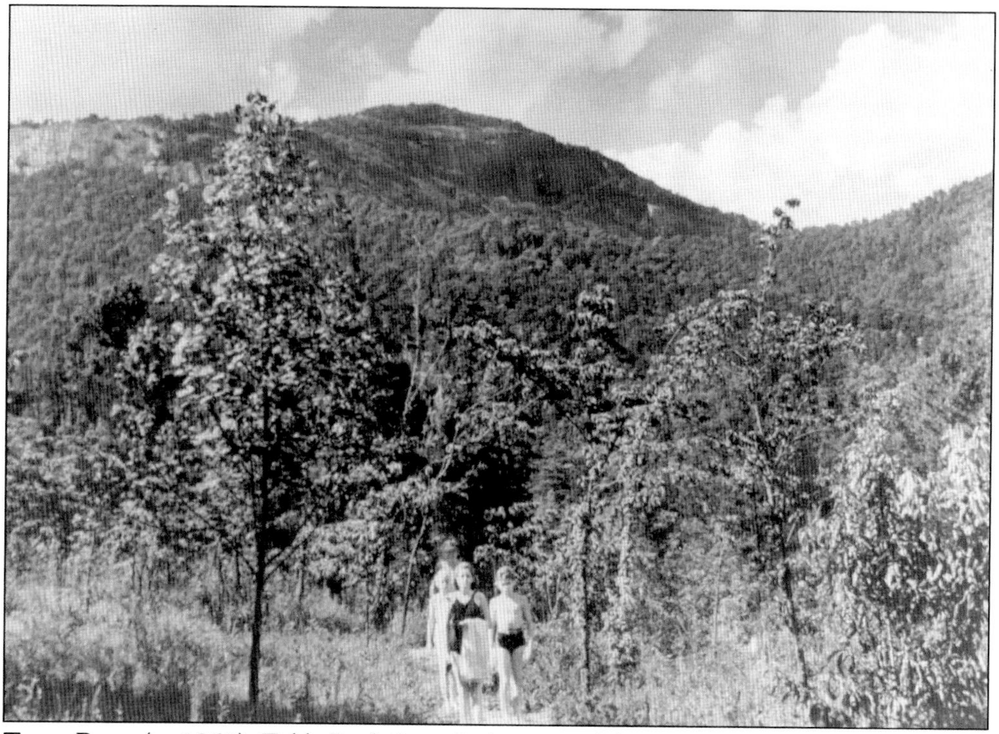

Table Rock (c. 1960). Table Rock State Park is one of the state's oldest parks and Keowee-Toxaway Park, located at the junction of S.C. 11 and S.C. 133, is one of the newer parks. South of the site of Keowee-Toxaway Park is the location of Keowee, now inundated. Keowee was the capital of the lower Cherokee nation. At the park is an interpretive center and boardwalk with artifacts and exhibits about the Cherokees. Another place for local sun and fun along the shore line is on S.C. 133. Mile Creek Park, the only county park, has 7 miles of shoreline, a beach area, nature trails, 25 picnic sites, and 69 campsites equipped with water and electric hookups. (Photo courtesy of the PDHRT.)

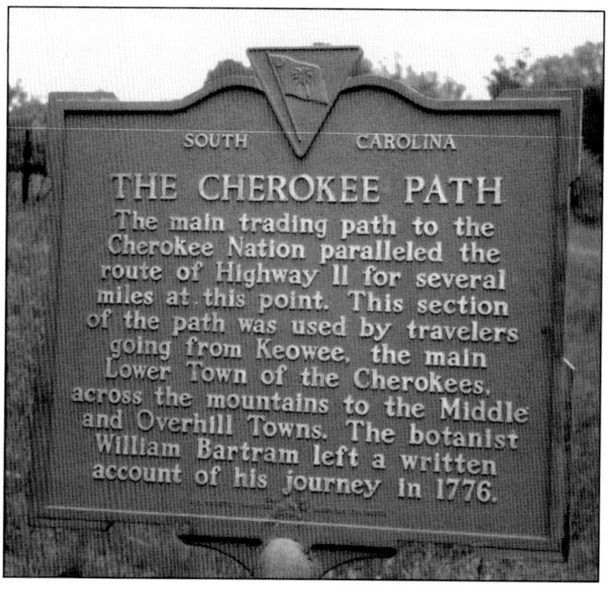

Cherokee Marker. Parts of S.C. 11 (Cherokee Foothills National Scenic Byway) follow an ancient Cherokee path from Oconee to Pickens counties. (Photo by P.E. Peters.)

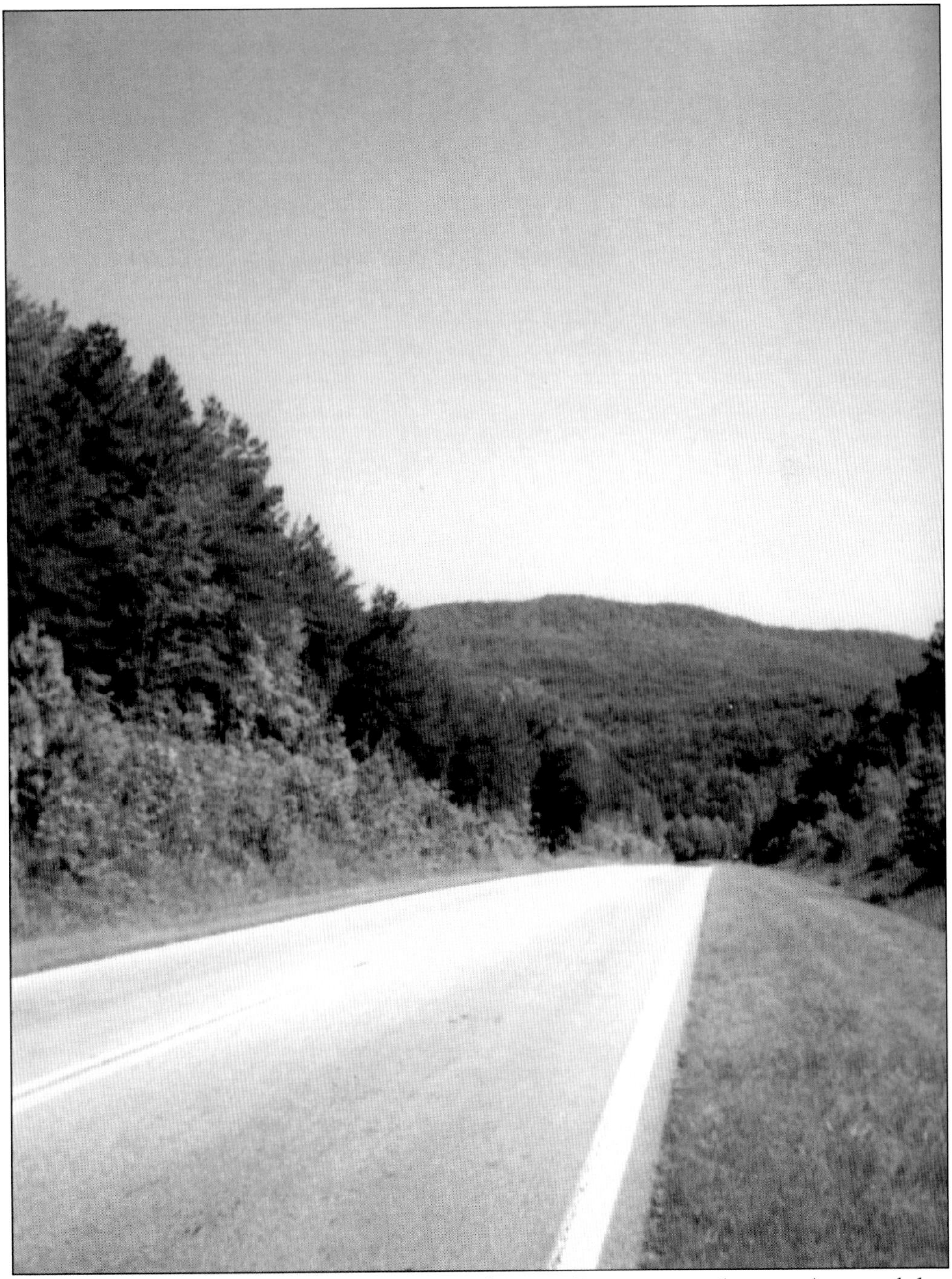

HIGHWAY 11. The Cherokee Foothills National Scenic Byway is a modern two-lane road that exits I-85 at the Georgia state line and makes a 130-mile arc north past several parks, over man-made Lake Keowee, through peach orchards, villages, and past Cowpens Battlefield. The highway rejoins I-85 in Gaffney, S.C. Residential and commercial developments along the road and mountains burden the environment, so the challenge for the residents of Pickens County is to preserve the land and waterways while managing urban development and the massive migration of individuals into the region. (Photo by P.E. Peters.)

Acknowledgments

This book would not have been completed without the generosity and support of the vivacious Donna Roper at the Pendleton District Historical, Recreational, and Tourism Commission (PDHRT); the indefatigable Christine Vissage and the Pickens County Library staff; the gracious Beverly Cureton at the Central Heritage Society; and the spirited Anne Sheriff and Susan Cooper at the Faith Clayton Room, Southern Wesleyan University. I also extend thanks to the team at the Strom Thurmond Institute, Clemson University Libraries, including Michael F. Kohl and my favorite "compiler" and amigo Dennis S. Taylor. I am forever in debt to the kindness and generosity of Beth Bilderback, my encouraging friend at the South Caroliniana Library, USC who has lifted my spirits through three arduous projects. And to my fellow pecan-lover Don Stewart at the SC State Museum, thanks for those E-mails! Lastly, I extend special thanks to Judy Alexander Black and her husband, Jerry Black, and the patrons of Garren's Café who contributed to this book while I ate my lunches.

I extend a special thanks to writers Fred C. Holder, Jane B. Morris, Dot Jackson a.k.a. Dot Robertson, A.V. Huff Jr., Michael Hembree, M.M.M. Allen, Julia J. Woodson and G. Anne Sheriff, Jerry Alexander, L. Ford, Ron Rash, Mark Steadman, and Kate Salley Palmer. I also researched a variety of materials from B.F. Perry, J.C. Calhoun, T.G. Clemson, Ben Robertson Jr., J.W. Shealy, N. Roberts, C.H. Neuffer, F.V.Clayton, Betty Hendricks, and Rick Littlejohn. The *Keowee Courier, Pickens Sentinel, Easley Progress, Liberty Monitor, The Journal SC Medical Association*, and articles from *Sandlapper* allowed me to obtain a great deal of knowledge and information pertinent to the development of Pickens County.

Lastly, I thank my husband Richard for his tireless support. I also thank Eric and Rachel Peters, Jo Ann Peters, C.D. Peters, Natalie Barrett, Lisa Looman, and Sharon Riedel for shelter, food, and laughs. And as always I greatly appreciate the hardwork of the Arcadia team, especially Sara Long, Mark Berry, and Doug Rogers.